ROSSINI

By the same author

Melinda
Don Juan/Salome
Il Metodo
A Siberian Encounter
Angelo La Barbera: The Profile of a Mafia Boss
Mafioso: A History of the Mafia
Insider Outsider
To a Different World
Luchino Visconti
La Donna nel Rinascimento
Il Lamento d'Arianna
Un' infanzia diversa
La vallata
The Story of R.
Incontri
Traviata
Motya: Unearthing a Lost Civilization

ROSSINI

Gaia Servadio

CARROLL & GRAF PUBLISHERS
New York

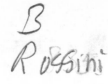

B
Rossini
.156 0485
10/1/03

Carroll & Graf Publishers
an imprint of Avalon Publishing Group, Inc.
161 William Street
NY 10038–2607
www.carrollandgraf.com

First published in the UK in 2003 by Constable,
an imprint of Constable & Robinson Ltd

First published in the USA in 2003 by Carroll & Graf Publishers

Copyright © Gaia Servadio 2003

ISBN 0–7867–1195-7

Printed and bound in the EU

Library of Congress Cataloging-in-Publication Data is available on file.

to Jonathan Kent

Rossini, of course was born and belonged to this world. But he perceived the avalanche of the incoming movement and, partly out of convenience, partly because he felt it, he moved towards it and contributed to the enrichment of Romanticism.

Isaiah Berlin

That poor man of genius.

Stendahl

Contents

ILLUSTRATIONS

ACT ONE

STENDHAL AND THE NEOCLASSICAL

Sous Napoléon, j'eusse été sergent; parmi ces futurs curés, je serais grand vicaire.   Stendhal, *Le Rouge et le noir*

[Under Napoleon I would have been a sergeant, amongst these future priests I would be a Vicar-General.]

I

SCHERZO

One crisp February evening, Stendhal came face to face with the composer he most admired and Rossini found himself talking to his future biographer. That meeting was said to have taken place in the winter of 1817; Stendhal himself admitted that he did not care much about dates or precise details. On his way from Rome to Naples, Rossini found himself at the post house in Terracina, a sleepy town set between the Bourbon kingdom and the Papal States, the two most reactionary states of nineteenth-century Italy. The inn was known for its jovial host and the wines it served, like the famous Moscato. Rossini and the seven tired and dusty passengers who travelled with him decided to take a rest and then dine. A fire was lit in the hall of the simple inn where a wooden table was prepared and wine poured in majolica goblets.

From the opposite direction another coach arrived. In it was Henry Beyle, a lover of music, an admirer of Italian life. Monsieur Beyle, who wrote under the pseudonym of Stendhal, was quite sceptical about Italy's political determination to free itself, although he was quick to hear the notes of rebellion from its best composers, especially those of the brilliant new star, Gioachino Rossini, whose music he was going to hear in Naples. But, an admirer of the sophisticated North, Stendhal shared the opinions of many travellers: 'In Italy, the civilized part of the country stops at the river Tiber. Midway across that river we begin to feel the energy and the extroversion of savages.'

At the staging post, horses were fed and rested – just like the travellers who would leave at dawn the following day. The innkeeper suggested that those coming from Naples and those aiming for Rome should dine together since they were all gentlemen. So Stendhal, then aged thirty-four years old, noticed that the group of travellers to Rome included 'a very fine-looking man, slightly balding, aged twenty-five or twenty-six'.

That was his first impression of Rossini. Stendhal's approach to taking notes during his journeys was that of a painter: broad lines to remember later, skipping the non-important detail, ignoring the shade: 'one writes with a pencil during those lost moments when waiting for fresh horses at a post house.' Did Stendhal recognize Rossini sitting at the same table among the group of travellers? Probably not. In all likelihood the room was dark, with a few candles throwing large shadows. Maybe a few diners had decided to play cards in a scene characteristic of Caravaggio or Georges de La Tour, painters who were out of fashion by then, their *verismo* had become shocking in an era that still sublimated the classical. Furthermore, Stendhal himself would have had to be discreet. He was politically suspect, a French expatriate who had fought for Napoleon and was still a fervent Bonapartist, travelling towards the country of those arch enemies, the Bourbons.

While the diners gathered around the table, Stendhal started talking to the unknown balding gentleman about music and opera in particular. Might he have the opportunity, he enquired, to see Rossini's *Otello* when he reached Naples? The gentleman smiled. Stendhal persevered: Rossini, he said, was the hope of Italian music. He was a brilliant composer of arias and a wonderful orchestrator. Still not disclosing his identity, a 'slightly embarrassed' Rossini continued to smile and to listen. 'It is crazy,' said Stendhal, 'that this unworthy country of yours is unable to produce a royal patron who would give him a pension of at least 2,000 scudi . . . Rossini is the man who, among all Italians, has most genius. Composers like him are so badly paid! They have to rush from one side of Italy to the other without a moment's rest, and the finest opera does not bring them more than 2,000 francs.' The conversation focused on musical events in Naples. Both men knew that it was better to avoid topics concerning political events there. Eventually discovering that the gentleman was Rossini himself, and having detected his sombre inner nature, Stendhal went on to ask a great many questions, to which Rossini answered 'with concepts which were clear, brilliant and pleasant.' Rossini explained to his inquisitive and knowledgeable new acquaintance how the Neapolitans required a style of music different from the Milanese.

It is surprising that Stendhal did not recognize Rossini immediately because by the time of their encounter there were hundreds of images of the composer on sale, especially at the main Italian opera houses – not only at La Scala in Milan, or La Fenice and San Moisè in Venice, but also at the Teatro Argentina, the Teatro Apollo and the Teatro Valle in Rome. Despite his youth the composer had become a superstar, acclaimed for his operas as well as his looks – a mouth all curves, curly hair and wide-open eyes. Indeed Byron described in a letter how Rossini was followed everywhere by admirers claiming a lock of his hair, girls shouting his name and craving a scrap of his clothes or an autograph. Souvenir images of Rossini were good business. Yet even at that stage, Rossini was still quite poor.

Stendhal told Rossini of his enthusiasm for *L'italiana in Algeri*, and asked him whether he preferred that opera to *Tancredi*. It was quite a question. It meant choosing between *opera buffa* and *opera seria*. Rossini was cunningly evasive in his response: he preferred *Il matrimonio segreto*, Cimarosa's opera. So Stendhal went back to a previous point. Why not ask for payment when one of his twenty operas was being played in theatres all over Italy? He was talking about copyright before that concept existed. 'He proved to me that during this period of disorder the matter would not even be possible to propose.'

As they talked, Stendhal became engrossed in 'that poor man of genius', finding him 'not very cheerful and happy'. 'It was the most pleasant of my Italian evenings,' Stendhal noted. 'We drank tea until past midnight.' Contradicting himself, he added that Rossini showed 'the happiness of a fulfilled man', although he detected melancholia in Rossini's music. Considering the composer's poverty, Stendhal declared that no one should reproach Rossini for writing an opera in eighteen days (the time he allegedly took over *Il Barbiere di Siviglia*). 'He writes on a nasty table, with the noise of the hostel kitchen in his ears and with sticky ink which is brought to him in an old pot used for pomade.' This is a lovely portrait of the young Rossini who, like Mozart, could work in any circumstance, whether in bed, standing up or, in this case, on a coach carrying him up the Italian peninsula.

The 150 miles which link Rome to Naples were bare and brigand-infested. On long poles hung arms and legs, the remains of robbers and murderers. Well-defended cities served as harbours to the papal and Bourbon forces, but the land was more hostile than the sea. Behind the narrow strip along which it was possible to travel – but only in daytime and provided there were armed guards and a post-illion, the Apennines rose steeply in a mysterious rocky plateau rife with bandits, or *banditti* as English travellers used to call them and whom Salvator Rosa painted in shimmering colours. Banditry meant lawlessness but also appalling poverty, combined with a lack of justice and a disregard for human rights which is still felt today. Prevarication was the law of the land and it was easier to be outlawed than to eat two meals a day. Nevertheless, Stendhal was looking forward to his journey. In Naples he would have the opportunity of hearing Rossini's new operas played well: the Bourbons' capital was famous for its excellent orchestras.

A few years later Stendhal was to devote a whole book to the man he met at Terracina. Rossini was only thirty-two when Stendahl's *Vie de Rossini* was published and commented that the biography was a mirror of the writer, not of him. As an old man, destroyed by depression, he snapped: 'A Frenchman, some time ago, wrote my biography and passed himself off as my friend.' The book was an immediate bestseller and went through various reprints. It was published in 1824. Rossini finished *Guillaume Tell* in 1829. After that, he did not write another opera. The question remains, why did the most successful composer of his time enclose himself in a world of silence for the remaining thirty-nine years of his life? What had happened to the man from Pesaro, who had become the star of European courts and opera theatres, one of the most appreciated wits of his time?

II

ADAGIO

Gioachino Rossini was born in Pesaro, on the Adriatic coast, a 'new town' of the Renaissance redesigned for its rulers, the Della Rovere papal family. Even its harbour was invented. In fact the Foglia, pompously called 'the river' but in fact merely a spring flood or *torrente*, was disinclined to allow a sheltered port and continuously changed course, blocking itself and the harbour with silt. Agricultural goods came from the well-irrigated hinterland and were shipped from the so-called harbour towards markets along the coast in round-bottomed boats of a type that can still be seen today. Built mainly of brick because there are no stone quarries nearby, Pesaro is situated south of the river Rubicon which brought it within the Roman Empire. Therefore, the inhabitants of Pesaro enjoyed the full rights of Roman citizenship. As for the legendary Rubicon, which Julius Caesar crossed at the head of his legions without the permission of the Senate, thus destroying the Roman Republic and causing a civil war, it simply is not known where the river bed actually lay. Don't believe the signpost which was merely planted by a Fascist *Podestà* to please the visiting Duce; the Rubicon and its historic bridge disappeared as alluvial sand changed the shape of the coastline.

In spite of heavy levies imposed by papal rule, Pesaro was quite rich. Artisans, traders and musicians seemed to prosper in the attractive city enclosed by pink walls within which the nobility built themselves villas and palaces. Pesaro was not a place in which to be poor. Unfortunately for Gioachino, his parents Giuseppe and Anna were just that –

not destitute but poor. Querulous and naïve, Giuseppe was not particularly gifted but he must have had strong lungs: he was a municipal trumpeter, the official who announced edicts in the squares and market place, rather like an English town crier. As an itinerant musician, he tried to make ends meet by finding work in rickety orchestras around Lugo, Ferrara, Imola and Pesaro. At times he also played the horn during the opera season at Pesaro's Teatro del Sole. His most reliable employment was with the military band of the Ferrara garrison; but that finished when he was placed under military arrest for being absent without leave. On his travels, he would always stay in cheap accommodation. On 14 March 1789, three years before his only son's birth, he applied for a job as trumpeter at Pesaro, saying that he had been particularly applauded during a previous Carnival opera season. The job was vacant and the town council accepted him; so Giuseppe was able to work in the city in which he wanted to settle because Anna Guidarini lived there.

Giuseppe was not originally from Pesaro, in the Marche region, but from nearby Lugo, in Romagna. Anna's mother came from Urbino which, at dawn, is almost visible from Pesaro. Anna Guidarini's father was a baker, and she was the eldest of four children. Her sister Annunziata figured in the Pesaro police files of 1798–9 as practising prostitution. In one instance, a certain citizen Ricci was accused of insulting Annunziata, calling her 'porca puttana', dirty whore. Ricci justified himself saying that Annunziata deserved all such names. Although Anna officially worked as a seamstress, it is likely that need had pushed her on the same path as her sister. The floor which the Guidarinis inhabited was often used as a modest *pensione*, probably a kind of bed-and-breakfast establishment with the occasional bonus of paid sex. Those who visited Pesaro on a temporary basis, like Giuseppe, would have found the Guidarinis' cheap accommodation ideal for every imaginable need.

Soon after their marriage, Anna and Giuseppe had to leave the overcrowded rooms in via Fallo that they had been sharing with other members of the family and moved to via del Duomo. They took over two narrow rooms on the first floor, which had belonged to an exiled Chilean Jesuit, the recently deceased Xavier Pugar. Their son was born in 1792, only a few weeks after Mozart's death and one year before the guillotine fell on Louis XVI's neck. The era into which Gioachino was born is the key to the composer's enigma: Baroque was melting into the well-proportioned colonnades of Neoclassicism, to be followed by the political upheavals accelerating the adventures of Romanticism. Poverty was to haunt Gioachino Rossini throughout his childhood and adolescence; his early life was a constant struggle, a stressful and breathless rush to earn enough to survive in a more or less dignified way. He is first recorded as having a job at the age of six, but he had certainly worked even earlier than that. Besides, his father was not clever with money. In fact, Giuseppe was not clever full stop. Enthusiastic, boastful, probably rather charming, Giuseppe was altogether a simpleton, somebody who scraped a living *vivacchiando*. In Pesaro, where everybody had a nickname, Giuseppe was called Vivazza – *Cittadino* Vivazza in Napoleonic Republican days. Responsibility for raising their child and supporting the family fell on Anna who was twelve years Giuseppe's junior. She was alone much of the time and had to fend for herself and her child; this state of affairs applied whenever her husband was in prison which, for one reason or another, happened quite often.

The need to earn caused Gioachino's parents to be constantly on the move around the province. Their child remained at home. He was partly looked after by his paternal grandmother Antonia, who came from Lugo specially to be with him. His maternal grandmother Lucia Guidarini also helped out. So if there is one well-established legend in Rossini's biographies which should be disclaimed from the very beginning, it is that he had a happy childhood. Not only was Rossini lonely and poor but also his lifelong preoccupation with money was a direct consequence of those years of deprivation. Soon after Gioachino's birth, his parents were in such need that they had to let one of their two rooms to a couple from Tyrol. Four adults and a baby living in this restricted space cannot have been comfortable for anybody.

Anna was a real beauty. She had a lovely soprano voice. 'She was ignorant about music but she had a prodigious memory. Her voice was beautiful and full of grace, sweet, like her appearance.' She could not read a note and probably had hardly any education. 'She sang by ear,' her son remembered. The remarkable musicality and intelligence that lit up Rossini's life came from her. His early good looks were hers as well: mother and son shared not only sparkling eyes and soft curls, but an almost identical, rather feminine mouth.

Why should Anna Guidarini, at nineteen years of age, both pretty and intelligent, marry a simple man like Giuseppe who was always in and out of trouble? The answer is simple. Anna was pregnant and it was unlikely that, with her bad reputation and lack of money, she would have been able to find another husband while carrying a baby. But was the baby Giuseppe's? 'I am the son of a horn,' Gioachino Rossini was to say (*Sono il figlio di un corno*: the pun is the same in English and Italian). This joke sounds bitter and the notion that Gioachino might not be his father's son or the certainty that he was not, must have weighed on a soul as sensitive as his. In any case Anna, five months pregnant, and Giuseppe, a man of thirty-two, married on 26 September 1791. It was a religious wedding, in the old cathedral and it took place before the tomb of San Terenzio, Pesaro's patron saint. One can do no more than speculate whether Anna went to confession at San Terenzio and, if so, whether she said anything about the father of the baby she was carrying. And it is equally uncertain whether Giuseppe was marrying her in the knowledge that she was expecting somebody else's child. (To this day, it is whispered of the noble Perticari family of Pesaro that a Perticari count had fathered Rossini.) Perhaps he received money for consenting to give his name to a baby conceived out of wedlock? On the other hand, Giuseppe might have accepted this as a useful marriage of convenience. He earned little and was getting on. As for Anna, she was grateful to have found a man, any man; she would finally leave the two rooms she shared with her parents and her sister's occasional clients. And Giuseppe was a good man. She may not have loved him, but he was a caring, decent person.

So Gioachino Antonio Rossini came into the world on the last day of February 1792, a leap year. His godparents were members of the nobility; one of them, Caterina Semprini-Giovannelli, was notorious 'for her inflamed Jacobin speeches'. There was nothing odd in the nobility agreeing to be at the baptismal font of an ordinary family (before becoming Verdi's wife Giuseppina Strepponi had also enjoyed the presence of aristocrats at the christening of her first illegitimate baby).

The political upheavals that overwhelmed the little city of Pesaro absorbed Rossini's life from its very beginning; he was four when General Bonaparte descended on Northern Italy. 'Had the French not invaded Italy, I would have ended up by being a chemist or an oil merchant,' he was to comment. The Napoleonic invasion was a cataclysm that changed the part of Italy which lived under the French in a far-reaching and astonishing way. Italy was ready for the change and, even if Napoleon ruled for a very short time, he brought with him a revolutionary tide which was to affect the Italians for ever. As Stendhal put it at the opening of *La Chartreuse de Parme*:

> On 15 May 1796, General Bonaparte made his entry into Milan at the head of that youthful army which but a short time before had crossed the Bridge of Lodi, and taught the world that after so many centuries Caesar and Alexander had a successor . . . A whole nation became aware, on 15 May 1796, that everything it had respected up till then was supremely ridiculous and on occasion hateful. The departure of the last Austrian regiment marked the collapse of the old ideas; to risk one's life became the fashion.

Even before the French arrived, the local patriots – Giuseppe Rossini among them – arrested the papal governor and voted to join Napoleon's Cisalpine Republic. But as it turned out, Giuseppe showed off his republican feelings too early and lost his position as municipal trumpeter. In effect Pesaro was hostile to the ruling clergy and had hardly contributed to the papal call when troops were mobilized to counter Napoleon's army. Disenchantment with papal rule was stimulated by the corrupt administration of the clergy. As soon as the French arrived, Giuseppe regained his former position. The *gonfaloniere* (mayor) Gian Francesco Mamiani, the papal legate Cardinal Francesco Maria Saluzzo and the bishop Monsignor Beni fled Pesaro. When 12,000 French troops under the command of Victor Perrin entered Pesaro on 5 February 1797, Giuseppe was among the patriots who welcomed them. In the riots that followed, the statue of Pope Urban VIII was demolished while anti-clerical feelings which had grown as taxation had increased exploded into joy. Titles were abolished and the municipality proclaimed that all citizens of Pesaro were to be equal. But, of course, some became more equal than others, especially if they were French. On the following day the new commander in chief, Napoleon Bonaparte himself, arrived in Pesaro and was lodged in the patrician Palazzo Mosca, not far from where the Rossinis lived. A tree of liberty was erected in the main square and the enthusiastic citizens tried to catch a glimpse of the general of the army of Italy, throwing flowers and cheering him as he passed. Napoleon left a few days later without making any official appearance; he was back in Pesaro on 20 February, but only for an hour. While cries of liberty, equality and fraternity echoed around the lovely squares, the narrow streets and the graceful doorways, Pesaro witnessed the other side of the Napoleonic coin. The French Commissariat emptied the public coffers, requisitioning hay for its horses and wheat for its army. All the churches were looted and everything of value was removed – silver and gold candelabra, holy chalices, paintings.

But *Cittadino* Giuseppe Rossini, a member of the local revolutionary governments, swore eternal allegiance to the Republic. And then, while Napoleon was temporarily on the retreat, Giuseppe was imprisoned. He was not freed until the victory at Marengo against the papacy's Austrian allies on 14 June 1800. Shortly afterwards, he was described in the *Gazzetta di Pesaro* as 'the excellent patriot Rossini known by the nickname of *Cittadino* Vivazza'; Giuseppe's republican enthusiasm was so staunch that he was given credit for a hymn which he had not in fact composed himself, 'Patriots, let's break the tyrant's chain'. Times were so volatile that the true author was too scared to claim the composition as his own. Indeed, the *Gazzetta di Pesaro* now announced Giuseppe's re-imprisonment. That was because fortunes were reversed in the Papal States. Vivazza avoided a longer term in prison by making 'a confession', implicating some of his old friends, which of course made him *persona non grata*.

With Napoleon's return, there were festivities and, as Giuseppe came out of prison, the eight-year-old 'Giovacchino' Rossini was employed as a kind of mascot for the revolutionary band. Observing his father going in and out of prison because of what he had said, rather than what he had done, made the child realize that he should keep himself to himself. This also taught Gioachino not to disclose his political stance, whatever his leanings. He knew that spies had reported to the police against his father at every change of regime. For example Giuseppe was accused of having liberated the Jews from the Pesaro ghetto in advance of the Napoleonic forces. A neighbour, the cobbler Arcangelo Sabatucci, a witness against Giuseppe, told the police that he had observed how Vivazza would shout: 'Free the Jews, open the ghetto doors, here are your liberators.' According to another spy, the barber Antonio Gennati, he would publicly praise the republican government and Napoleon. His music should express everything except his own thoughts; to think was highly dangerous, especially if you were an obscure musician who had to struggle to earn enough to keep a tiny family just above starvation level. 'From the little we know of his traumatized childhood,' writes Bruno Cagli, 'which he passed among the upheavals of the French invasion with which his papa, Vivazza, had got himself mixed up so blithely . . . we cannot imagine that much time was spent in singing lullabies and telling tales by the fireside.'

Having attended the local *scuola comunale*, Gioachino was sent to board with a butcher in Bologna; it was there that his formal musical education began. He was taught by three priests and then by Giuseppe Prinetti, 'a strange fellow', Rossini remembered, who 'never owned a bed – he slept standing up'. Prinetti taught him to play keyboard instruments. Probably because he was often drunk, Prinetti was also often tired: 'Sometimes when he hadn't rested enough, he'd go to sleep while I was working at the spinet.' Noticing that his teacher's eyes were heavy with sleep, the boy would slip back inside his own warm bed. Small wonder that he later admitted having learnt little from this man.

How Anna managed to find the money to provide for her boy is something of a mystery. Perhaps she found another protector. And she continued to eke out a living as a singer. Defying the papal ban on women singing on the stage, she appeared in secondary roles in the splendid little theatre of Iesi, for example, and, during her husband's prison terms, rose to more important roles. The fact that she appeared on the stage underlines that Anna did not have much of a reputation to defend. She also made appearances with her son, for example in Mosca's *L'impresario burlato* at Imola.

Following Napoleon's misadventures, which in papal territory became ever more complex as a result of special treaties between Bonaparte and the Holy See, Giuseppe and Anna Rossini decided to move to Giuseppe's native town of Lugo. From 1802 the family was to be found at via Poligaro Netto, where they rented two rooms from the Marocchi family. Giuseppe asked a certain Don Giovanni Sassoli, who had already helped them to find lodgings, to act as a kind of musical agent for Gioachino. Having become skilled in many musical activities, including singing, accompaniment on the harpsichord, rewriting scores and tuning keyboard instruments, the young boy now had earning power. His real breakthrough, however, came when Canon Giuseppe Malerbi, who lived in Piazza Padella in Lugo, taught him composition and singing.

How the Rossinis became acquainted with the grand Malerbi is easy to imagine; in Lugo there can't have been much choice of company and the itinerant family would have offered much better conversation than the average local citizen. So the three Rossinis were often invited to dine at Casa Malerbi, where there was an excellent cook. Indeed Gioachino ate there almost every night. Furthermore, Malerbi gave him harpsichord lessons. And because Don Luigi, the canon's brother and also a priest, was a composer, Casa Malerbi was full of scores which Rossini read and played. Thus he immersed himself in the music of Mozart and Haydn. These composers became so fundamental to his style that, when he first emerged on the Italian musical scene, he was nicknamed 'Il tedeschino', the little German. He also studied scores by Bach, Handel and Gluck and learnt how to accompany singers, *suonar d'accompagnare*. In those days contemporary German music was almost ignored in Italy, so that access to the Malerbi library would have made a strong impression. It does not need much imagination to understand how the two priests, celibate and sensitive, might have taken a fancy to the good-looking boy.

By 1803–4 Gioachino was beginning to write his own compositions. No doubt his family and Canon Malerbi were thinking of early employment for him. Opera companies needed composers to edit scores; it was also customary to add a cavatina to suit a particular voice and at times whole acts were lifted from one opera and transposed into another to suit the company. The young Rossini could do all this. The composer, who was generally required to conduct from the harpsichord, was then a lesser figure than the singer; not only castrati but even 'normal' sopranos earned more than composers.

On 22 April 1804 Gioachino and his mother appeared at Imola's Teatro Comunale, playing duets together in a programme that included a cavatina composed by the child prodigy. Can one possibly imagine the magic of such moments? To witness his mother, lit by the special theatre lighting, her over-painted cheeks and glittering eyes glowing, wearing colourful clothes designed for an operatic princess or queen; to hear her beautiful voice, indeed to sing with her, must have been thrilling for the boy. In the semi-darkness, he would imagine the attentive faces of the public listening to him. He would also watch that beautiful woman so familiar and yet so magical, Anna, the angel who had looked after him. Gioachino was stage-struck and also mother-struck. The strong link he had with his mother was to last all his life.

It was around this time that Anna had a row with Francesco Maria Guidarini, her brother-in-law. Gioachino's miraculously fine voice could be kept as a *voce bianca* with a simple operation, he suggested. The Rossinis needed to make money and castrati were in vogue; Gioachino could be trained as a castrato. 'My brave mother would not consent at any price,' he was to recount. The suggestion actually tempted Giuseppe. In later life Rossini would recall the risk he had run:

> I came within a hair's breadth of belonging to that famous corporation – or rather let us say de-corporation. As a child, I had a lovely voice, and my parents used it to have me earn a few paoli by singing in churches. One uncle of mine, a barber by trade, had convinced my father of the opportunity that he had seen, the breaking of my voice should not be allowed to compromise an organ which – poor as we were, and as I had shown some disposition towards music – could have become an assured future source of income for us all. Most of the castrati in fact, and in particular those dedicated to a theatrical career, lived in opulence.

Rossini himself was enamoured of the castrato voice; it was a sound, he wrote, whose 'purity, miraculous flexibility and, above all, profoundly penetrating tonality moved and fascinated me more than I can tell. I should add that I myself wrote a role for one of them, Velluti, one of the last but not the least. That was in my opera *Aureliano in Palmira*.'

By 1805 it was clear that the future of the family rested on Gioachino's potential earning power. Anna's voice had become weakened by strain and tonsillitis, while Giuseppe had never been a satisfactory breadwinner. At the age of twelve, Gioachino was invited by Agostino Triossi, a wealthy merchant of twenty-three, to pass the summer at Triossi's villa. Many delightful evenings were spent making music in the villa's moonlit garden. It was during this holiday that Gioachino composed six sonatas for two violins, cello and double bass. In later life Rossini would make fun of his early compositions. As his fame increased, many manuscripts emerged from the dust of time with requests to be authenticated; not all were his own, but of his six

Triossi sonatas he attested: 'First violin, second violin, violoncello and double bass parts for six horrendous sonatas composed by me at the country house of my friend and patron Agostino Triossi, at a most youthful age and not even having had a single lesson in thorough-bass.' Rossini was being unduly modest: these quartets are in fact astonishingly beautiful, showing a sense of liberty and an early streak of melancholy.

Triossi had accumulated his wealth as a result of the Napoleonic Wars. He and his cousins had acquired the villa when the church was compelled to hand over some of its possessions to the state. In fact the cultivated Triossi traders represented the new Italian middle class created by Napoleon. By the time Gioachino and his parents moved to Bologna, the family hardly constituted a family. And Anna's health declined further.

But Bologna was a great capital of music.

III

AGITATO

At sunset the skyline in Bologna melts into the red roofs of the city. Under the arcades that curve around some of the oldest churches in Italy, people stop and talk to one another. They often chat about food and how to prepare it. And about music. Not for nothing is Raphael's sublime painting of Santa Cecilia in Bologna. In summer, the shade of the arcades keeps the pavements cool and the arcades themselves retain their convivial and social role, and in autumn they afford shelter from the rain which, in the fertile plain, is plentiful. Bologna has always been rich and is known by other Italians as *Bologna la grassa*, 'Bologna the fat'. It is generous because it could always afford its extra rolls of fat. The study of music flourished in Bologna which for centuries was the intellectual centre of the Holy See. Its university, the oldest in the world, trained some of the greatest intellects of the West since the Middle Ages. Monastery after monastery – so many that the post-war Communist administration, and indeed the Bonapartist regime, did not know what to do with them – enclosed learned clerics who, from Bologna, would be dispatched all over the world. Bologna was the brain that Rome needed to contain a population which became more and more demoralized spiritually.

It was at the time of the Counter-Reformation that Pope Marcellus decided that music was to become the voice of God. Palestrina dedicated one of his best-known masses to this pope, who appreciated the emotional and mystic influence of music. The grandiosity of melody was no longer to be the monopoly of monarchs, to be staged during banquets and spectacles: choruses and singers were to be exploited in the churches so long as women did not use their sensual vocal cords in holy places. The soprano voice was taken by castrati and by highly trained *voci bianche*. The severe Gregorian chants, the Council of Trent decreed, were to be replaced by compositions which could agitate the soul. Severity in music, simplicity, were to be left to Northern heretics like Calvin and Erasmus who called for the whole congregation to join in – women included. The church was to be the guardian of great Italian melodies. This was the tradition to which Rossini came to contribute in an exemplary way.

The Rossinis moved to Bologna, with the intention of ending their peripatetic travelling and of giving Gioachino a musical education. He started singing in churches as a soloist, also acting as a repetiteur and continuo player in orchestras. Little is known about these years because it was a period of penury and despair for the family and because Rossini did not like to talk about sad moments of his life. He also pretended gaiety and happiness when there was none. There are different versions about these early times, especially as Rossini contradicted himself in later years. He always aimed to present a smiling face to his public, who therefore became used to seeing him as a laughing cavalier.

In Bologna Anna and Gioachino lived in one room, near the ghetto. When you turn into Strada Maggiore, two towers – one of them leaning – come into view; these used to bar the Bologna ghetto. Walking towards them you pass by the ornate palace where King Enzo, son and heir to Frederick II, was kept a prisoner by the papacy until his death in 1272. In one of the narrow pink and red streets, the Rossinis lived on a second floor, not too close to the smelly pavements and the open sewers which, in summer, attracted flies and rats.

Meanwhile the map of Northern Italy was changing once again. In 1802 Napoleon reorganized the Cisalpine Republic with a new constitution and made himself its president. When he decided to establish an hereditary empire in December 1804, he crowned himself emperor and Italy had to follow suit. In 1805 Northern Italy was transformed into a kingdom within the empire and Napoleon placed the iron crown of the Longobards on his own head with the famous phrase, uttered in perfect Italian, 'Dio me l'ha data, guai a chi la tocca!' ('God gave it to me, woe befall whoever touches it!'). With his stepson

Eugene de Beauharnais as viceroy, he started a series of important public works. Keeping an eye on the important port of Naples, Bonaparte signed a treaty with the Bourbons in October 1805. A month later the Austrian-born Queen Carolina broke the truce by admitting British and Russian troops into her husband's kingdom. Napoleon resolved to 'hurl this criminal woman from her throne' and, as French troops closed in, the royal family of Naples sailed to Palermo for what was to be a long exile; indeed, Carolina died in exile. The Bourbons made the crossing on Nelson's flagship and, according to her lover, Emma Hamilton was the only passenger not to be sick.

These events were to colour Rossini's life; Napoleon's presence in Italy changed everything for everybody. Even if Bologna was to bounce back and forth between the Holy See and Napoleon, Gioachino would never been admitted to important musical institutions had it not been for the populist reforms that had swept Northern Italy because of the Bonapartist regime. His father's enthusiasm for the republican cause, which had already led to his imprisonment, was increasing, even though the cause itself was turning monarchical. By the time of the victory of Marengo, Napoleon had won back Piedmont, Liguria and Lombardy. Bologna and part of the Papal States had been returned to the French (28 June 1800) and many of the convents and monasteries were turned into academies. Opera theatres started performing new works – Anna Rossini sang at the Teatro Marsigli-Rossi in Gazzaniga's *Don Giovanni*. This theatre was an important cultural centre, as was the Accademia Polinnica, notable for having a woman director, Maria Brizzi Giorgi, who was also a virtuoso pianist. Tickets became cheaper in order to encourage the poorer levels of society to attend; the Napoleonic order was keen on spreading culture.

Gioachino was working full time. Indeed, his talents had been recognized to such an extent that at the age of twelve he had won the title of *Maestro* at the Accademia Filarmonica of Bologna. He went on to sing the part of Adolfo in *Camilla*, an opera by Napoleon's official composer Ferdinando Paer, an important role in which he was seen to embrace the soprano in an over-seductive way. His early career also took him round smaller centres, mainly with second-rate orchestras. In 1807 he was in Faenza, the city of ceramics, where he played in Guglielmi's *La serva astuta* and in April 1809 he sang in operas by

Paer and Cimarosa. As he played and sang, so he learnt. He was amazingly precocious and very handsome – a kind of Mozart's Cherubino slipping in and out of beds, maybe not yet visiting the scented sheets of the prima donnas, but certainly those of the *comprimarie*. His auburn hair curled near his almond-shaped hazel-coloured eyes; his pale hands and svelte body could have allowed him to become one of Bologna's most sought-after gigolo. But Gioachino Rossini was no *cicisbeo*: he had no time to court rich ladies and accompany them to the theatre in their gilded coaches; he was in a hurry to make money. In Senigallia, then an important market town of the Marche, he overstepped the mark when Adelaide Carpano improvised a cadenza on the stage which should have been avoided. Adelaide was a pretty soprano and, like all sopranos, she had a 'protector'. He was Marchese Cavalli, an able and intelligent impresario, who financed the company. If he did not enjoy Adelaide's misguided cadenzas on the stage, certainly he enjoyed her in his bed. What happened that night became notorious: hearing the unbearable notes which he was meant to accompany on the harpsichord, Gioachino laughed so loudly that the whole audience echoed his merriment and applauded his negative but ebullient judgement. It was a scandal – everybody in Senigallia talked about the assurance of the young maestro and everybody mocked Adelaide. Covered with ridicule, the young soprano, in tears, went to Marchese Cavalli who was not amused by Rossini's cheek. This episode, however, was not to hamper Gioachino's career, quite the opposite.

Whilst travelling around Emilia and the Marche in order to earn as much as he could to support his ailing mother and inept father, Gioachino was also studying music privately with Padre Angelo Tesei. There was hardly time for such subjects as Italian grammar, mathematics, geography and foreign languages. In fact Rossini's Italian orthography remained faulty and eventually he wrote better French. Literature, foreign languages and mathematics, he learned from life. He was, for instance, to develop a real love and understanding of Dante Alighieri's *Divina commedia*, often quoted in his letters.

In Bologna in 1805 Rossini met the tenor Domenico Mombelli, a friend of Anna's who was then in his mid-fifties and knew everyone of any importance in the world of music. His first wife had been Mozart's first Contessa in *Le nozze di Figaro* and his second wife was Vincenza Viganò, the niece of Boccherini and sister of Salvatore Viganò; hugely admired by Stendhal and Beethoven, Salvatore Viganò had choreographed Beethoven's *Prometheus* for its première in Vienna in 1801. The Mombelli family formed in fact a touring opera company rather than just a family. A musician to the core, Domenico Mombelli recognized a musical genius when he met one and instantly picked out Gioachino from among the many Bolognese who jostled to catch his attention. The Mombelli company was performing an opera by one Marcos António Portogallo. One of Rossini's rich and admiring patronesses asked him to obtain a copy of one of the love arias. However, neither the copyist nor Mombelli agreed to copy it out for the teenager. Angered by the refusal and keen to provide his passionate lady-friend with what she wanted, Rossini told Mombelli that he would pay for his ticket, listen to the opera, and return home in order to write it all down from memory. He did just that; in fact, as we shall see, Rossini did just what Mozart had done at more or less the same age and in the same city. When Mombelli saw what the teenager had produced after his second visit to the theatre, he sceptically refused to believe that Rossini had not been in collusion with the copyist. Eventually he had to acknowledge that the thirteen-year-old had an extraordinary ear. This episode launched the friendship between the two and the start of Rossini's operatic career.

Rossini was asked to write music for verses by Signora Mombelli and in particular for a libretto called *Demetrio e Polibio*. Although it was not performed until 1812, the composition of this two-act *dramma serio* was a clear demonstration of Rossini's talent. 'These songs were the first fragile blossoms of Rossini's genius,' writes Stendhal, 'the dawn of his life had left the dew still fresh upon them.' The opera's title refers to the kings of Syria and Parthia, fathers to a pair of young lovers. Rossini produced the music piecemeal, without even being given details of the plot.

In April 1806 Rossini was admitted to the coveted Liceo Musicale where he was to study singing, cello, piano and counterpoint with Padre Stanislao Mattei. That the director of such a famous institution would himself teach the young Rossini underlines the fact that Gioachino was considered a musical phenomenon. Maybe Padre Mattei thought that he had found an equal to the young Mozart who had been brought to the same Liceo Musicale in 1770, when its director was Padre Martini, after whom several of the most highly regarded musical institutions in Bologna are still named. To qualify at the Liceo Musicale was considered vital for any young musician. The personal collection of 17,000 volumes that Padre Martini left to its library remain an invaluable source of knowledge and learning (at that time printed music was extremely rare).

Years earlier the young Mozart was drawn to Bologna to earn a valuable qualification from the world centre of musical scholarship and to add yet another distinction to his already prodigious collection of honours, he was interviewed by Padre Martini himself. A pre-requisite for gaining admission to the Liceo Musicale was to write a composition from memory. Mozart's choice of Allegri's *Miserere* was audacious. The papacy had refused to allow any copy of this score to leave the Sistine Chapel on pain of imprisonment. The hauntingly beautiful composition by Gregorio Allegri (1582–1652), based on Psalm 51, the most penitential of all, was traditionally sung on Ash Wednesday in the Sistine Chapel. Clerics would walk in the dark chapel at Vespers, each of them singing and carrying a candle. By the time the whole chorus had entered, darkness had turned into light and the soprano voice would break into his high C, reaching Michelangelo's ceiling and beyond. Mozart, locked in a room of the Liceo Musicale, having heard it only once (at the age of twelve), wrote it out from memory for the examination set by Padre Martini. This must have caused a certain degree of scandal but Mozart was not punished for his daring. Maybe he was admired for his gall, just as Rossini had been for clandestinely memorizing Portogallo's opera at the same age and in the same city.

Rossini learnt more harmony from studying Mozart's and Haydn's scores than from Padre Mattei and his student compositions show how much he absorbed from Mozart in particular, whom he described as 'the admiration of my youth, the despair of my maturity and the consolation of my old age'. And echoes of Haydn's quintets can be found in Rossini's later compositions. In fact it can be said that the combination of Italian melodic verve inherent in Rossini with the seed of harmonic genius planted by Mozart and Haydn in those Bolognese days created the Italian school of the nineteenth century.

Italy was on the whole cool towards any form of imported music and symphonic orchestras hardly existed because the concept of music without voice was unpopular. There was scope for solo instrumental writing and for chamber music, but orchestras were restricted to the operatic repertoire. As the members of such orchestras were often assembled at the last minute, they played badly; at one stage Rossini was so enraged by the sounds they produced that he threatened to beat them all with a stick.

In 1808 Rossini composed *Il pianto d'Armonia sulla morte d'Orfeo*, a cantata for tenor, chorus and orchestra which won him an academic prize and was performed in Bologna on 11 August that year. Critics found an excessive German influence in the phrasing but, as Richard Osborne has pointed out, the work includes 'some characterful orchestral writing, with lovely wind solos and a glimpse of Rossini's new-found love, the solo cello'. As a student in Bologna, Rossini also wrote a number of overtures and instrumental variations, some of which have survived through being re-used in such operas as *Il Signor Bruschino* and *L'inganno felice*. During those years Rossini took every opportunity to hear the stars of *bel canto*, as well as some of the world's last and greatest castrati, who made regular appearances in the city.

Among the singers Rossini heard at this time was the soprano Isabella Colbran, who had first visited Bologna in 1807 and was highly acclaimed for the agility of her voice and its extraordinary range. Born in Madrid on 28 February 1784, she was seven years Rossini's senior, and came to have a decisive influence on his life. Her father Juan (later called Gianni or Giovanni) was trumpeter to the royal guard of Charles IV, King of Spain. She had her first singing lessons from the Neapolitan composer Marinelli and went on to study with the castrato Girolamo Crescentini. Stendhal wrote of her that hers was

> *a beauty in the most regal tradition: noble features which, on stage, radiated majesty; she had eyes like those of a Circassian maiden darting fire; and to crown it all, a true and deep instinct for acting tragedy . . . Off stage she possessed about as much dignity as the average milliner's assistant. But the moment she stepped on to the boards, her head encircled with a royal diadem, she inspired involuntary respect even among those who a moment or two earlier, had been chatting with her in the foyer of the theatre.*

Rossini and Colbran certainly met in Bologna, where they were both admitted to the Accademia Filarmonica. The beautiful singer, rich and experienced, must have fascinated the young maestro who never missed an opportunity to woo and bed a woman. While in Bologna Isabella's father bought a villa in the area of Castenaso. A graceful and rather grand Neoclassical house, it was surrounded by good agricultural land and it came cheap because its previous owner, the Collegium Ispanicum, a clerical institution, was forced by the new Napoleonic laws to sell some of its properties in a hurry. The house would be the perfect dowry for his daughter, Juan thought. It would be ideal for Isabella, by now grand and famous, to inhabit a villa fit for an aristocrat.

Little did Rossini know that Castenaso would one day become his residence. But in 1810, the rebellious youth was getting fed up with the dry discipline of academe at the Liceo Musicale. Conventional, decent and dull, Padre Mattei was not the ideal teacher for Rossini who later confessed: 'I would have had greater interest in cultivating a stricter, more serious type of music if my counterpoint teacher had been someone who explained the purpose of the rules to me. But when I asked Mattei for explanations, he would always reply: "This is the way it has been done."' So, when Mattei, whose round face and pink cheeks reminded Rossini of a castrato, suggested to the eighteen-year-old a two-year course in musical canon, the student knew that he had had enough.

IV

PRESTISSIMO

Having abandoned Padre Mattei and the Liceo Musicale, Rossini's good fortune was to stumble across Giovanni Morandi, composer and conductor. Passing through Bologna, Giovanni and his wife, the mezzo-soprano Rosa, stopped to call on Anna. The Morandis were on their way to Venice, where they were to join the impresario Marchese Cavalli. They were to perform at the tiny Teatro San Moisè for a season of *farse*. Generally in one act, lasting an hour or just over, the *farsa* was popular in Venice in the late eighteenth and early nineteenth centuries; a typical programme at the San Moisè would include two *farse* and two ballets. Later the Viennese operetta was to achieve a similar popularity, offering its public sugary confections, while Gilbert and Sullivan fed a more ironic London public in the same way. Because there was a continuous need for new pieces of this sort, perhaps there would be a chance for a young composer to go with the Morandis to Venice, it was suggested. Gioachino needed little persuasion, he was ready. Besides, Venice was the city of *farse*, of opera, of Carnival, of beautiful and bored women. Since La Serenissima had been occupied by the Austrians, the Venetians had tried to forget their lost thousand years of independence in an orgy of music, balls and masquerades. La Fenice, the San Benedetto, the San Cassiano and the San Moisè were not the only opera houses that distracted Venice from its sorrow.

Success for *farse* seemed to be guaranteed if their melodies were played at the Caffè Florian or the Caffè Quadri in Piazza San Marco, both of which still provide music for tourists and pigeons. The latter was a meeting place for Austrian officers; in Napoleonic times, French officers took their place. The Florian was instead filled with conspirators and Venetian nobility. Which side would Rossini take? If Napoleon, the very embodiment of the French Revolution, had let so many people down, to whom could he and the Venetians turn? For a short time Venice was back in Napoleon's control, but the French behaved as occupiers; more masterpieces by Veronese and Titian left for the Louvre than the Venetians could count.

As he settled in Venice, Rossini wrote to his mother frequently, letters in brown ink and full of spelling mistakes. He longed to send her good news. He was like a pointer, waiting for his chance. And it came. When Marchese Cavalli's season ran into difficulties, the impresario was easily persuaded by the Morandis to engage the young maestro to compose a new *farsa* for his dwindling season; a German composer had backed out and a new score was needed immediately. Rossini, who shared accommodation with the composer Stefano Pavesi, a crazy chap with curly black hair and a smiling face, couldn't have asked for a better opportunity. The San Moisè was used not only as a theatre but as a meeting place where families would play tombola and gamble. The theatre company was good and it could afford to take risks. Its orchestra was reduced to the barest minimum – an average of twenty players. In short, Rossini could feel confident about making his operatic début, showing off his talent and his considerable fantasy in a not-too-demanding place.

The libretto, written in a hurry by Gaetano Rossi, was *La cambiale di matrimonio*, an early example of opera making fun of the American in Europe, although the wealthy simpleton is mocked with benevolence. It concerns a Mr Slook, whose intention is to buy a wife from an English merchant called Thomas Mill. The Englishman (a touch of Napoleonic anti-British propaganda here) thinks of nothing but trade; his daughter Fanny is no more than another piece of merchandise to him. But clever Fanny and her penniless lover Edoardo, a typical protagonist of the conventional *farsa*, outwit the generous and innocent Slook in a predictable happy ending. The music is characterized by Rossini's energy and wit; the comedy, as in all successful comedies, brushes the reality of life, the sad side of existence. From the start Rossini made women his protagonists; they are not romantic heroines who faint; they are altogether much smarter than their menfolk, whom they seduce while pretending not to. 'I have all the ills of womanhood, I lack only the uterus,' he was to say later, when he was no longer a winner like his wily comic heroines Rosina or Isabella. Herbert Weinstock wrote of this work, first performed on 3 November 1810:

> *Rossini's originality as a stylist of musical farce lay chiefly in his melodic and rhythmic brio, in the disenchanting lack of sentimentality with which he selected from a libretto those story elements which were nonsensical, absurd, preposterous, and then gave them apt musical revelation. Nothing exactly like the dash, the propulsive rhythmic and melodic onrush of* La cambiale di matrimonio *had been heard earlier. In it, as in his later comic operas, he seized upon every chance for pell-mell involvements, for swift purely musical illustration.*

For this *farsa*, an enormous success, Rossini received 'forty scudi, an amount that I never had seen brought together that way, one on top of the other.'

Success projected the young man into an easier life and, when in 1811, he returned to Bologna to conduct and coach the Accademia orchestra for Haydn's *Die Jahreszeiten*, his reputation was made. Around this time he also composed *In Morte di Didone* for Ester Mombelli, his new innamorata, but she did not make use of it until 1818.

Meanwhile an impresario who was planning a new season for the Teatro Corso in Bologna asked him to compose an opera for the libretto by Gaetano Gasbarri. *L'equivoco stravagante*, a two-act *dramma giocoso*, followed the Mozartian pattern of ensembles rather than solo arias. It was staged on 26 Ocotober and caused a huge scandal. The Bolognese liked the novelty but the libretto did not please the clerics. In fact it so offended them that the Holy See sent its police to close the theatre down after only three performances. The opera tells the surrealistic story of the poor tutor Ermanno, who has fallen in love with his student Ernestine. She, the daughter of Gamberotto, is a blue-stocking. Ernestine and her father are taken in by an odd character called Buralicchio, a silly man; to discourage him, Ermanno convinces Buralicchio that Ernestine is a castrato in disguise and, worse (especially in 1812), a deserter from the army. The libretto is full of *doubles entendres* and naughty expressions much underlined by Rossini's music. A contemporary review states that the music of *L'equivoco stravagante* was well received, that Signor Rossini had been called on to the stage and that some of the arias were encored. It goes on to clarify why the police were driven to ban further performances:

> *That the libretto is, permit me, vicious is demonstrated by the resolution taken by the very watchful prefecture, which has forbidden further performances. Only out of regard for the composer had it allowed three performances to be given after correction and recorrection – despite the mutilations thus inflicted – there are expressions that, when sung, produce an impression not to be tolerated. But as the argument of the libretto revolves around a supposed mutilation that necessarily allows room for many equivocal expressions, to mutilate some pieces does not suffice but it is necessary to cut the root of the scandal by suppressing the libretto.* (Redattore del Reno, 29 October 1811)

The fact was that what could have been composed for Venice was not acceptable in Bologna, which was back in papal hands. Apparently some of the words and gags which had been censored were reintroduced for the spectacles. Indeed, walking in his father's steps, the composer was arrested, probably *pro forma*, as a note from the police prefect says that he would let Rossini free.

The prima donna who sang Ernestine was Maria Marcolini, a curvaceous young woman with auburn hair and a wonderful stage presence, especially when in trouser roles. The former mistress of Napoleon's brother, Lucien Bonaparte, Maria was ready to fall into Rossini's arms – and he into hers; she was a coloratura contralto with a wide range. Diva of an opera called *Il trionfo*, she sang an aria that Rossini composed for her, making a spectacular entrance on the stage on a white – the English would say grey – horse.

Rossini then returned to Venice, which was to become the stage for his greatest success so far, *L'inganno felice*. First performed on 8 January 1812, this opera was then performed in Bologna, Florence, Verona and Trieste; then it was to travel further afield – to Paris, which might have given Rossini food for thought. Although labelled *farsa*, the work is closer to a *dramma semiserio*. The libretto by Giuseppe Foppa had already been set to music by Paisiello, a sequence that was to be repeated with *Il barbiere di Siviglia*, but with a very different result as by that time Rossini had become too famous a musician for Paisiello's fans not to react. *L'inganno felice* tells the drama of the Duchess Isabella, who has been wronged by two men whose rehabilitation occurs in a set of strange mining galleries. As Richard Osborne noted:

> *The* buffo *duets are reserved for the villains . . . This is an excellent early example of the conspiratorial buffo duet in which words are subject to manic repetition and where the music reproduces the gossipy lunacy ('Oh, che ciarle, che pazzie') with repetitions and alliterations of its own.*

The success of *L'inganno felice* was hailed by the release of pheasants, canaries and doves from the loges of the theatres. In a letter to 'Carissima Madre', dated 9–10 January 1812, he wrote:

> *Before going to bed I am going to tell you about my* farsa. *A great success – furore in grande – while from the overture to the last note of the Finale there was nothing else but great cheering. I was called to the stage not only last night but tonight; to conclude, I am the idol of the Venetians – and I am to write the* opera seria *for La Fenice and maybe tomorrow I shall sign the contract. All this will merit my dear parents' affection.*

The young man's joy sparkles throughout. Even his impresario wrote a letter to Anna congratulating her: her son was an 'ornament to Italy'.

Since it was to be staged during Lent, Rossini's next opera took the form of a semi-sacred piece, *Ciro in Babilonia*. The story is based on the biblical Belshazzar's feast. Rossini gave the tyrannical king incredibly difficult arias with which to express his fury when he threatens the wretched and beautiful Amira. The work was a flop on its first night, in Ferrara on 14 March 1812, and was rarely revived. As usual Rossini pretended to make a joke of it all and, when he returned to Bologna, he ordered a marzipan ship and invited friends to eat it. 'On the pennant there was the name Ciro. The ship's mast was broken, its sails were in tatters and the whole thing lay shipwrecked in an ocean of cream. Amid great hilarity, the happy gathering devoured my shattered vessel.' Gioachino's new passion, the mezzo-soprano Maria Marcolini, was present at the dinner; the two were soon living together and this new liaison was the talk of musical Italy. 'It was at her side, upon her piano, and within the walls of her country house at Bologna' that Rossini, inspired by Maria's voice, wrote his finest scores, wrote Stendhal; he added that Rossini made her into 'the finest musician you might hope to find in the whole of Italy'. She created roles not only in *Ciro in Babilonia*, but in *La pietra del paragone*, *l'italiana in Algeri* and *Sigismondo*. Without Maria Marcolini, Gioachino couldn't have reached La Scala so early in his career. Indeed, with the baritone Filippo Galli (who had sung in *L'inganno felice*), Maria pressed her protégé on to the impresario of La Scala, Domenico Barbaja.

Rossini's first score for La Scala demanded for its central character a highly developed voice and technical ability such as only the mezzo-soprano Maria could deliver. His preference for the darker shades of the contralto and mezzo-soprano is slightly strange, given that his model, his mother Anna, was a soprano. With a hilarious libretto by Luigi Romanelli, *La pietra del paragone* (1812) is still in repertoire, and includes music that Stendhal judged to be the funniest Rossini ever wrote. Rossini was conscious of the attention that his first opera in Milan would attract and took great care over its preparation. By this time the city, with an expanding population of 150,000, was the capital of the kingdom of Lombardy which Napoleon had created in 1805. It is worth stressing that the viceroy Eugène de Beauharnais, had transformed the city to a considerable extent: he was responsible for the eventual completion of the cathedral, the building of canals, new roads, sanitation and the establishment of *lycées*, high schools open to everybody, an education policy which still holds in Italy. La Scala, owned by its shareholders, was a crucial centre of social activity; not only opera, but gambling, intellectual exchange, love-making and conspiracies all took place within its walls. The poet and art collector Samuel Rogers, who visited it in 1814, wrote:

> *The house is vast and simple in design, the boxes circling in parallel lines hung with blue or yellow silk alternately from the floor to the roof; and all receiving light only from the stage; except for a few instances; where the figures being illuminated from within, the glimmering and partial lights had a very visionary and magnificent effect.*

Stendhal's observations of La Scala focus on people chattering in boxes, men and women calling on each other and then more people gambling in the foyer than listening to the music inside the auditorium. There was even sudden shouting as people demanded a famous aria or greeted the arrival of the star.

La Scala's set designs were superb, grand and famous all over the

operatic world; those of Alessandro Sanquirico, who combined monumental Neoclassical designs with intricate attention to detail, introduced new standards. It was Sanquirico who introduced the dimmed
light in the auditorium during performances – and not Wagner as is
often believed. Another personality who gave status to La Scala was the
choreographer Viganò, mentioned above. But at the centre of it all was
Alessandro Rolla, conductor, viola player, composer and violinist, who
saw to a fine execution of the scores and to an orchestra which could
play well – and together – something by no means usual at that time.
Rolla, who was in charge of La Scala from 1803 to 1833, had taught
Paganini. In Rossini, Rolla immediately recognized the brilliant orchestrator, the virtuoso and the innovative composer.

La Scala was the largest opera house for which Rossini had
composed so far and indeed he had to think about the special sonority
of the auditorium. There were also some hiccups because he was ill
and had not finished some pieces for *La pietra del paragone*. On 11
September 1812 the Minister of the Interior Luigi Vaccari wrote a
letter, marked *Pressante*, that rumours were exaggerated about 'parts
still missing from the opera which Maestro Rossini is writing'. The
fact that a minister should write about such a matter shows the
importance given to the completion of an opera for La Scala and
the attention concentrated on the young maestro. *La pietra del
paragone* was an enormous success and ran for fifty-three performances in its first season, a record which was not beaten until 1842,
when Verdi's *Nabucco* clocked up fifty-eight nights. For this opera
Rossini finally received a satisfactory payment; the public began to
flock to anything Rossini composed. Even more importantly, Rossini's
success at La Scala guaranteed him exemption from military service at
a time when the majority of the 90,000 Italian conscripts were lost in
Napoleon's Russian Campaign. But was this exemption really due to
his musical talent? I am more inclined to believe that a woman was
involved. As a former cherished mistress, Maria Marcolini, would
have had the ear of Lucien Bonaparte and could well have asked him
for this favour. There is supposed to have been a letter, now said to be
apocryphal, in which Bonaparte asked to exempt a man who, at the
age of twenty, might become a mediocre soldier but should be
preserved as a first-class composer.

It is hard to imagine – and impossible to describe – the musical
activity of this period in Rossini's life. Not only was he composing

prolifically and at great speed, but he was also conducting. In this area, he learnt a great deal from Rolla. Unfortunately there is little record of Rossini's conducting apart from dry descriptions and his threatening to beat with a wooden stick those musicians who did not follow his directions. He was also planning programmes for Bologna's various impresarios, writing the occasional aria to be added to a weaker score or for Maria Marcolini to shine in, and reading stories for possible librettos, where he would rewrite whole sections or change words to suit his music and temperament. And, of course, he invariably found time for his busy love life.

The success of *La pietra del paragone* brought Rossini a fame which was soon transformed into social success. The grand salons of Milan opened their doors to the handsome young man whose wit and charming manners were becoming legendary. Already renowned for his extraordinary voice, which could cover tenor and baritone parts, he was often asked to sing. His dandy looks, his *bons mots*, his mannerisms, became the fashion; crowds followed him including girls wanting to catch a glimpse of the new star, just as they would later with Hollywood stars or pop singers. 'This opera,' wrote Stendhal, 'created at La Scala a period of enthusiasm and of joy. Crowds hastened to Milan from Parma, Piacenza, Bergamo, Brescia, and all the towns within a radius of twenty leagues. Rossini was the first citizen of the land. Everyone was eager to see him. Love took it upon herself to reward him.' Stendhal was always attentive to the amorous side of life – his own included. Was he hinting at a new love of Rossini's with Princess Belgiojoso, to whom the composer dedicated a cantata, *Egle ed Irene* in 1814? It was while staying with the princess that he wrote to his mother: 'I'm really going through a lovely kind of life . . . Madame Amelia Belgiojoso, who is My Darling, returns the greetings that you kindly sent.' From Milan Rossini returned to the San Moisè in Venice, where he had two new commissions, *L'occasione fa il ladro* (24 November 1812), which he called 'my music of eleven days' since he took less than two weeks to compose it, and *Il Signor Bruschino* (January 1813). Both of these are *farse*, a genre that Rossini marked with a bitter and, at times, even offensive humour, castigating new money (journalists, lawyers, rich foreigners), sweeping away the vulgarity of *buffo*. But the greatest test for the composer was the *opera seria*, in which Rossini had not yet made his début. It was La Fenice that approached him first.

V

VIVACE AGITATO

Rossini's choice, in 1813, of Voltaire's tragedy *Tancrède* (1760) for his first *opera seria* is significant. In the Neoclassical style and tradition and one of the many derivations from Tasso's *Gerusalemme liberata*, this text has more than a touch of nationalism which could not escape the humiliated Venetians. The first version of *Tancredi* was arranged into verses by Gaetano Rossi, whose libretto is by no means as bad as has often been claimed.

Tancredi made Rossini a household name from London to St Petersburg. Its protagonist is a *cavaliere* from Syracuse (contralto *en travesti*) who makes his entrance at night on board a boat, landing incognito to visit his secret love. Tancredi's opening recitative hails his beloved *patria* and then develops into a cavatina in which his thoughts turn to his lover. Then a famous cabaletta turns into the joy of anticipation at the thought that he will soon set eyes on her – and she on him: 'Mi rivedrai, ti rivedro' ('I shall see you again, you will see me again'). I will spare my readers the many anecdotes which have accompanied the discussion of this aria, anecdotes to which Rossini either consented or even added and which all sound equally untrue. The passionate anticipation of the young man whose hopes are soon to be dashed is translated into throbbing palpitation ('Di tanti palpiti'). With this opera and this aria in particular Rossini became 'the reluctant architect of Italian romantic opera', as Julian Budden aptly put it. The cabaletta became so widely circulated (and hummed and whistled) that

Byron was confident his readers would understand his allusion to it in *Don Juan*:

> Oh! the long evenings of duets and trios!
> The admiration and the speculations;
> The Mamma Mias! and the Amor Mios!
> The Tanti Palpitis on such occasions.

And Balzac made his Marquis Raphael de Valentin descend the stairs in *La Peau de chagrin* (1832) whistling 'Di tanti palpiti'. It is not at all surprising that this sensuous song took the public by storm. *Tancredi* marks an important stage in the development of opera through the innovations that Rossini brought. With self-assurance and guts he introduced changes now often taken for granted: the recitatives are short and linked to the context of the arias; there is a new and masterful balance between the dramatic, the lyrical and the musical; and the chorus makes its first important appearance in an *opera seria* (in fact the cast includes *nobili, guerrieri, paggi, cavalieri, guardie, scudieri, popolo, damigelle* and *saraceni*, quite a crowd!). Rossini dedicated *Tancredi* to the Mombelli sisters, Ester and Anna, his favourite interpreters until the arrival on the scene of Isabella Colbran. One of the Mombelli singers was for a time Rossini's mistress – or maybe one of Rossini's several simultaneous mistresses.

The version of *Tancredi* first staged on 6 February 1813 at La Fenice allowed the protagonist to survive reunited with his beloved. In Lent the same year, a second version was staged in Ferrara. This time Rossini asked Luigi Lechi, whose left-wing sympathies would make him stress the thread of patriotism and hopeless love implicit in the music of *Tancredi*, to restore Voltaire's original tragic ending. Bruno Cagli used the simile of a marble bas-relief for the Ferrara version where Tancredi, mortally wounded, enters accompanied by a mournful chorus. In other words, the opera emulated a Neoclassical image, a Canova. Richard Osborne has commented that the Ferrara ending 'is a sobering and finely judged resolution to this sad, touching, exquisitely imagined heroic idyll.'

But the romantic solution did not please the audiences; it was not part of the accepted convention to end an opera tragically, even if it was an *opera seria* or *melodramma eroico*, as Rossi labelled his libretto. Further changes were made later in 1813 at the new Teatro Re in Milan, but the version of *Tancredi* usually heard today has the happy ending. When *Tancredi* opened, the two protagonists were ill. The *Gazzetta dell'Adriatico* noted that it was difficult to judge this latest work by Rossini because of 'a fatal illness' caught by both 'the excellent' contralto Adelaide Malanotti and the soprano Elisabetta Manfredini.

The opera is set in Syracuse at the time of the First Crusade. A chorus of knights celebrate the end of an internal feud; Amenaide has sent an anonymous letter to her beloved and exiled Tancredi, asking him to return to see her without knowing that he has decided to come to Syracuse in any case. Meanwhile Amenaide's father has promised her hand to Orbazzano so that the struggle against the Saracens may be resumed. Misunderstandings, imprisonment, danger, betrayal and treason, fatal love and doomed lovers – it is all there. In the words of the philosopher Arthur Schopenhauer:

> the intimate essence of each piece of music unrolls before us like a paradise that seems very familiar to us and yet remains eternally afar, understandable and yet incomprehensible, reflecting as it does all the impulses of our innermost secret selves, but without their reality, and keeping its distance from any torment.

Had Rossini developed the individualistic determination of a Romantic, he would have certainly stuck to the tragic ending, but as a Neoclassicist he wanted to please, to do what people wanted, not to provoke or shake. Besides, contemporary Italian audiences were not yet prepared for the Romantic wave which had begun to sweep Northern Europe.

Rossini probably travelled back and forth from Ferrara to Venice by boat, first on the river Pò, then sailing the short stretch on the Adriatic. That would have given him time to work on urgent new scores.

Rossini became legendary for the speed with which he completed a piece – two weeks, eleven days, eighteen days. In the process he would accumulate a host of musical ideas; and, when he had composed quite a number of operas, he started borrowing from his own works, pasting one aria from a previous opera to a new one but often changing orchestration and key. Furthermore, the printing of musical scores was reserved for very few composers; the autograph scores were generally kept by the impresario who had commissioned the opera and were eventually destroyed. Copyright did not exist and the first music publishers were only just being established. One of them was Giovanni Ricordi, who had worked as a copyist for La Scala and had met Rossini in Milan. At that time he had received a letter written by Isabella and her father Giovanni Colbran asking Ricordi to pass a note on to 'Il Maestro Rossini'. Isabella, by then the toast of Naples, was hoping to lure Rossini to that city; she was certainly writing on behalf of her lover, the impresario Domenico Barbaja.

But at that time Rossini had other engagements. In fact after Ferrara, Rossini was back in Venice for *L'italiana in Algeri*, commissioned for the Carnival season, the most important time for music, festivities and clandestine love-making. Its libretto appealed to the current taste for things oriental and to a special fascination with Roselana, Suleiman's Italian wife, whose 'biography' had just appeared. Because of its trading history, the Venetian Republic had a perennial love–hate relationship with the East and with the Ottomans in particular.

Venice had suffered tremendously; its independence and pride had been crushed by Napoleon who, on his first arrival in 1797, had been treated by La Serenissima as a *parvenu*. He retaliated: 'I will stand no more Senates, no more Inquisitions; I will be an Attila for the Venetian state.' And so he was. The doge was forced to resign and the oligarchic government which had ruled La Serenissima for a thousand years was dismantled. When even the four horses of San Marco were looted, Samuel Rogers remarked: 'How inhuman to rob them of the only four horses they had.' Then Napoleon handed Venice to the Austrians; the city was neglected even further and in 1807, the French got it back. On his visit there in 1812, when it was again under Austrian rule, Shelley was appalled: 'The Austrians take 60% in taxes and impose free quarters on the inhabitants. A horde of German soldiers, as vicious and more disgusting than the Venetians themselves, insult these miserable people.' But Venice never lost its great artistic pulse, providing a true home for the stage works of Vivaldi, Gozzi, Goldoni and Da Ponte.

L'italiana in Algeri had already been set to music in 1808 by Luigi Mosca, for La Scala. The version that Anelli wrote for

Rossini was in fact for the Venetian Carnival, when theatres were open all day long with non-stop performances; gondoliers were allowed free admission to any opera. When Rossini arrived for his *L'italiana*, banquets were organized in his honour in palazzi which reflected themselves with trembling luminosity in the water of the Gran Canal. As usual, he had been recalled in haste, because the Teatro San Benedetto suddenly found itself with no new opera and too many flops. Rossini's request for 700 lire, a large sum, was accepted without discussion. How much time he took to compose the new opera is uncertain; some sources say twenty-seven days, others eighteen. Angelo Anelli reworked his original libretto considerably, following Rossini's specifications, and with the composer adding his own onomatopoeic touches. The part of Isabella, the *italiana* of the title, was created for Maria Marcolini who was still by Rossini's side. At the première, postponed on account of her being ill, Rossini himself was more vociferously acclaimed than ever; he was covered in a cascade of flowers floating down into the pit and little pieces of paper containing verses lauding his genius and confessing total love – a custom which was generally reserved for the prima donna. *L'italiana in Algeri* was played throughout June and saved the San Benedetto from bankruptcy. 'I thought that, after hearing my opera the Venetians would treat me as a lunatic; they have demonstrated that they are even more mad than I,' he wrote.

After the overture, which Stendhal described as 'charming, but ... too frivolous', *L'italiana in Algeri* opens with a chorus of eunuchs attempting to console Elvira. Women, in a place like Algiers, are born to suffer, sings Elvira, wife of the Bey Mustafà; she is about to be discarded – in fact she bores him to death. ('My dear you've shattered my eardrums, I don't know what to do with you.') Mustafà resolves to give Elvira as wife to Lindoro, an Italian slave; he will send Lindoro back to Italy a free man and thus regain his own liberty as well. Mustafà asks his captain Haly to find him an Italian girl, and Haly answers complaining that his pirates have only a meagre catch. Of course Lindoro is Isabella's lover and she has just been captured herself. Accompanied by Taddeo, her *cicisbeo*, she has been searching the seas for Lindoro. At her first appearance on the shores of Algiers, Isabella demonstrates how she can dominate menfolk. In the meantime Haly learns that she and Taddeo are niece and uncle – a connection she has just invented. He also asks the two new prisoners, Isabella and Taddeo:

HALY: Di qual paese?	From which country?
TADDEO Di Livorno ambedue.	From Livorno, both of us.

HALY:
Dunque italiani?
. . .
Ah non so dal piacer dov'io mi stia.
Prescelta da Mustafà sarete, se io non
   sbaglio
la stella e lo splendor del suo serraglio.
	Then, Italians?
	. . .
	I'm so delighted and relieved
	Selected by Mustafà, if
	   I'm not mistaken, you'll be
	the star and splendour of
	   his seraglio.

When Taddeo is tricked into becoming a Kaimakan and Mustafà joins the Grand Order of the Pappataci, promising to eat, drink and sleep while Isabella and Lindoro behave as they wish, music and words entwine into a hilarious knot. Stendhal, who labelled this masterpiece a work of 'organized and complete madness', perceived the mockery which makes fun of formal and pompous power, showing the emptiness and pomposity of the Napoleonic new titles. Rossini's 'comic Muse brushes close against the least attractive monarchy', he commented.

Although Rossini had felt confident enough to play with the sound of words beforehand, never is this ploy so prominent as in this opera. He clearly derived huge pleasure from playing with the syllables of his language. Isabella's three suitors, who by the end of the first act are under her total control, watch her as she finishes dressing. She sings 'Per lui che adoro' ('For him whom I adore'), leading each of them – Mustafà, Lindoro and Taddeo – to think that the one she adores is himself. The finale of the act explodes in 'organized madness', each singer comparing his feeling to a sound which corresponds to a percussion instrument:

ELVIRA

Nella testa ho un campanello	In my head I've a bell
che suonando fa din din.	ringing ding ding dong.

ISABELLA AND ZULMA

La mia testa e' un campanello	In my head I've a bell
che suonando fa din din.	ringing ding ding dong.

LINDORO E HALY

Nella testa un gran martello	In my head a great hammer
mi percuote e fa tac ta.	is beating bing bang bong.

TADDEO

Sono come una cornacchia	I'm like a crow that's been
che spennata fa cra' cra.	plucked crying craw craw.

MUSTAFÀ

Come scoppio di cannone	Like cannon fire my head's
la mia testa fa bum bum.	going boom boom.

Isabella's strength lies not only in the fact that she will save the situation but that she is a patriot – something that did not escape the humiliated Venetians. 'Pensa alla patria,' she sings to the Italian slaves in a rondo judged subversive enough to be changed or omitted whenever the opera was performed outside Venice. The ear of the censors was not sharp enough, however, to catch that the little chorus preceding Isabella's aria, a short melody played by violins and flute, echoes the French Revolutionary anthem, *La Marseillaise*.

Although critical of the Bonapartist regime, Rossini was aware of the political changes and followed his father in his sympathy for the left. He had known clerical rule at Pesaro and Bologna too well not to be aware of the advantages that the French offered Milan. Even if the Austrians and the papacy were back, what the Italians had glimpsed – free education, free press (almost) and even free love – could not be taken away between one day and the next, nor could it be easily forgotten. A new liberal wave was sweeping the Venetian canals as well as the arcades in Bologna and Rossini, attentive to the spirit of the time, did not miss this opportunity, but his next two commissions took him back to Milan.

VI

CANTABILE

While Rossini was in Milan, the Austrians were on their way back to Lombardy, Napoleon having been defeated at the battle of Leipzig. The news of Napoleon's abdication in April 1814 did not take the Italians by surprise; but, tired as they were of being exploited by the French, they still preferred their Latin cousins to the German horde which was preparing once again to take over the peninsula. In *La Chartreuse de Parme*, Stendhal described the return of the Austrians and the clerics to Milan and how the old order re-established its rule through an omni-present secret police.

Those Italians 'contaminated' by Bonapartist ideals or by liberalism were gathering in cafés and salons and the secret societies were gaining new converts especially from the ranks of the professional classes, the newly formed Napoleonic bourgeoisie. Having left the court, opera could be used as a vehicle to voice the dreams and aspirations of this new bourgeoisie and was beginning to express the middle-class vocation for nationalism. The masses were being prompted into rebellion against foreign invaders, absolute monarchies, dictatorial governments. Music developed into a political weapon; operas could be political manifestos, triggering revolts if not revolutions. When Rossini arrived in Milan, La Scala had to receive the Emperor of Austria and Prince Metternich; those spectators who belonged to the middle class and some of the aristocrats protested by wearing their hats in the presence of Franz II causing general approval in the upper tiers.

Rossini was back in Milan because La Scala had commissioned another *opera seria* from him, *Aureliano in Palmira*, for the Carnival season of 1813–14. One of the three central characters, the Persian prince Arsace, was conceived for the flamboyant castrato Giambattista Velluti, who took such liberties with the music that Alessandro Rolla and Rossini quarrelled with him. The première took place on 26 December 1813 and delighted the singers but not the public. On the other hand, *Tancredi* was concurrently enjoying an enormous success at the Teatro Re. In a letter to his mother, Rossini recounted that while *Aureliano* had been a flop 'everybody says it is divine music but that the singers are dreadful so I don't lose credit. *Tancredi* is bursting out in the theatre they have just opened here; I am very happy if everybody is having a great time with my music in one or the other theatre, so who cares?'

Milan was delighted to welcome Rossini back. In April 1814, while overseeing the Milanese première of *L'italiana in Algeri* at the Teatro Re, his *Il turco in Italia* opened at La Scala; the former was resoundingly successful, but the latter was coolly received. Both the story and the music of *Il turco in Italia* have a strange, almost surreal, character. Prosdocimo, a sad *buffo*, is the poet looking for a story while walking along 'a lonely beach near Naples'; (I like to think that Rossini was including autobiographical elements in this character). In his wanderings, Prosdocimo encounters some gypsies; at their camp he meets Zaida, who has been abandoned by a Turk, and Fiorilla whose '*capricci* have been put on the stage by poets of all kind'. Finally he sees Geronio, Fiorilla's betrayed husband who is a gentleman. There is also a *cicisbeo* and, naturally, the Turk in question, Selim. When the poet discovers that Selim is Zaida's former lover, he knows that he has a story for the opera and exclaims: 'E'un bel colpo di scena, il dramma e' fatto!' ('a fine *coup de théâtre*, there's my plot!').

POETA	POET
Atto primo	Act one
il marito con l'amico . . .	enter husband with the lover . . .
scena prima,	scene one,
moglie . . . turco . . . grida . . . intrico.	wife . . . Turk . . . shouts . . . plot thickens
no: di meglio non si dà.	no: there's nothing that can beat this.

The game that Fiorilla is trying to play goes all wrong. Don Geronio does not want his wife back, the poet is up in arms, Selim judges the seduction too easy and, when he finds himself alone with Fiorilla, embarrassment is all they have in common. Besides, Fiorilla is not made of the same stuff as Isabella in *L'italiana*; she is insecure and somewhat silly. At the masked ball Fiorilla, who had planned to elope with the Turk, is approached by two other identical Turks (Geronio and the *cicisbeo* in disguise). Nobody recognizes anybody else and the wrong couples form. It is significant that the poet has no aria or duet, but sings entirely in recitative; the trios and quintets show Rossini's increasing involvement in ensemble writing, sometimes witty, sometimes serious. The character of the Turk is a metaphor for difference, and how modern – maybe too modern – that theme has become. Maria Callas, who was not its ideal interpreter, insisted on singing the role of Fiorilla, with which she might have felt a personal affinity: her 'Turk', the man who was different, was Onassis; her Don Geronio was Meneghini, the gentlemanly husband. And there was Zaida, of course, the gypsy from New York (Callas called her a witch) who took her Turk away. Too many poets were watching in order to tell her story, though none of Rossini's calibre.

In November 1814 Rossini was back in Venice for another *opera seria* with a text by Giuseppe Foppa, *Sigismondo*, which is little more than a mishmash of pieces from his earlier work; La Fenice paid him 600 lire for it. After its opening night on 26 December, Rossini told the composer Ferdinand Hiller: 'I was really touched by the Venetians who were at the première of *Sigismondo* which bored them a lot. I could see how happily they would have given voice to their annoyance; but they restrained themselves and kept quiet.'

On 16 May 1815, some two months after Napoleon's escape from Elba, Rossini wrote to Angelo Anelli from Bologna: 'This Carnevale I go to Roma and I want a *buffo* writing from you full of *capricci*, understand? Galli, Remorini, Donzelli tenor, and a good prima donna will certainly enhance our work.' These were famous singers. A month later and still in Bologna, a slightly impatient Rossini wrote again:

Carissimo Amico.
    I have to compose a new opera and you offer an old libretto, where is your genius gone and your fantasy? . . . Choose some good old plot or

choose one which fits my needs. Those are: for the tenor, a heroic-comic part.

For Galli, an exaggerated personality.

For Remorini the opposite.

And for the woman, a cock which could fit the so-called pussy of the woman who will fit our parts.

Rossini reflects his mood during this time in Bologna, where he relaxed and earned well by giving music lessons to Napoleon's niece, the daughter of Elisa, Grand Duchess of Tuscany. The libretto from Anelli never arrived and Rossini had to ask Cesare Sterbini to provide him with a text for Rome.

With Napoleon's escape and first successes, Italy felt *Un peu d'espoir et beaucoup de désespoir* ('a bit of hope and a lot of despair'), as the Neapolitan Finance Minister aptly commented. Following Napoleon's abdication, his brother-in-law Prince Murat, who had kept his Neapolitan throne by sending messages of goodwill to the British government, waited for the decisions of the victors – the British and Metternich. (From 1808 to 1815 the King of Naples was Murat, the handsome Gascon who was married to Caroline, Napoleon's youngest sister.) Hearing of Napoleon's first victories Murat turned coat again and, without waiting for the Emperor's reply, or declaring war on Austria, started hostilities in March 1815 and marched towards Milan announcing that his army counted 80,000 men. As his columns rushed north, Murat found no opposition and went on appealing for 'the high destiny of Italy to be fulfilled'. He hoped to unite the peninsula under his rule. But his and Bonaparte's rule had worn the Italians out.

As Murat's march reached Rimini, on the Adriatic coast near Pesaro, there was a popular uprising against the Austrians in Bologna. Since Rossini was at hand, and since he was the composer of *L'italiana in Algeri*, the opera that had stirred many Italians, he was asked to compose a cantata, a hymn to welcome the victorious Murat. The resultant *Inno d'indipendenza* was sung for the first time in Bologna on 15 April 1815, in Murat's presence. The two men met: the handsome cavalry sergeant who had become a prince and the composer, who by then had become the prince of music. Rossini wrote of this work: 'it was performed under my baton at the Contavalli Theatre. The word independence is in this hymn which, although not so poetic and sung by my own voice at the time!, was repeated by the people, chorus, etc., and aroused great enthusiasm.' Indeed, as Raffaello Monterosso pointed out, his hymn was so enthusiastically received that, for a short time, it was called the Italian Marseillaise; its performance was accompanied by cries of 'Viva l'Italia!'

The words were only recently rediscovered. Their predictably patriotic tone caused subsequent invectives against Rossini.

Sorgi Italia, venuta è già l'ora:	Italy, arise; the time has come,
l'alto fato compir si dovrà	high fate will come true
dallo stretto di Scilla alla Dora	from the straits of Sicily to the Alps
in sol regno d'Italia sarà.	and there will be only one Kingdom.
Del nemico alla presenza	When you take up arms in the presence
quando l'armi impugnerà	of the enemy, shout:
un sol regno e indipendenza	a sole kingdom, independence,
gridi Italia, e vincerà.	Italy and victory will be yours.

When the Austrians took the offensive at Carpi, Murat issued the Rimini declaration, calling the Italians to rise. Nobody did. Then, at Tolentino on 3 May, he lost all his artillery and 4,000 men were taken prisoners. He had no choice but to retreat back to Naples. So, a few days later, using the same Rossinian tune, the populace started singing:

Tra Macerata e Tolentino	Between Macerata and Tolentino
è finito il re Gioachino.	king Gioachino is finished.
Tra Chieti e Potenza	Between Chieti and Potenza
è finita l'indipendenza.	independence is all over.

The cynical adaptation of the music to mark Murat's defeat suggests that the tune was a good one; the words convey the people's tired disappointment in empty patriotism. The day after the first performance of the *Inno d'indipendenza*, the Austrians retook Bologna. Rossini was immediately listed as a subversive revolutionary. His name remained on the Austrian black list for some twenty years.

With the Austrians back in Northern and Central Italy, Rossini needed a change of climate. Conveniently, he was able to unearth an invitation to work for the most reactionary of all Italian rulers,

Ferdinand of Naples. Advised by his humble servant, the impresario Domenico Barbaja and probably by Isabella Colbran as well, the Bourbon king wished to avail himself of Rossini's services. Had Rossini not accepted this contract, mean as it was, there is no question that he would have been imprisoned, just as his father had been, and for the same reasons. 'I'm off to Naples, you'll write to me there,' he wrote to Anelli.

VII

ACCELLERANDO

N aples at this time was the second largest city in Europe, the most densely populated and also one of the most backward. Rossini's advantage in going there was that he would be working in a city ruled by Murat's enemies; this would exonerate him from his enthusiasm for the Bonapartist cause. King Ferdinand had vouched that, on his return from exile, he would take no revenge on those who had worked for the abominable regime of his Bonapartist predecessor. The Austrians and the Holy See took a different view. In June, one month after Rossini's arrival in the kingdom, Napoleon was defeated at Waterloo.

Rossini saw Naples as a city of sunlit terraces over a blue harbour, the kind of Naples epitomized in Mozart's *Così fan tutte*. The tempestuous sea of Europe seemed to have settled down after the Congress of Vienna and Waterloo, travellers – especially British aristocrats on the Grand Tour – flocked to Naples attracted by the blue sky, the gentle breeze and Vesuvius smoking in the background. Such nobility attended salons, the most intellectual and socially desirable of which were those of Marchese Berio, an Anglophile bachelor, and the Archbishop of Taranto, at the time a social monument as famous as Pompeii. Sipping iced wine on the terrace Gabriele Rossetti *père* could be seen talking to Lady Morgan. Such visitors invariably wanted to attend the famous San Carlo opera house. 'All of London was there,' remarked Stendhal. The vanquished French were fairly bitter about the wave of British travellers taking over their cultural territory. English earls and eager lady diarists revelled in the architectural features, ranging from Castel dell'Ovo, the fortress overlooking Marechiaro, to the crennelated monastery of San Martino, from which one could look down on the many churches and the maze of streets teeming with life and fantasy. The huge royal palace, its gardens hanging over the turquoise sea, had first been renovated in the Neoclassic style by Joseph Bonaparte and then by Caroline Murat, who plundered Versailles for her Neapolitan palace. The San Carlo opera house stood adjacent to it and, in the year of Rossini's arrival, the square had been closed to incorporate the hideous church of San Francesco di Paola, top-heavy and incongruous. The restored Bourbon king provided the money for its design, by Niccolini, and for its construction, intending the church as a thank-you present to his saint protector for welcoming his dynasty back to its capital city. By now a widower, the king had retitled himself Ferdinand I of the Two Sicilies. The death of his wife, Maria Carolina of Austria, Marie Antoinette's sister, was mourned by few. Talleyrand wrote to Louis XVIII, 'The Queen of Naples is scarcely regretted. Her death seems to have put M. de Metternich more at ease. The question of Naples is not solved. Austria wishes to place Naples and Saxony on the same level, and Russia wants to make them objects of compensation.' Ferdinand could now not only live openly with his mistress but marry her, bestowing the fanciful title Duchess of Floridiana on her. In spite of being a philistine, Ferdinand (affectionately known as Nasone, 'Big Nose') knew that with opera he could keep his subjects happy – or almost happy.

So Naples was endowed with many theatres and became the operatic capital of Europe. The main theatres were the San Carlo, the Fondo (later the Mercadante) and the Nuovo. Operas, which were lavishly staged, could also be seen at the Teatro dei Fiorentini and at the San Carlino. The orchestra of the San Carlo was considered the best in Europe – probably today one could claim the reverse. The city also became renowned for its conservatoire, which trained such musicians as Bellini and Spontini and, much later, Riccardo Muti. Maintaining a high opinion of itself, the Neapolitan school damned whatever came from outside. Rossini was initially made to feel unwelcome, especially by the composers who reigned in Naples like Ferdinando Mayr, Valentino Fioravanti, Mosca, Cimarosa and Paisiello; this last had already attacked Rossini's music as 'licentious'.

Naples was far too conservative to be ready for Rossini's inventions. It would certainly have objected to the overture of *II Signor Bruschino*, where the score requires string players tap their bows on their music stands.

Rossini had not been consulted about the subject of his first Neapolitan opera, *Elisabetta d'Inghilterra*, but its libretto was waiting. In the story, Elisabetta forgives and forgets; she is the benevolent and wise sovereign who knows how to turn the page and continue to rule – there are echoes of Titus in Mozart's *La clemenza di Tito* and of King Ferdinand who, back in Naples, had forgiven those who had followed Murat, Rossini included. The message did not escape anyone.

Rossini intended his first Neapolitan opera to please the English visitors and the Bourbons in particular. The story revolves around Queen Elizabeth's love for the Earl of Leicester and the title role was conceived with Isabella Colbran's exceptional vocal ability – and temperament – in mind. After the first performance, on 4 October 1815, even Stendhal could only praise the diva whom he otherwise loathed because of her Bourbon connections:

> The music was a kind of catalogue of all the resources of this magnificent voice, and we could hence judge what flawless interpretation she can achieve in music.

Happy with the success of his opera, Rossini wrote first to his father, mentioning that he 'stood for eight minutes to receive the cheering', and then to his mother:

> FURORE   Oh! what music! what music! Naples claims. It's impossible for me to explain the degree of enthusiasm produced by my music . . . But I must add that I have also toujours [sic] been called on the stage to be thrown oranges in my face.

As *Elisabetta* was being hailed at San Carlo, Rossini had cleverly seen to it that the Neapolitans were also being exposed to his earlier successes; concurrently, *L'italiana in Algeri* was being played at the more popular Teatro dei Fiorentini. Naples no longer resented Rossini; if anything, resentment turned into jealousy. He now started to delight the Neapolitan drawing-rooms with musical entertainment, singing and accompanying himself on the piano. Outside, the street musicians, conjurors, water-ice sellers, puppet booths performing night and day, and crowds assembled, cheering.

Storytellers and 'philosophers' recited the stories of Tasso and Ariosto in every corner of the smart *passeggiata*, the Riviera di Chiaia, and Mergellina. Lady Blessington remarked that 'The gaiety of the streets of Naples at night is unparalleled . . . groups of three or four persons with guitars, were seen seated on a terrace, or on a bench before their houses singing Neapolitan airs and barcaroles, in a style that would not have offended the ears of Rossini himself'. In Naples the English found what the puritan North denied them. But it took Dickens to warn the 'lovers of the picturesque' that behind the screen of songs was 'the miserable depravity, degradation and wretchedness, with which this gay Neapolitan life is insuperably associated'.

The Naples that Rossini first saw was full of the Neoclassical buildings that had sprung from the rediscovery of Pompeii and Herculaneum. The style had been adopted by the Bonapartist regimes; Murat had also used those symbols of the Roman Empire so dear to Napoleon. The order and clarity of Neoclassicism influenced the poetry of Rossini's contemporaries Vincenzo Monti and Ugo Foscolo, the music of Cherubini and Paisiello, the sculpture of Canova, the triumphalist paintings of the young David. Metternich's neoclassical attempt at the Congress of Vienna to impose order and clarity on Europe, was political but was also part of the same movement.

All Neapolitan theatres ran smoothly thanks to Barbaja. Even the critical Berlioz had to recognize that in Naples 'for the first time since coming to Italy, I heard music'. The French composer loved the 'zest, fire and brio' of the Neapolitan *opera buffa* and was impressed by the quality of the voices. Barbaja was a very shrewd individual who had amassed a fortune by operating gaming tables in the foyer of La Scala. He had also invented a patented concoction of hot coffee and chocolate whipped with cream, the *barbajada*, which he served in his own Milanese café; but his wealth actually derived from catering for the Napoleonic forces stationed in Milan. Having arrived in Naples in 1809, he was to dominate the Neapolitan musical scene for thirty-one years. He and Isabella lived in a Neoclassical palace at Posillipo, where he kept race-horses and paintings by Old Masters.

But soon he also kept Rossini, the most important treasure of his collection. He employed so many singers and composers that he often forgot whom he had engaged. Indeed when he offered a contract to a celebrity tenor (his company was teeming with tenors, hence Rossini's over-use of them in his Neapolitan operas), the celebrity answered that he was already in his employment. 'Then go to Donizetti and tell him to write a new part!'

The flamboyant Barbaja wanted Rossini to fulfil the terms of his contract and exceed it. In the end Rossini was producing, coaching singers, training the orchestras for his own and other productions as well as becoming a skilled artistic director, an experience that stood him in good stead when he got to Paris. When Rossini was absent from Naples, Barbaja was under no obligation to pay him. But whenever he was there, Rossini was expected to do everything, from conducting and composing to selecting singers and designers, with a lot of socializing too. 'Had he been able to, Barbaja would have put me in charge of his kitchen!' Rossini quipped. It was not just the kitchen that Barbaja would have liked Rossini to look after; maybe he actually intended the young composer to look after his domineering mistress as well.

Soon Naples was gossiping – not only had Barbaja's daughter quarrelled publicly with Colbran but Barbaja, Colbran and Rossini seemed to have set up a *ménage à trois*. Isabella had fallen in love with the dashing Gioachino, who was composing especially for her with more dedication than passion. As for Barbaja, he was not lacking in other distractions, he had all the stars and starlets to pick from and he certainly exercised this *droit de seigneur* all too often. He was not going to give Isabella up as his star and *agent provocateur* just because she had fallen in love with Rossini. Besides, Barbaja had already lent her to many people – including Nicolò Paganini and maybe the king himself. In a letter of 1 July 1818 Paganini wrote:

> I had a great time in the company of Madama Colbran who is as beautiful as Hebe and made me fall in love with her when we sang a duet ... Through Madama Colbran, Mr Barbaja invited me there, promising me the use of all his theatres without paying if I arrive before the end of September.

Badly treated not only by Rossini's biographers but, in the late years of their marriage, by Rossini himself, Isabella was then a superstar – she commanded a much higher fee than Rossini. In fact, Gioachino was grateful for the attention of such a successful – and rich – prima donna. Rossini had conquered Naples – and La Colbran.

VIII

GAVOTTA

The journey from Naples to Rome was notoriously dangerous, the frontier between the Neapolitan kingdom and the Holy See guarded by corrupt officials and infested with spies. Several passports and letters were required, coaches were plagued with insects.

The Russian writer Alexander Herzen gave a vivid account of what it was like to cross the frontier at Terracina:

> A Neapolitan carabinier came to the diligence four times, asking every time for our visas. I showed him the Neapolitan visa: this and the half carlino were not enough for him; he carried off the passports to the office and returned twenty minutes later with the request that my companion and I should go and see the brigadier. The latter, a drunken, old, non-commissioned officer, asked me rather rudely:
> 'What is your surname and where do you come from?'
> 'Why, that is all in my passport.'
> 'I can't read it.'
> We conjectured that reading was not the brigadier's strong point.
> 'By what law,' asked my companion, 'are we bound to read you our passports aloud? We are bound to have them and to show them, but not to dictate them; I might dictate anything.'
> 'Accidenti!' muttered the old man, 'va ben, va ben!' and he gave back our passports without writing anything.

All those travelling between Naples and Rome at this time would have had similar experiences. Terracina was guarded by corrupt officials and infested with spies; for those making the journey, coaches were expensive and plagued with insects.

In November 1815 Rossini was in Rome, of which Stendhal wrote: 'Here all is decadence, all is memory, all is dead; effort is unknown, energy without purpose, nothing moves with haste.' It is still so.

Napoleon had tried to convert the decaying city into a capital when he restored the Pantheon and created the Piazza del Popolo, the latter deliberately reminiscent of a Parisian square. Of the countless English visitors to Rome in the early nineteenth century, Shelley was particularly enchanted by the Colosseum, 'overgrown by the wild olive, the myrtle and the fig tree', while Lady Morgan's diary declared that the avenue of San Giovanni in Laterano had 'no parallel in the history of desolation and that the corridors of the Teatro Argentina were used as a public pissoir.' Rome was like a large village, made up of scattered palaces built from the remains of the past, temples and ancient buildings used as though they were quarries. 'Quel che non fecero i barbari, fecero i Barberini' ('What the barbarians didn't destroy, the Barberini did'), the Romans used to say. The Barberini were a nouveau riche papal family who destroyed a whole ring of the Colosseum in order to build their own palace.

In 1815 Rome was once again the capital of a state ruled by Pope Pius VII who, exiled in 1809, had suffered the ignominy of being imprisoned by Napoleon. Under his newly reinstated regime, the papal censorship regulations became increasingly oppressive; Stendhal was furious when his copy of Montesquieu's collected works was confiscated at the border with the Papal States. But it was Cardinal Consalvi, the Vatican's Secretary of State, a man who had never taken holy orders, who was really in charge. That year, a momentous one for Europe, the cardinal had represented the papacy at the Congress of Vienna. His success was illustrated by a popular print showing him surrounded by four pretty maidens who represented the regions of Romagna and the Marche and the cities of Pontecorvo and Benevento. This scene, watched by a Minerva-like Austria, was intended to show that the sharp-witted cardinal had secured those territories for the Church. Although no liberal himself, Cardinal Consalvi knew that the Napoleonic policy of liberalizing institutions could not be arrested; in the face of opposition from other cardinals, he aimed at restoring a more flexible form of government. Indeed Rossini's presence in Rome would not have been possible without Consalvi's relatively enlightened attitude to the arts in general and music in particular. Rossini, the man that every impresario now wanted, had been commissioned to write *Torvaldo e Dorlinska* for the Teatro Valle, 'a foul little theatre' according to Lady Morgan, and notorious for its bad orchestra.

Rossini had rented rooms in via del Leutario, near the Pantheon, and, as was the custom, every morning a barber would call on him and gossip while shaving him (just as Figaro does at Dr Bartolo's). During one of these visits, the barber mentioned that they would meet again later that day. Rossini was puzzled until the barber revealed that he not only shaved people's chins but, in his spare time, was the first clarinet of the orchestra scheduled to rehearse *Torvaldo e Dorlinska* in a matter of hours. Rossini was alarmed. How could a barber be any good as a first clarinettist? How could a decent orchestra employ somebody whose day-time job would prevent him from practising and studying music? Moreover, were Rossini to correct the clarinettist's playing during rehearsals, he might risk offending the man who every day held a knife to his throat. Rossini soon realized that all the members of the orchestra were amateurs. According to Donizetti, the Valle's orchestra included jewellers, decorators and carpenters whose musical activities were reserved for their leisure time. So Rossini feared for *Torvaldo e Dorlinska*. The first performance, on 26 December 1815, was coolly received. His next letter to his mother included a coded message about it: a *fiasco* drawn on the envelope which needed no further comment; as the flask was only medium sized, Rossini was hinting that he did not regard this opera a total flop. Besides, he was already working on what was to become his most celebrated and loved opera, *Il barbiere di Siviglia*.

In November 1815 Duke Francesco Cesarini-Sforza had asked Rossini to write an *opera buffa* for his theatre and the contract was soon signed. The duke was the owner and impresario of the Teatro Argentina. Papal Rome regarded theatres as places of sin; the Vatican pretended they did not exist in the holy city. Theatres were therefore built as precarious wooden frames, as if they were temporary structures: such hypocrisy was fed also by the fact that theatre owners were invariably lay members of the community, generally aristocrats who hired impresarios, but never members of the clergy who nevertheless regularly attended performances. Music was often twinned with gaming (forbidden in Rome) and whoring (not forbidden in Rome).

The terms of the contract for *Il barbiere* were quite generous. Rossini agreed to submit the score by the middle of January, although the subject of the opera had not yet been discussed. The contract, one of the few surviving documents of its kind, specified:

> *Maestro Rossini will be obliged to conduct his opera according to custom, and to be present in person at all the vocal and orchestral rehearsals, whenever it will be necessary; and also undertakes to be present at the first performances given consecutively, and to direct the performances from the keyboard. In recompense for his labours Duke Cesarini-Sforza undertakes to pay him the sum of 400 Roman scudi once the first three performances have taken place, which he will direct from the keyboard. The impresario will provide lodgings for maestro Rossini for the duration of the contract.*

In spite of Cardinal Consalvi's liberal influence, the choice of a subject, especially one for an *opera buffa* (the genre which offered most possibilities to be subversive) was more difficult in Rome than in Naples. Rossini then asked Cesare Sterbini to write a libretto based on Beaumarchais' play, a choice probably inspired by Mozart's *Le nozze di Figaro*, second in the French playwright's trilogy of incendiary comedies. In order to avoid comparisons with other settings of the play, Rossini and Sterbini gave the opera the title *Almaviva ossia L'inutil precauzione* and in the printed introduction Rossini showed an exaggerated respect for Paisiello, whose *Barbiere* was still performed; indeed, in a 'Notice to the Public', Rossini explained the change of title as coming from 'a feeling of respect and veneration which motivates the composer of the present opera towards the very famous Paisiello who has already set this subject to music under its original title.' The latest setting, by Francesco Morlacchi, was premièred in Dresden in April 1816, shortly after the première of Rossini's version in Rome. But the fact was that the old school was not so much fearing yet another *Barbiere*, as resisting the impact of the new weapon that Rossini was constructing. Paisiello's music, after all, represented the antithesis of Rossini's wild innovations. After having called him 'il tedeschino' ('the little German'), the ultimate insult, Paisiello's fans nicknamed Rossini 'il Signor Baccano' ('Mr Clamour'); 'Signor Crescendo', 'Signor Chiassoni' ('Mr Noisy'). Pretending indifference, Rossini's answer was 'And this is so. I make such a din that no one falls asleep during my operas.'

The plot revolves around Count Almaviva who, enamoured of the pretty Rosina and having difficulty in entering the household of her guardian-tutor Bartolo, engages the city's barber as his fixer. Figaro, like all barbers of the day, calls on his clients, making a business of knowing everything and everybody. It is Figaro who suggests what to do in order to conquer Rosina and defeat her tutor's pretentions; all ends well.

On one occasion Rossini said that he composed *Il barbiere* in thirteen days, on another, nineteen. But most of this opera had probably been in his mind over a longer period. He took the overture from his *Elisabetta d'Inghilterra* and there are a few other self-borrowings. Rossini wanted to offer his audience at the Teatro Argentina a truly sparkling comedy with superb music. He had at his disposal a competent orchestra – not so good as the one at San Carlo, but certainly not as bad as the one at the Teatro Valle – and he also had excellent singers, among whom was the tenor Manuel García, Maria Malibran's father.

The first night of Rossini's *Il barbiere di Siviglia*, on 20 February 1816, turned into something that resembled a riotous football match. Geltrude Righetti-Giorgi, as Rosina, was booed at her very first entrance. García, who was singing Almaviva – a role for which Spanish voices seem to be specially suited – showed his despair. A cat walked on the stage – no doubt encouraged by the 'opposition'. Luigi Zamboni, the baritone who sang Figaro, attempted to chase the cat off stage, with little success, causing the audience to imitate its miaows. One of the singers fell on a loose board – no fortuitous happening either – and hurt himself very badly. From the keyboard, Rossini, resplendent in a new saffron jacket with gold buttons, was seen trying to encourage the disheartened singers. He was vociferously accused of applauding himself and mocked for his showy garment. Of course many first nights were filled with claques generally paid by the singers themselves who would not so much cheer as try to destroy a rival's performance, but on this occasion the partisans of Paisiello, who represented the old school so averse to Rossini, were out in force to hiss and jeer. The organized opposition wanted to ruin Rossini's opera. They were so noisy that it became practically impossible to hear anything during the first act.

The characters which Rossini developed in *Il barbiere* were those he had observed and met all over Italy: the rogue priest, the charlatan notary, the miser who talks about the-good-old-times and the pert, sharp Rosina who always knows what to do (rather like Isabella of l'Italiana in Algeri). They would not be found in Seville but sprang from the characters of the *commedia dell'arte*. They endure in the people who crowd the streets of Naples and around the Pantheon in Rome – irritating and dangerous but also lovable and crafty. And, of course, *Il barbiere di Siviglia* survived the catastrophes of its opening to become one of the most popular works in the operatic repertoire. Singling out Figaro's cavatina 'Largo al factotum' for particular praise, Stendhal wrote: 'What a wealth of wit, fire and delicacy in the passage: "Per un barbiere di qualità." What an abundance of expression in the phrase: "Colla donnetta, col cavaliere." ' Figaro is a character who pursues his aims with determination.

Don Basilio the priest suggests what can best destroy a man. The weapon is calumny, *la calunnia*, a snake which crawls through the streets of the city (the Italian words are suggestively onomatopoeic) and then explodes 'like a thunderstorm, a cannon-ball'; the bass drum on the words 'un colpo di cannone' make one jump. When the symbol of calumny is crushed, the music calms down and from the tempestuous sea of destruction emerges a placid horizon ready to raise again the opaque waves of gossip and *calunnia*. One can even feel sympathy for Dr Bartolo as the disguised Count Almaviva makes a fool of him, repeatedly calling him by the wrong name. Also Berta, Bartolo's tired and underpaid servant, who is Rossini's invention, is a semi-tragic figure. Berta sings the *aria del sorbetto*, so called because it was given to a minor interpreter while the audience left their seats for a water-ice and on the stage the scenery would be changed. As Berta mops up the rain drops which have percolated through the roof, she complains of her old age and watches how, in spite of the rain, love is setting the house on fire.

Fearing another protest for the second night of *Il barbiere*, Rossini barricaded himself in his room. His impresario, wanting to let him know that this time there had been an immense ovation, found him asleep. He insisted that Rossini should get dressed and hurry to the Teatro Argentina – a short walk from his lodgings – because the public was overwhelmed and wanted to thank him. 'Fuck the public!'

declared Rossini – maybe the only time in his life he expressed his true feelings. Contrary to the impression he wanted to project, that of a self-assured man confronting a humiliating experience with total nonchalance, Rossini suffered a great deal. The fact that the disastrous first night was immediately followed by a triumph did not lessen Rossini's bitterness. To his mother he poured out his initial reaction in this previously unpublished letter:

> *Carissima Madre*
>   *Last night my opera was performed and was solemnly booed; oh what mad things, what extraordinary things are to be seen in this country. I will tell you that in the midst of it all my music is very fine and already people are talking about its second performance when the music will be heard, something that did not happen last night. From the beginning to the end there was a constant noise that accompanied the whole performance . . .*

At this point the letter breaks off. He did not complete it until he was able to continue with better news: 'I wrote that my opera was booed, now I can write that, on the second night and all following performances, they cheered this work of mine with an enthusiasm for which I came out five, six times to receive applause of a totally new kind and that made me cry with pleasure.'

In reality, with the attack on *Il barbiere*, a work in which he had put so much of himself, Rossini's faith in the public had been broken for ever. In later years he would disclose to Angelo Catelani, a composer who was also to suffer from depression, that he had hidden his own state behind a mask of gaiety. Rossini pretended to take flops in his stride. In fact he learnt to conceal the rage he felt, especially when he knew that he had delivered something good. He had to compose in order to survive; furthermore, his parents and grandmother were increasingly dependent on him. But his overall desire was to become rich. He also wanted to fool the public by presenting a debonair version of himself – and both public and biographers were duly cheated.

On his return to Naples early in March 1816, Rossini found the Teatro San Carlo gutted; it had been destroyed by fire a few weeks earlier, on 12 February. Although people blamed the Jacobins and the troops were ordered to take up arms, it was in fact caused by sparks from a lamp. But the empty space next to the royal palace was immediately crowded with builders and artisans; the San Carlo was feverishly rebuilt so as to reopen in time for King Ferdinand's birthday in January, as he had wished. That wish came true, largely thanks to Barbaja, who gave the money for the reconstruction, and the theatre was ready within a year. Why doesn't La Fenice in Venice have a Barbaja today! Rebuilt in the Neoclassical style, reminiscent of the Napoleonic period, the San Carlo reopened to a delighted audience. Stendhal wrote: 'My eyes are dazzled, my soul is ravished. Nothing is more fresh yet nothing is more majestic, two qualities which are not easy to mix.' The auditorium was silver and blue, the boxes lined in dark blue and their balconies adorned with golden torches entwined with the Bourbon lilies. On the ceiling Giuseppe Cammarrano whom Harold Acton calls 'a ponderous exponent of neo-classicism' had been commissioned to paint Apollo presenting Minerva to the world's most celebrated poets, from Homer to Alfieri.

In his recently expanded responsibilities in Naples, Rossini was now obliged to compose pieces to celebrate such events as a royal wedding, birth or coronation. The first of these was *Le nozze di Teti e di Peleo*, a Neoclassical cantata composed for the marriage of the hereditary prince's eldest daughter to the Duke of Berry, a dynastic marriage which was to link the two Bourbon houses, French and Neapolitan. Maria Carolina, daughter of the crown prince Francesco, was to be married on 24 April 1816 to the second son of the Count of Artois, brother of Louis XVIII of France. (As Louis had no issue and was famously impotent, his brother was next in line to the throne of France which indeed he eventually inherited. Later Rossini would be called upon to write another cantata for the same king who took the name of Charles X.) The religious ceremony was celebrated by proxy, though members of the royal family and the entire court attended that night's performance of *Le nozze di Teti e Peleo* at the Teatro del Fondo. The soprano part was sung by Isabella Colbran, and a contemporary lithograph by G. Carloni shows how beautiful she was, Neoclassical in style and resplendent in her revealing Empire dress, a shawl demurely draped over her shoulders. The portrait was made when she was about thirty.

Rossini attached considerable importance to *Le nozze di Teti e Peleo* as it represented his début as the official composer of the Bourbons. But, as it was intended for only one performance, he incorporated the Rondo of *Il barbiere* and later also transposed several numbers of the cantata.

Le nozze di Teti e Peleo was therefore staged in a new auditorium in the gardens of the Neoclassical Villa Caprile during the Pesaro Festival of 2001, a delightful setting among cypresses and Roman pines. The ample stage was crowded with graceful followers of Venus, Love and Hymen, as if once again preparing for the marriage of the Duke of Berry to Maria Carolina of Naples. When Peleus invokes the gods to help him find Thetis, the sea goddess arrives escorted by maritime divinities. Rossini included this last detail to stress that the Neapolitan royal house derived its power from the sea. Deity after deity appears and Ceres, patron of the Kingdom of the Two Sicilies, foresees the glory of the newly united kingdom – a prophecy which was soon to be shattered.

IX

CRESCENDO

D uring 1816–17, with continuing ingenuity and irrepressible energy, Rossini moved between Naples, Rome, Milan and Bologna, though Naples remained his base. These were astonishingly productive years. Incessant work and dangerous travel became something of an obsession; he raced around as if he knew that his creative life was going to be curtailed.

Rossini's next *opera buffa* was *La gazzetta*, first performed at the Teatro dei Fiorentini on 26 September 1816. Based on Carlo Goldoni's *Il matrimonio per concorso* (1763), conceived for the French public. This version was written in Neapolitan dialect and mocks the new Neapolitan bourgeoisie and the power of the press. 'I don't really understand the shape of the dialogue and the development of this action,' Rossini wrote to his mother. He was indeed lost with the dialect, which were often ad-libbed. The principal character, Don Pomponio Storione, was played by the actor-singer Carlo Casaccia, a Charlie Chaplin of his time. *La gazzetta* was not a favourite among the Neapolitans and, apart from Casaccia's contribution, the public was disappointed with the long-winded action and undue length of the recitatives. Rossini himself was not too keen to see *La gazzetta* staged again because it contained a lot of music that he intended to use elsewhere. In any case, he remained the toast of Naples, where young girls collected reproductions of the many portraits of him, paintings as well as lithographs and aquatints. Kand's lithograph, based on a contemporary drawing by Jausse, encapsulates the essence of Rossini as a young Werther and other images idiolized him into the icon of an early dandy.

Rossini's next Neapolitan commission was for an *opera seria*. He decided to base the work on the story of Otello, the Moor, in its original Venetian version. By then only twenty-four, he had already written nineteen operas and with this bold choice he seemed to be shifting away from the Neoclassical movement. (Shakespeare's *Othello* was almost unknown in Italy at this time; Verdi's setting is much later, 1887.) Rossini asked Marchese Berio di Salsa to provide the libretto. According to Stendhal, Berio was 'a charming companion in society but unfortunate and abominable as a poet'. The latter observation is confirmed by Berio's verses, while Lady Morgan's diaries endorse the former: at Palazzo Berio 'a congregation of elegant and refined spirits' formed his intellectual salon. Rossini attended that salon increasingly on his own terms, no longer merely entertaining the elite with his piano playing and singing, but as an equal. This was part of the modern, post-Napoleonic era: the artist was to become an equal, even a prince of society; he would dress eccentrically – Byron had led the way sporting Albanian costume and turbans, confounding conventional society left behind in England. The artist was unique. Should he be unsuccessful, he would become a desperate, misunderstood and even sought after individual. Soon the successful artist would be regarded as a slave to despotism – as would happen to Rossini. Byron, incidentally, was shocked by Rossini's *Otello*, especially by the fact that in the opera a love letter substitutes for the handkerchief. In a letter to Samuel Rogers, Byron wrote:

> *They have been crucifying* Othello *into an opera . . . Music good but lugubrious – but as for the words! – all the real scenes with Iago cut out – & the greatest nonsense instead – the handkerchief turned into a* billet doux, *and the first Singer would not black his face – for some exquisite reasons assigned in the preface. Scenery – dresses – and Music very good . . . The author (of the libretto) does not know his job.*

The libretto was – and is – often panned. Stendhal remarked: 'some petty consideration of backstairs patriotism (which earned him great favour in Venice) induced our worthy poet to revert to the original Italian legend which had provided Shakespeare with the basic plot of his tragedy.' Nevertheless, he was spellbound by the music: 'In *Otello*, we are so electrified by the magnificent musical quality of the songs, . . . so overwhelmed by the incomparable beauty of the theme, that we invent our own libretto to match.'

The protagonist of Rossini's *Otello* is undoubtedly Desdemona, the fragile victim, while for Verdi it is Iago, and for Shakespeare it is, of course, Othello. Rossini's Desdemona is particularly moving in the third act and her last lament, delivered in the knowledge of her imminent death, almost invariably brings listeners to tears. Rossini insisted on retaining the off-stage gondolier's song, one of the most poignant melodies in the opera; in a misty and gloomy Venice, the boatman quotes Francesca's words of misery in Dante's *Inferno*: 'Nessun maggior dolore che ricordarsi del tempo felice nella miseria' ('There is no greater pain than to remember happy times gone by in days of sorrow'). Berio objected that no gondolier would know the *Divina commedia* by heart.

Among the composers hugely impressed by *Otello* were Schubert, who referred to its 'extraordinary genius' (1819) and Meyerbeer:

The third act of Otello *established its reputation so firmly that a thousand errors couldn't shake it. The third act is really godlike, and what is so extraordinary is that its beauties are quite unlike Rossini. First-rate declamation, continuously impassioned recitative, mysterious accompaniments full of local colour and, in particular, the style of the old romances brought to the highest perfection.*

Alfred de Musset, writing in 1839, thought that Rossini's *Otello* was a masterpiece, 'impossible to overpraise. Shakespeare's *Othello* is a living portrait of jealousy, a horrifying vivisection of the human heart. Rossini's is [. . .] the sad tale of a slandered girl who dies in innocence.'

Rossini had little time to enjoy the furore following the first run of *Otello* (which opened to a packed house on 4 December 1816) because he had to travel once again to Rome. It is at this point that he met Stendhal at Terracina. As already noted, these were dangerous journeys. A few years earlier Isabella's father, Juan Colbran, had written to Giovanni Ricordi, the music publisher, saying that he and his daughter were determined to stay in Naples 'because the road from here to Rome is infested with bandits who are not satisfied with robbery but also murder those who fall into their hands.' Another traveller, the Englishman Henry Sass on the same route, stumbled 'on a sight shocking to humanity and disgraceful to the government in whose territory it occurred. Strewn in our path and stretched in the arms of death, lay a traveller, the victim of assassination.'

At the time of his meeting with Stendhal, Rossini was on his way to Rome for a new opera, *La Cenerentola*. Within a matter of weeks he was expected at La Scala for *La gazza ladra*; before the end of 1817 he was due back in Naples for an *opera seria* and in Rome again for *Adelaide di Borgogna* – enough to kill a horse. What did Rossini tell Stendhal? How did he explain his music to a stranger at an inn when he barely had time to breathe between one masterpiece and the next? How did he manage the frenetic pace? Among the other diners there were probably one or two spies – most likely two, as every stage coach usually had one each. Maybe Rossini told Stendhal that it was not the king who paid him but Domenico Barbaja, a famous impresario, semi-literate, brilliant and a crook. Stendhal certainly knew about Barbaja. Who didn't? Barbaja was more famous than any singer and richer than the Bourbon king himself. While discussing the famous composer Rossini and still unaware that he was addressing the man himself, on this occasion Stendhal evidently did not mention 'the laziness of that beautiful genius nor his numerous plagiarisms'. By this time, Rossini had written more operas than Bellini did in his whole life – no one could accuse Rossini of laziness in 1816–17. Stendhal's mention of plagiarism is also odd, first of all because Rossini 'stole' only from himself and almost always from operas which had been dismissed by the public, works that he thought would not be heard again.

Stendhal had no reason to make up this detailed encounter, even if he was wrong about his dates; the meeting cannot possibly have taken place in February 1817, as Rossini had reached Rome by then. It is likely that the composer, who met hundreds of different people every day and was surrounded by fervent admirers, soon erased the Terracina encounter from his mind. Furthermore, Rossini later clashed with Stendhal about what angered him most, to be mistaken for a reactionary.

Stendhal's *Vie de Rossini* has a whole chapter, treated as an apologetic digression, on the 'wars' between harmony and melody. In summary, Stendhal preferred melody ('the sweet succulence of the peach'). The chapter also conveys a sense of the Enlightenment slipping away from a world threatened by the dark clouds of Romanticism. Rossini's music was paving the way for that movement which was to change the century.

When Rossini and Stendhal met two years had passed since Waterloo; everything had changed. Still divided between the Austrians and the Bourbons, with countless little states including leftovers from the Napoleonic empire and the Church, Italy's dream of unification remained remote. Napoleon had given Italy a national flag, a legal code and education for all, women included. He had pulled down the walls of the ghettos, an act to be reversed by the Austrians; but even if he had looted and had sent thousands of young Italians to their deaths in his imperial campaigns, the germ of liberty was left behind him. Liberty was an infectious idea, the one utopia which was absorbing students, intellectuals and women, some of them turned this iconoclastic cause into a religion. Some joined secret societies which proliferated among the middle classes whose aim was the unification of Italy and liberation from injustice, topics which were widely discussed in many salons – the cafés having become nests of spies. The salon became a secure place for liberals to confront their ideas both in Naples and Milan. It also gave educated and well-to-do women a new niche and a new social eminence.

The voice of liberty was not to be found in Italian newspapers and journals, which were severely censored, but in music which surreptitiously introduced the new Romantic concepts: the rights of the single individual, the idea of the motherland, of the nation, of a unified common cause. While the Roman Church could still convince the peasantry that the more they suffered in this life, the happier they would be in the next, this bribe was beginning to lose its sway among the educated. Music could distract them, indeed, Stendhal and Byron alleged that opera had become the opium of Italian inventiveness. The Italian 'genius', as they called it, was unable to involve itself in most of the literary arts because of suppression or censorship, and therefore turned towards music. That was why music – and at that time music in Italy meant opera – was dominated by Italians. There was no need for the novel to flourish, as in nineteenth-century France and England, the middle classes were entertained by opera.

When in Rome, Rossini found that the ecclesiastical authorities had censored the libretto as the impresario Pietro Cartoni had proposed so a new libretto had to be found. Jacopo Ferretti (who had failed Rossini over a libretto for *Il barbiere* and was now keen to make amends) wrote a delightful – though probably not reliable – account of how the choice of subject came into being. Shivering from a cold winter's night just before Christmas, the three men – Cartoni, Rossini and the poet – sat and drank tea, dismayed at finding themselves without a libretto for an opera which was to be performed the following month. They began to think of 'twenty or thirty subjects'. Some were discarded as being too serious for the opening of the Carnival season, others too complex for the company available at the Teatro Valle. After several hours, exhausted, Cartoni went to bed. Ferretti was half asleep and Rossini had wrapped himself in blankets when the poet murmured: '*Cenerentola?*'

> ROSSINI (sitting upright like Dante's Farinata degli Uberti): Do you really feel like writing a *Cenerentola* for me?
> FERRETTI Would you have the courage to set it to music?
> ROSSINI When can I have the outline . . .?
> FERRETTI You can have it in the morning if I go without sleep tonight.
> ROSSINI Good night! (Wrapping himself in the blankets and falling asleep 'like Homer's gods'.)

Ferretti drank another cup of tea and, after waking the impresario to haggle over his wage, he ran off home to write a synopsis for a work which turned out to be Rossini's most popular *opera buffa* for years to come. Ferretti's recollections were to mythologize Rossini as the distant and unconcerned composer. In fact Ferretti was not creating a new libretto but drawing from two existing settings of Perrault's tale. The sensitive and forgiving Cinderella, in whom one can find traces of Rossini's mother, was very much the composer's creation. Indeed *Cenerentola* departs from the norms of *opera buffa* because its main character, Angelina, is a person who suffers. She despairs when she falls in love, unable to utter a word because she is confused; unlike her two stepsisters, or Dandini the prince's valet, Angelina is a real and humane character. She is what the English call an underdog; she is favoured by the prince in disguise not because morality thus dictates, but because everything is upside down in this crazy version of the story. *Cenerentola*'s real theme is that of madness. In the delirium which moves the characters, the audience accepts the surrealism of several situations in the opera. For example, at the court ball we don't question why only two young ladies seem to have been invited while a third and uninvited guest appears later – a fateful addition who will steal the prince's heart. We accept such invented words as 'dindolar' for their onomatopoeic evocation of pealing bells; instead of gossiping, the stepsisters emit a repeated 'ci-ciu ci-ciu'. In his brilliant analysis of the work, Bruno Cagli stated that

> *in a different world, in an impenetrable world in which reason is disturbed at every step, the protagonists are doomed to plunge into madness, to twist and untwist without any way of escape. Hell is represented by the irrational, the punishment is to be overwhelmed by dark forces that reason cannot even disentangle, let alone conquer. Having left myth and illusion behind him, the sceptical Rossini brings everyone's destiny down to the same level in his comic opera. It represents the absolute summit of Rossini's achievement in opera buffa.*

The première of *La Cenerentola* on 25 January 1817 was noisily received. Followed by twenty consecutive performances in Rome, it was then replayed all over Europe. Indeed, it was the first opera to tour the world, without copyrights, of course, and subject to changes that singers and orchestras imposed on it. Professor Cagli continues:

> *Thus Rossini brought to completion his work of demolishing the old Neapolitan opera buffa . . . replacing it with a world exposed to the blind caprices of fate, in which not even the mental brilliance that had carried on the game . . . could be of use any more. It is no coincidence that, whereas* Il Turco in Italia *and* Il Barbiere *are partly set in a bourgeois atmosphere, with* La Cenerentola *we return to a fictitious ancien régime made up of rulers, nobility and titles, all crumbling like the walls of the palace of Montefiascone, home of the tipsy Don Magnifico.*

It is no surprise that *La Cenerentola* would be Rossini's last Italian *opera buffa*. After this amazing *tour-de-force* nothing could be added. His later French comic operas would follow a very different route.

Now his reputation in Italy was really established and, on 11 February, Rossini left Rome for Bologna – another long journey but not as dangerous as that between Naples and Rome. Passports were not needed since Bologna, the Holy See's intellectual seat, was within the Papal States. Although he wrote to them frequently, Rossini had not seen his parents (who no longer lived under the same roof) for two years; and Isabella Colbran had a magnificent villa just outside Bologna. Rossini was still sharing Isabella with others and she likewise. Sex was completely open in those days, especially in theatrical circles. Not until later in the nineteenth century did sopranos marry dukes and marquesses; at this time singers were courtesans, whether male or female. Falling in love, love-making and courting were central to any social and artistic endeavour.

At this stage Rossini had not yet introduced Isabella to his parents. He was not ashamed of her, a woman who, although a star, was known as a grand courtesan; but he was ashamed of his parents' simplicity. Rossini knew that Anna had neither the clothes nor the sophistication to be shown off; for example, he would not dream of taking her to Berio's salon or to the premières of his operas at which the king, the court and Isabella herself were present. Anna had not had any opportunity to learn the ways of polite society; she had spent part of her life with a simpleton as husband.

The prospect of being back in Bologna had the further appeal of re-establishing contact with the friends of his childhood. He wrote to one of them wondering whether a certain Clementina would still receive him: 'Does she remember me? does she think I'm a fool? were it to be so, I forgive her because I'd die without the hope that she might not look after me.' Besides La Colbran and Clementina, whoever she might have been, there was an endless succession of prostitutes; avoiding attachment to a single woman is typical of a son who adores his absent mother. Rossini certainly preferred prostitutes to *grandes dames*, although there are episodes which suggest that grand ladies lost their heads over him, even abandoning husbands, children and households for his sake. The onset of the gonorrhoea which was to plague him in the 1830s and the 1840s probably dates from this time.

The brief visit to Bologna was merely a stop-over *en route* to Milan. When Rossini reached Milan, Bonaparte's institutions, palaces and schools were being demolished by the Austrians. There is nothing left of Napoleon's imperial palace, which had been frescoed in Neoclassical style by Appiani; it was in the very heart of the city near Castel Sforzesco, in what is now called the Foro Bonaparte. Yet Napoleon left a stronger mark on Milan than on any other Italian city. The newly emerged middle class was modelled on the French; cosmopolitan, rich and culturally impressive. Being averse to Austrian rule, many of them became professional conspirators. 'In the café various habitués of the revolution were sitting with dignity at a dozen little tables, looking darkly and consequentially about them from under wide-brimmed felt hats and caps with tiny peaks,' observed Alexander Herzen. On his arrival there, Byron was immediately introduced to Ludovico de Breme, a distinguished young man, invariably dressed in black, the son of a former Minister of the Interior for Napoleon's Italian kingdom. 'Lord Byron is amiability itself,' de Breme wrote to Madame de Staël. Another Milanese revolutionary, Silvio Pellico, whose name was given to many Italian streets, described the twenty-year-old Byron as having 'the most modest . . . aspect and manners, a prodigious knowledge and with this, they say, an infernally malicious spirit'. (Pellico and several other Milanese intellectuals translated Byron's poetry into Italian.)

Milan was full of spies. Around the tables of famous cafés like Martini's or Cova's sat elegant conspirators within earshot of police informants pretending to be conspirators in order to hear all the plotting and scheming. Spies were also widely distributed among the boxes at La Scala, some trying to enter de Breme's box, known to be a focal point for opposition to the Austrians. Stendhal was often de Breme's guest and, at his famous box, would meet Vincenzo Monti, Byron, Pellico and other left-wing intellectuals. 'I bring to these gentlemen news of France, on the retreat from Moscow, on Napoleon, the Bourbons; they pay me back with news from Italy.' Rossini, too, was to frequent this circle. Salons were safer than cafés because the grand and not-so-grand ladies who opened their houses knew who was to be welcomed and who, on the other hand, had sold their services to the Austrians. The latter were generally gamblers who needed to refill their empty purses with Austrian *svanzich*. And yet, the return of the Austrians had meant that gambling had been banned from the foyers of all theatres and free speech had also been stamped out (not that, under the French, speech had been totally free). Secret societies centred around the Caffè degli Artisti, the Osteria della Scala al Teatro Grande, the nearby Caffè Cova and the Martini. According to Count Hubner, an Austrian diplomat writing in 1840, 'The Caffè Cova is the breeding place of conspirators and we still have not the courage to close it down.' The success of the cafés was also a direct consequence of the success of the middle class; but palaces and salons existed alongside. The Milanese salons reproduced the French model insofar as they did not only belong to aristocratic figures like Princess Belgiojoso, Countess Carcano and Countess Saimoyloff, but also to rich middle-class ladies with radical sympathies like Elena Viganò and Clarina Maffei. Viganò held her salon on Wednesdays between 11 p.m. and 2 a.m. Rossini and Stendhal met there for dinner, an occasion that the composer could not deny because there were many witnesses. Countess Saimoyloff, a Russian beauty who had been the tsar's mistress, was many times married and famous for bathing in milk, like Poppaea. However in her case, the milk which had touched her body was then taken to the Caffè Martini and avidly drunk by her admirers. Exotic and promiscuous, Giulia Saimoyloff was almost unique in keeping a salon which was pro-Austrian – 'simpatie tedesche', as the Milanese labelled it. There was also Giuseppina Visconti, a dark beauty who, during the Napoleonic Cisalpine Republic had been the mistress of Marshal Berthier, living between Paris and Milan. Clarina Maffei, who opened her salon around 1825, was emphatically pro-revolutionary and her soirées had a musical emphasis. Music was an excuse for groups of people to gather and, since the Austrians censored most publications, musical gazettes turned into a vehicle for discontent. By reading between the lines, people could follow international news as well as pick up forbidden information. Milanese society at this time revolved around Stendhal, the champion of Neoclassical ideas, Byron the poet of Romantic rebellion and Rossini, the musician of the future.

While enjoying the pleasure of Milan but avoiding the dangerously left-wing cafés, Rossini was there to produce *La gazza ladra*, a work which would appeal to that sophisticated Francophile city and was indeed based on a French play. He did not want to risk mediocrity, so there is no self-borrowing in this score; nor did he want to risk being accused of repeating himself, as had happened with *Il turco in Italia*. Rossini wanted to astound, and he succeeded. Tailored for a Milanese audience, *La gazza ladra* was neither *opera seria* nor *opera buffa*, but what was then called *semiseria* (the *dramma giocoso Don Giovanni*, for example, belongs to the same genre). The protagonist of *La gazza ladra*, a modest servant girl unjustly accused of theft, was based on a real character who, unlike the fictitious heroine, finished her life hanged at Palaiseau. The story verges on tragedy since the servant Ninetta is accused of a theft committed by a magpie and risks being executed. Nevertheless, at the eleventh hour, in this version she is rescued. The libretto offered Rossini the possibility of including martial instruments in his score, and the rarity caused an uproar. The overture – then called sinfonia – still stirs with threatening drums as if we were to know that the scaffold was ready for the weak and the poor at all times.

Stendhal attended the first performance of *La gazza ladra*,

> *and it was one of the most glittering, the most single-minded triumphs that I have ever witnessed and it continued for three months on end! . . . What to say of the overture of* La Gazza ladra*? In fact I wonder whether there is anyone who is not already totally familiar with this most picturesque little sinfonia. Rossini's innovation of scoring for the drums as a major part of his instrumental pattern creates an atmosphere of realism, if I dare use the term . . . Again, it would be almost impossible to describe the enthusiasm and the delirium of the Milanese audiences on first hearing this masterpiece.*

By 'realism', Stendhal meant 'Romanticism'. Rossini himself was pleased with the sinfonia and wrote to his parents: 'I can't remember a similar *fanatismo*. It starts with such a divine symphony that everybody is enchanted; they were intoxicated by two drums that, from the opposite parts of the theatre, responded to each other like an echo.'

Rossini conquered several Milanese beauties but kept aloof from politics and subversive talk. Consequently some of the intellectuals began to criticize him as a cynic and he became nicknamed 'le Voltaire de la musique'. On the other hand, Rossini knew that back in Naples his pay-masters belonged to a right-wing regime that had supported him generously and sheltered him from political trouble. And that is where his next commission would take him.

X

Vivace con brio

Although the San Carlo had been rebuilt in only eleven months and was larger and more splendid than before, it was not enough to placate the Neopolitans. Political dissent was now sweeping the kingdom. Like all those who are successful, Rossini was grateful to the regime that had recognized his qualities to such an extent that he had his contract renewed by the crown. In these circumstances he did not want a change of regime and he kept away from the 'professional' revolutionary. He would have probably agreed with Herzen's description:

> In addition to naive people and revolutionary doctrinaires, the un-appreciated artists, unsuccessful literary men, students who did not complete their studies, brief-less lawyers, actors without talent, persons of great vanity but small capability, with huge pretensions but no perseverance or power, all naturally drift into this milieu.

But even in the salons the Carbonari were thriving. According to Harold Acton there were 30,000 of them in Naples: 'the rebels' chief objects were to impose a Constitution and to obtain the independence of Italy, or rather these were the objects of its educated leaders, for the majority of its members were frustrated rebels with a passion for conspiracy.' The Carbonaris' 'shops' were divided into grades, *ap-prendisti*, *maestri* and *gran maestri*; the clandestine members mainly belonged to the new middle class. The Neapolitan Left could not bear

British interference in their affairs; the Sicilians instead wanted separation from Naples while Naples itself wanted a constitution which would grant more power to the people and weaken the absolutist monarchy. Metternich's repressive Holy Alliance (which Britain refused to join) had engulfed most of Europe in further unrest. As a result, the first revolutionary waves, in Spain, Portugal, Walachia and Italy, were beginning to shake the status quo.

Rossini was back in Naples to work on *Armida*, with which the San Carlo was to reopen on 11 November 1817. He loved the newly rebuilt theatre as it could accommodate his ambitions to write for a larger orchestra than before, moreover, it could equally accommodate bigger audiences. But there were many who were critical of the restored building, among them the composer Louis Spohr; 'The house is too large,' he wrote, 'if the theatre was really so sonorous before the fire, the improvements sought in the new construction have not materialized.' Isabella, now joining Gioachino on most of his travels (in July 1817 they were together on the island of Ischia which they found 'a very boring place'), was crucially involved in the composition of this new work, Rossini's third Neapolitan *opera seria*. In fact she wrote her name under his on the score, as if to emphasize the extent to which she was involved in the composition of the masterpiece, which glows with sensuality. She of course sang the title role. 'Her measureless power, the important events that could spring into being at a single word of hers, were all reflected in her Spanish eyes – so beautiful and at a certain moments, awe-inspiring,' Stendhal commented. Based on an episode in Tasso's *Gerusalemme liberata*, the libretto by Giovanni Schmidt was ready for Rossini on his arrival. Isabella was ideally suited to sing the sorceress who ensnares the Christian Rinaldo and the other Paladin knights with her magic. The only female role in the entire opera, Armida is the vamp, the precursor of the *femme fatale*, indeed, the character Armida fascinated composers ranging from Jommelli, Lully, Handel, Gluck, Haydn and even Dvořák. In a letter to Giuseppe Rossini, Isabella described the opera as containing 'angelic music'; Gioachino added a postscript saying that he was 'immersed in glory'. He was aware that he was creating a superb role for her, but perhaps not that this would cost Isabella her voice. By now Rossini and Isabella were so close that Isabella hovers in this most erotic music while Rossini's letters begin to discuss her frequently, as if he wanted his *carissima madre* to become accustomed to Isabella's name. By then Isabella was writing to Anna directly, addressing her as 'Mia buona Mamma'. Inflamed and inspired by love, she herself composed; but only one song dedicated to her father Juan has survived.

Isabella's supremacy at the San Carlo became a matter of politics. While the king and the court were her enthusiastic supporters, the liberal constitutional wing was hostile, which meant that Rossini was also tarnished. Like so many of his generation, the young Gioachino, once a fervent liberal, was joining the increasingly large party of Italian cynics. He was close to believing in nothing except music.

Rossini's next masterpiece was *Mosè in Egitto*, first performed at the San Carlo on 5 March 1818. When Stendhal heard the work, he approached it 'with a marked lack of interest for the plagues of Egypt', but 'before I had heard twenty bars of this superb introduction, I could imagine nothing more profoundly moving than a whole population in captivity.' Some scenes, for example the parting of the Red Sea, a Cecil B. de Mille's type of scene, were so clumsily staged that people scoffed and jeered. Andrea Leone Tottola's libretto is derived from the Old Testament struggle between the Jews and Pharaoh that culminates in the Exodus; in the opera the narrative of course incorporates a love story. The central theme – the attainment of the Promised Land – naturally stirred the Italian left; the dictatorial Pharaoh became a symbol for the Bourbon king or any of those tyrants who kept Italy divided. Like Verdi's *Nabucco*, the biblical lament in *Mosè* struck a chord in the heart of captive Italy. It was indeed a tale of liberation from tyranny and of the longing for nationhood; works such as these could and did inflame the public. 'People stood up in their boxes and leaned over the balconies, shouting to crack the vault of heaven,' wrote Stendhal. 'I have never known such a triumph – which was all the more tremendous since everyone had come expecting to laugh or jeer . . . Who can deny that music can provoke an immediate physical nervous reaction?'

In June 1818 Rossini was on the move again, this time bound for Pesaro, where he had been nominated an honorary member of the academy by its vice-president, Count Giulio Perticari (the nobleman rumoured to be Rossini's brother). The mayor of Pesaro had also extended an invitation, asking Rossini to stage anything he wished at the Teatro Sole. He chose *La gazza ladra*, and took particular care that this work should be performed in his native city as well as possible, taking responsibility not only as artistic director and impresario but also as stage manager. He even rearranged the disposition of the orchestra in the pit to accommodate the complexity of his score. The performance was to take place in May the following year. His former home town extended a warm welcome – yet there was trouble looming.

Besides the Perticaris, there were several cultivated families in Pesaro. Count Perticari himself was married to Costanza, the beautiful daughter of the poet Vincenzo Monti. Rossini found her 'an odd character', prone to making terrible scenes after which the count would beg Rossini to placate her. Soon there was gossip in Pesaro about a love affair between hostess and guest; in fact it was the countess's wish, but not Rossini's desire. Costanza (who plainly did not do justice to her name) had him followed and would lie naked on his unmade bed. Maybe Costanza was like her father, a fickle political poet who changed sides as often as new armies descended on Italy – but a wonderful translator of Homer. Count Perticari's palace stood near the house where Rossini was born; but, unlike his step-brother's, the rooms in which the Rossini family had lived were small and simple. An early life of intense hard work, study, commitment and nervous activity, coupled with overwhelming talent, combined to make Rossini's return to Pesaro a triumph and he loved the experience. He was in huge demand everywhere. The Perticaris, however, warned him against the salon of their *bête noire*, Carolina Brunswick, the estranged (though not yet divorced) wife of the Prince Regent, later George IV of England. The noisy and vulgar Princess of Wales had rented Villa Caprile, a beautiful Neoclassical house, in order to set up home with her lover, Bartolomeo Bergami. They made a horrible couple; she was fifty-six and he, much younger, invented a fake title for himself. Caroline's insistence on being treated like royalty alienated the couple from Pesaro society and with it, from the Perticari family. But, as soon as he arrived, the famous Rossini was invited to attend the princess's musical soirées. Declining these invitations, in one instance he mocked the princess by answering that 'certain rheumatic afflictions in my back prevent me from practising the bows prescribed by court etiquette'. It was a slight which would not be easily forgotten. By now exhausted from too much travelling and overwork, Rossini fell ill and rumours circulated that he was dead and some found their way into various Milanese publications. The news caused so much grief that Rossini himself had to publish a letter informing his admirers that he had no intention of dying so early in his life. He was soon well enough to attend a grand banquet given by Perticari, to which neither the semi-obese Caroline nor her unpleasant lover had been invited. At the same time he started working on the staging of a very special *Gazza ladra* for 'his' Pesaro; it is interesting to see Rossini work as artistic director and impresario of his own opera and to observe how the busy composer did not spare his energies and attended to every detail. Rossini's alleged laziness is often cited at this stage but it is difficult to imagine anyone applying himself to his commitments as he did. He even rearranged the position of members of the orchestra because, as he wrote to Perticari, the score of *La Gazza ladra* was complex.

The summer of 1818 found Rossini in Bologna, where he spent time with his parents and received a commission from a Portuguese patron for his last *farsa*, to be called *Adina*. Giacomo Leopardi, the greatest Italian poet of the century, who was leaving Neoclassicism and moving speedily and tragically towards Romanticism, together with Ugo Foscolo (who was exiled in London), lamented Italy's servitude: 'Oh, my Italy, I see your walls, your arches, but I do not see your glory.' For expressing the same ideas, Foscolo had to flee.

Rossini returned to Naples and started working on both *Ricciardo e Zoraide*, to be premièred on 3 December 1818, and *Ermione* (27 March 1819). By November 1818, Rossini and Isabella were almost a married couple in spite of his infidelities; he even admitted to an infidelity in a letter describing how he composed a famous piece from *Mosè* almost while making love to a certain lady, but this boast smacks too much of bravado. In Naples Rossini faced mounting criticism. He was accused of being politically too conservative and musically too avant-garde.

Of *Ricciardo e Zoraide* Stendhal wrote that 'the style, as a whole, is impassioned and full of oriental grandeur.' It is scored for such vast vocal and orchestral resources (including *banda sul palco*, a stage band) that it is seldom staged. Despite its lack of success, Rossini knew the qualities of this opera and, according to the French music publishers Leon and Marie Escudier, withdrew the score from Barbaja with the words: 'you will encounter it again sooner or later and perhaps then the Neapolitan public will recognize its error.' *Ermione*, Rossini's only opera for Naples that digs into the Homeric pot beloved of

Neoclassicists, was dismissed by Stendhal as 'an experiment in which Rossini tried to explore the genre of French opera.'

After those disappointments, Rossini went to Venice for a so-called new opera *Edoardo e Cristina* (24 April 1819), in fact a mishmash of self-borrowings; but the Venetians didn't know that and were delighted with the piece. In a letter to John Cam Hobhouse, dated 17 May 1819, Byron was lavish in his praise: 'There has been a splendid opera by Rossini who came in person to play the harpsichord. The people followed him about, crowned him, cut off his hair for memory, he was shouted and sonnetted and feasted and immortalised.'

Now Pesaro was finally ready for the performance of *La Gazza ladra* and, as planned, Rossini returned to the Teatro del Sole in May. This gave Caroline of Brunswick and her lover the opportunity to ensure that her bravos would wreak revenge on her behalf for Rossini's snub of the previous year. Rossini was staying at the Hotel Posta because Count Perticari was in Rome and Rossini clearly did not want to be anywhere near Costanza. When, on the day, he arrived at the opera house, the atmosphere was so frenzied and the thugs so aggressive that the management had to smuggle him out and put him on a coach to leave through the city gates in the middle of the night. The citizens, who by now had made a cult of their Rossini, were distraught and escorted the composer with torches and words of encouragement. But Rossini, on whom any manifestation of crowd violence provoked a deep nervous crisis, never set foot in Pesaro again. This is the first sign of a condition which was to plague the composer with a form of pathological panic that developed into a grave nervous disease.

A letter sent to Count Perticari described the events of 24 May:

> the people who had gathered in the theatre in a large number to celebrate the arrival of this illustrious townsman had to endure the shame of Rossini's entrance through the stage door, the thugs of the princess of Wales were able to forestall the citizens' applause and greet him with the most horrible whistling . . . as the thugs scattered about in several parts of the theatre and showed that they were ready to use their knives and pistols.

What happened that night in Pesaro wounded him deeply; Rossini had consumed so much of himself in offering one of his best operas at its very best and yet the hisses of the paid thugs drowned out every single note of his score – as had happened on the first night of *Il barbiere*. The citizens of Pesaro should have known better, they should have prevented what happened; he was hurt, even though Perticari mentioned that when they talked about the incident in Rome only a month later, 'as usual [Rossini] laughed about it all.'

On his return to Naples, Rossini discovered that a libretto he was expecting had not materialized, so he needed to find a substitute. A young winner of the Prix de Rome called M. Batton told Rossini about his admiration for Walter Scott's poem *The Lady of the Lake*. 'Lend me the little book,' Rossini asked. It was a French translation. 'I want to see if it will do for me.' Two days later he announced that the six cantos full of mist and unrequited love, of rural descriptions and winds blowing on the chilly waters of Scottish lakes, would suit his purpose perfectly. Indeed, no novelist or poet did more to 'launch' romantic Scotland than Scott did; his evocations of spooky castles and heather captured the imagination of a whole generation and were a decisive influence on the Romantic movement. Rossini was the first composer ever to set Scott's work to music, his example being followed by Donizetti, Pacini and Berlioz. Rossini's *La donna del lago*, premièred on 24 September 1819, met with a lukewarm reception. Stendhal was more perceptive than most of his contemporaries, and noted how the composer introduced 'an unsuspected dynamic force', adding that Rossini could be 'physically ill when one of his works was whistled off the stage . . . this is saying a great deal of a man whose outward bearing is one of supreme indifference.' Leopardi wrote: 'This music, executed by astonishing voices is a wonderful thing and even I could be moved to tears by it, if the gift of tears had not been withheld from me.' Today the opera stands 'amongst Rossini's most visionary creations, taxing the audience's everyday capacity for understanding them', as Carli Ballola put it in *A Utopia of Happiness*. In the words of Fedele d'Amico, the work represents 'A unique and unrepealable moment of an absolute romanticism, all the more disturbing in its historical solitude, which would condemn it to misunderstanding and neglect.' For the programme accompanying a magnificent production at Pesaro in 2001, Alberto Zedda wrote: '*La donna del lago* is a very beautiful opera, fascinating and mysterious, among the best of a composer to whom mediocrity was a stranger. It is run through with pre-romantic throbbing, dear to worshippers of *Sturm und Drang*, and imbued with passions free from any banality.'

People began to notice a strange detachment in the otherwise sparkling light of the young composer's pupils and some started talking about Rossini's indolence, an odd thing to say about a young man who had composed an amazing quantity of music, who had rushed up and down the peninsula and had seen to the staging, the sets, the quality of the orchestras, not only for his own operas, but also for those of other composers. To underline his laziness even Stendhal described an episode in which Rossini, composing in bed, could not be bothered to rise from his warm blankets in order to look for the completed sheet of notes that had fallen to the floor. He preferred to compose an entirely new piece. Stendhal did not understand the classic behaviour of the depressive who refuses to get out of bed to face the day.

Rossini was soon to abandon Naples altogether. Abandonment, retirement, staying in bed: depression was knocking at Rossini's door. But now he had to rush back to Milan.

XI

CABALETTA

M ilan was decaying; gone were the days when it could boast of being the capital of the new Cisalpine Republic and a centre of cognoscenti and wits. The Austrians and the clericals were by now entrenched in the city. After the fall of Napoleon, the old order quickly re-established its rule with an all-embracing secret police.

The new opera for La Scala was *Bianca e Falliero*, first performed on 26 December 1819. Four main characters inhabit a politically stormy Venice. Father, daughter, lover and suitor were the staple diet of *opera seria* and Rossini constructed a web of melodies and coloratura which were guaranteed to please the Milanese; the sets were designed by the great Alessandro Sanquirico but, in spite of these ingredients and some of Rossini's finest music, the critic of the *Gazzetta di Milano* launched an attack on Rossini's musical language. On the other hand the public soon decided otherwise and *Bianca e Falliero* was on for thirty-nine performances.

By now, Stendhal, who was also in Milan, disliked Rossini the man but still admired Rossini the composer; not only had Rossini become right wing but, even worse, he also pretended not to recognize him. Probably Rossini had heard that Stendhal was writing his biography and wanted to let everybody understand that he hardly knew the Frenchman who tried to frequent the same Milanese salons. Stendahl wrote, 'Barbaja supports this great man and supplies him with a carriage, room, board and a lady friend. The divine Colbran who is, I believe, only 40 or 50 years old, is the

delight of prince Jablonowsky, the millionaire Barbaja and the maestro.'
Not very kind about Isabella's amorous activities – or about her age.

The young French dragoon, Henri Beylei, had arrived with Napoleon; later, because of his anti-Austrian writings, he used the pseudonym of Stendhal but was expelled from Milan all the same, accused
of being a spy. He was called 'the Chinese' because of his squashed
face. Stendhal was no beauty but he was constantly in love, with Italy,
with opera and with beautiful ladies. Ladies succumbed to him
because of his tenacity, his twinkling eyes, his availability and because
he loved them. Rossini, on the other hand, although a womanizer, was
rarely in love; he did not know the tempestuous flames which set
Stendhal alight in every other box of La Scala.

Nina, Elena Viganò, daughter of the choreographer Alessandro,
was Stendhal's love of the moment. Elena, his 'Nina', kept a musical
and literary salon. Stendhal suffered at the thought that Rossini was
going to dine at the Viganòs almost every night while he himself had
not yet been invited. 'Her piano will serve as Rossini's headquarters.
Yesterday, upon his arrival, Rossini was invited to dinner for ten days
out of every week.'

By now, too, European sentiment was changing. The Romantic
movement was well under way: Byron had published *Don Juan*
(1819–24) and Walter Scott *The Bride of Lammermoor* (1819).
And Géricault, bypassing his contemporaries with a jump worth
two centuries, unveiled to an amazed public the *Raft of the Medusa*
(Salon of 1819). What could be less like Canova's icy Neoclassical
beauties? While Goethe and the Germans had discovered the greatness
of the classical past, for the French Italy was the sole source of aesthetic
form. Even Frances' nationalistic soul, shaped by the Revolution and by
Napoleon's inflammatory rhetoric, could not do without her poorer
cousin – and this is true today, when Italian influence on France is
stronger than on any other European country. In *Rome, Naples et
Florence* (the third of his books in which he used his *nom de plume*)
Stendhal called Italy 'the garden of Europe'. This is neither a guidebook
nor a diary, just as Stendhal's future biography of Rossini is not a
conventional biography but a compendium of thoughts on music, Italy
and contemporary politics. The term 'Romantic', employed by Madame de Staël in her *De l'Allemagne* of 1810, was beginning to be given
such a wide application that it came to be synonymous with the word
'contemporary'. To define Romanticism is a contradiction in terms or,

rather, to find a definition is unromantic. Many have attempted to do so, with varying degrees of success. Asa Briggs, for example, described the Romantic movement as follows:

> *rejection of rationalism; preoccupation with the self; the cultivation of feelings; fear of age; the flight from the artificial and the pursuit of the primitive and the simple, the reckless and the strange, the picturesque and the grotesque; the urge towards untrimmed individual freedom; tension between desire and achievement or circumstance; the longing for the unattainable; delight in genius, not least misunderstood genius, as a 'force of nature' and in nature as a source of solace and of inspiration . . . These different aspects, tangled and even incompatible, wild-flower or hot house, acquired what unity they possessed not through the mind but through the heart or the soul.*

But for Isaiah Berlin:

> *The importance of romanticism is that it is the largest recent movement to transform the lives and the thought of the Western world. It seems to me to be the greatest single shift in the consciousness of the West that has occurred . . . the other shifts which have occurred in the course of the nineteenth and the twentieth centuries appear to me in comparison less important, and at any rate deeply influenced by it.*

As for Friedrich von Gentz (Metternich's agent), Romanticism was one of the heads of the Hydra, the other two being Reform and Revolution.

Although lionized in the Milanese salons, Rossini was working hard. Physically he had changed: he was a bit fatter and his forehead had become broader or, rather, his hairline had receded. Not quite twenty-eight, he was losing his youthful looks too early but he was bursting with energy and everything was going his way. Yet, as Stendhal wrote to his friend Adolphe de Mareste on 2 November 1819, Rossini 'wishes to retire at 30'. This sounds like a firm decision. Whether Rossini himself discussed the matter with Stendhal or whether he heard the rumour spreading around the Milanese salons, cannot be established. (Meyerbeer also mentioned Rossini's early desire to retire; and his overwhelming impact on Milan.) But Stendhal boasted 'I spend my evenings with Rossini and Monti; all things considered I prefer extraordinary to ordinary men.' He might have disliked Rossini but still craved to be seen with the composer.

A note from Giuseppe Rossini, dated 4 January 1820 and including an unusually reverent reference to his son as 'Maestro Rossini', shows that around this time the composer stopped at Bologna on his way back to Naples, where he was rehearsing Spontini's *Fernando Cortez* on 12 January. Under the Neapolitan sky he could forget the traumatic events in Pesaro. Furthermore, he had been asked to sit for the Roman sculptor Adamo Tadolini; the bust had been commissioned by the Accademia Pesarese in the hope that his native city would be forgiven. 'Naples! thou Heart of men,' wrote Shelley, 'Naked, beneath the lidless eye of heaven! Elysian city, which to calm enchantest the mutinous air and sea . . . metropolis of a ruined paradise.' The awe mixed with enchantment still takes one's breath away at the sight of that lidless eye, that ruined Paradise. Nevertheless, habit had probably lessened Rossini's enchantment with the city. The mutinous air disturbed him. The atmosphere of revolution, anger and discontent could be felt not only around the poverty-stricken Neapolitan districts but was escalating to include the elite. In spite of trying to avoid politics, Rossini found that he was being criticized by both right and left for his lack of commitment – and for his success outside Naples. Yet he remained sought after there too. On 9 May 1819 the king welcomed Austria's emperor and Prince Metternich with a cantata by Rossini sung by Colbran, Rubini and David. The emperor marvelled at the sumptuous scenery and Metternich wrote to Rossini: 'You have been the author of a new science more than a reformer of an ancient school.' Finally, Rossini might have thought, somebody understood his music.

Rossini's next Neapolitan commission, from the Arciconfraternita di San Luigi, was for a Mass. Fully aware that he had no time to complete it, he asked a friend, the composer Pietro Raimondo, to work with him and for him. The *Messa di gloria* was duly sung in the church of San Ferdinando on 24 March 1820. Stendhal, who claimed to have been there, related that at the end of the performance a priest cried: 'Rossini, if you knock on the gates of Heaven with this Mass, St Peter will be unable to delay opening it despite all your sins!' Rossini's sins, in the eyes of the priests, were enviable: all those women! If even half the figure attributed to him was realistic, Rossini must have been the busiest of sinners.

Meanwhile, in April 1820 Isabella's father died at Castenaso; she felt an immense sense of loss because he had been her main admirer and protector, her source of security. He left her a very substantial sum of money plus land in Sicily and the lovely property at Castenaso with its land and farms. Now it was up to Rossini to look after her. Rossini wrote to Tadolini, the sculptor for whom he had been sitting a few weeks earlier, asking whether he would design a funerary monument for Giovanni Colbran's tomb, showing 'the daughter at the foot of the mausoleum weeping the loss of her father; at the other side a singer chanting his glories'. This Neoclassical image recalls Canova's mausoleums for the Habsburgs and was probably never erected.

The première of Rossini's next opera, a two-act *dramma* entitled *Maometto II*, in which he was deeply involved during the summer of 1820, had to be delayed: in July some army deserters and leaders of the Carbonari marched and captured Avellino, a mountain city east of Naples. Five of them then descended on Naples and their leader, General Guglielmo Pepe, demanded to be received by the king. Ferdinand was firmly asked to give the Neapolitans a constitution like the one granted to Spain in 1812 otherwise, revolution.

General Pepe and Padre Luigi Minichini, an insurgent priest, led their troops into the city, shouting glory to God and proclaiming the constitution. With that Neapolitan flair for involuntary comedy, they scared King Nasone, who wanted only to be left in peace, either sitting on his throne or sleeping in the capacious arms of his duchess. She was so frightened that she appealed to the British; after all, a few years earlier Nelson had saved the very same Bourbon king. The king duly gave in, so that on 6 July (1820) the Neapolitans woke up to a constitutional monarchy rather than an absolutist one. They came out in their thousands, with no idea of what the constitution was; they gave thanks to San Gennaro and went back to their wretched *bassi* with their stomachs as empty as before. The aristocracy remained in their palaces, trembling – and so did Rossini. The middle classes – lawyers, students and bankers – joined the Carbonari and decided that they would change the world. Having resigned as commander of the rebel army, General Pepe became inspector general of the militia and civil guard, a reminder of Jacobin terror. Sir William A'Court, the British envoy in Naples, described Pepe going about the city 'at the head of an immense mob of people armed with guns, knives, sticks, clubs, swords etc carrying a tricolour flag which had previously received benediction from Carbonari priests, filling the streets with tumult and chanting "King and Constitution" and "Liberty or

Left: The composer's father, Giuseppe Rossini, nicknamed Vivazza, came from Lugo near Pesaro and worked as an itinerant trumpeter and horn player.

Below left: Anna Guidarini, Rossini's mother, couldn't read music, but had a lovely voice and a beautiful stage presence.

Below right: Disease and hard work turned the young beauty into a precociously elderly woman. When she died, in 1827, Rossini was distraught.

When he arrived in Naples in 1816 in the service of the Bourbons, Gioachino Rossini was a Byronic hero, the conqueror of all hearts. In his birth certificate he was Giovacchino but Rossini himself preferred Gioachino, more rarely Gioacchino.

Isabella Colbran at the time of her Neapolitan triumphs. She became Rossini's wife in 1822. His parents, by then separated, were present at the wedding.

Right: Henry Beyle wrote under the pseudonym of Stendhal; he spent his post-Napoleonic days roaming around Italy in search of operatic bliss. His *Vie de Rossini* was a bestseller.

Below left: Domenico Barbaja was the brilliant impresario who engaged Rossini for Naples and rescued him from a political impasse.

Below right: Marietta Marcolini, a famous coloratura contralto specialized in cross-dressing roles and had been Eugene Beauharnais' mistress while he was Viceroy of Milan. She became Rossini's ideal interpreter and ideal lover.

Marietta Marcolini

Non è l'Euganea sola
Testimonio giocondo
Della virtù di lei: n'è tutto il mondo.

Set designs were lavish. Alessandro Sanquirico, admired all over Europe and Beethoven's favourite set designer, reigned at La Scala. The set for Maometto Secondo's Second act.

Left: The Teatro Rossini is where the Pesaro Opera Festival stages its stunning productions; it was rebuilt during Rossini's lifetime and renamed after Pesaro's most illustrious son.

Below: The interior of the San Carlo was renovated after a terrible fire in 1817; it was all in blue and gold and even Stendhal was stunned.

Right: An admirer of Rossini's music, Honoré de Balzac wrote a great deal about his friend and his compositions and tried to cure his 'melancholia'.

Below: It was the Teatro alla Scala with La pietra del paragone that launched Rossini's international career, although his *Tancredi* at the Venice Fenice had made hearts palpitate all over Italy.

This pamphlet of three printed 'melodies' by Rossini sold all over Europe. Rossini's scores began to be printed by Ricordi and, later, by French music publishers. Rossini fought to establish the concept of copyright and protect his music from the then customary abuse and misuse of singers and orchestras.

Death".' In short, virtually an operatic scene, but one recalling the French Revolution, the memory of which still terrorized or elated those Neapolitans who, after all, had lived under the rule of a Bonaparte and a Murat.

Rossini, who belonged to neither persuasion, merely foresaw a scenario in which his life could change dramatically: his well-being was derived from the court and he preferred the pomp to what he had left behind in Pesaro and Bologna. Maybe in his late teens or early twenties he would have liked to change everything; aged twenty-eight, he wanted comfort and security. Indeed his paunch was growing to such an extent that the top buttons of his trousers often had to be adjusted. This was no bad thing: extra weight was a sign of affluence and hence of beauty; thinness indicated poverty and disease, and was considered unaesthetic. He continued to be in demand, but had begun to look forward to slowing down, to no longer being harassed by the need to deliver compositions, arrangements and orchestrations on top of all his other musical activities. Yet he enjoyed seeing friends and foes alike vying for his company. He was a wonderful conversationalist, ready to outwit anybody.

If General Pepe hoped to unleash a civil war, he was unsuccessful: the Neapolitan revolution proved bloodless. It did coincide, however, with a rising in Piedmont and the proclamation of a republic in Sicily. A Turinese politician claimed that these events marked 'the first revolution in which two Italian peoples worked together at the two extremities of our peninsula', a nationalistic sentiment which Metternich could not tolerate. The newly elected Neapolitan parliamentary representatives were mostly professional people, even some priests and noblemen; they began to meet in an orderly way and promulgated moderate laws. People like Rossini and Colbran began to come out of hiding and wondered how long this parliament could last. Most deputies were monarchist so it could not be said that the new parliament was as revolutionary as the French. But those inside the grand palaces continued to be apprehensive: no more San Carlo and open salons for them. *Maometto II* was still waiting to be performed.

Those Neapolitan events undermined the very principles of the Congress of Vienna. The moderation of Pepe's parliament was more worrying for Metternich than a bloody and disorderly revolution might have been; the success of this type of movement was threatening. Therefore Metternich called a meeting of the Great Powers,

Austria, Prussia and Russia. The current political situation had to be reviewed and the Congress stated that international intervention in such a case would be acceptable. 'Fate', Metternich said, 'has laid upon me the duty of restraining as far as my powers will allow a generation whose destiny seems to be that of losing itself upon the slope which will surely lead to its ruins.' It was on that occasion that Metternich explained to Tsar Alexander how revolutions were never the work of the mass but of groups 'of ambitious men, among them paid state officials, men of letters, lawyers, and individuals charged with public education.'

Although the city of Naples had not been mentioned, King Ferdinand was terrified and secretly wrote to Metternich asking for an excuse to flee his city. The Great Powers obliged by deciding to stage yet another congress to which Ferdinand could be invited, his attendance would not be construed as abandoning his kingdom. Naïvely Pepe's government allowed the king to go to Laibach (1 January 1821) but extracted from him the promise that he would not accept any modification of the constitution without the consent of the democratically elected Neapolitan parliament. No sooner had Ferdinand left than he recanted, saying that he had been constrained by force to accept the constitution and asked for Austrian intervention. Metternich, despite being averse to sending troops because he knew that some of the Great Powers, Britain for one, were against provoking armed conflicts, nevertheless complied: Ferdinand was the Austrian emperor's father-in-law. On hearing that the constitution was in danger, the Neapolitan parliament determined to fight. Every man in Naples was called to arms, Rossini included. But by the end of March 1821 the imperial Austrian army had entered Naples, cheered by the same people who hailed every change of government. 'This is the third time I'm putting King Ferdinand on his feet . . . he still imagines that the throne is an easy chair on which he can sprawl and fall asleep,' complained Metternich. This was a pyrrhic victory for Ferdinand: from then on the name of the Neapolitan Bourbons was soiled; many protested in Britain and, on the next call, the British navy was to help Garibaldi against the Bourbons – not the other way round. In the repression that followed his reinstatement, Ferdinand showed the vicious streak of the absolutist monarch and even those who had remained loyal to the dynasty were imprisoned; many Carbonari were executed publicly. Even Metternich protested and demanded that

Prince Canosa, the king's cruel minister of the interior, should be dismissed.

In these circumstances, it is not surprising that *Maometto II* made slow progress, though the nature of the upheavals and delays may well have contributed to the quality of Rossini's music. A parliamentary motion had decreed that 'the Asiatic pomp of the theatre of San Carlo, worthy only of a nation of slaves', was going to be obliterated. Barbaja was temporarily removed from his post and, for a time, there was no theatrical activity in Naples. Even before it reached the stage on 3 December 1820, rumour spread that *Maometto II* was a masterpiece. The text is not based on Voltaire's *Mahomet* (as is often assumed) but on a lost drama by Marivaux from which Cesare della Valle, Duke of Ventignano, had drawn the story of the conqueror of Constantinople from his own drama, *Anna Erizo*. It is not a good libretto, but the music has the sparkle of genius. Anthony Arblaster in *Viva la libertà* described *Maometto II* as follows:

> [It] consists of only two long acts, each lasting around an hour and a half. These extended spans are not mosaics of many small scenes but are constructed from a small number of greatly extended musical numbers. What is more, some of these do not reach a full close, but run directly into the next. Rossini's concern with forward momentum and dramatic continuity is evident.

The work was received coolly. Once more Rossini's best music failed to be understood. In addition, public opinion identified the composer with all that it wanted to dislike. For the conspirators and would-be revolutionaries, he was the tool of the reactionary Bourbons; for the aristocracy he was a former republican and hence a dangerous left-winger; and, for the musical lobby, he was an iconoclast. Small wonder that Rossini was now disenchanted with Naples, a city that had once delighted him. Its blue skies and turquoise bay, the smoking Vesuvius, the sing-song Neapolitan accent, all now conspired against him. Furthermore, the recent trials were also, in Rossini's eyes, barbaric events. The orchestra might have been the best in Italy, but there were other orchestras and other kinds of public north of the Alps.

There is an understandable note of panic in the letters that Rossini now wrote to Giovanni Battista Benelli, impresario of the King's Theatre in

London; he wanted to find a new employer and a new city – London, Vienna – he would go anywhere, but he must leave Naples! Rossini asked Benelli to spread a rumour that he had already been engaged for London. Benelli also asked for a new opera for the Londoners. Rossini wanted a contract binding not only him but also Isabella, whose voice was beginning to fail, a knowledge which must have reached the impresario. In fact on 22 December she cracked at a revival of *Maometto* and was described by Lord Mount Edgecumbe as 'entirely passée'.

But before leaving Italy Rossini still had other commitments to honour. First there was an opera for Rome, *Matilde di Shabran*, which opened the Carnival season on 24 February 1821 at the Teatro Apollo. The story of how the libretto was put together defies description. It went through so many hands and there were so many changes that the conductor died of apoplexy during rehearsals. Who would take over? Nicolò Paganini suggested himself as conductor. The virtuoso violinist could turn his hand to all aspects of music making; at Lucca he had led the court orchestra of Princess Elisa, Napoleon's sister; and in Rome he had played in a quartet with Ingres, who gave him a drawing of Paganini made on this occasion as a gesture of thanks. On a Carnival night Paganini and a group of friends, including Rossini, Antonio Pacini and Massimo d'Azeglio, future prime minister of Italy and *bel homme*, dressed up and went around begging and singing:

Siamo cechi; siamo nati	We are blind; we were born
Per campar di cortesia.	To surive on courtesy.
In giornata d'allegria	On this festive day
Non si nega carità.	Don't refuse us charity.

Between them they gathered quite a tidy sum that night. Rossini had good reason to ask for money as he had not been paid the 500 scudi owed for *Matilde di Shabran*. According to Prince Torlonia of the Teatro Apollo, Rossini's *Matilde di Shabran* was not entirely Rossini's – and in this he had a point; some of the music had been composed by Pacini. Rossini retaliated by going to the theatre and removing all the orchestral scores so that there could be no second performance. When Cardinal Consalvi intervened, the money was paid and *Matilde di Shabran*, which has sublime moments but also great weaknesses, enjoyed a long run.

The group of friends had great fun, as the memoirs of Massimo d'Azeglio relate:

in the evening I often found myself with [my bachelor friends] and their mad contemporaries. Carnival was approaching and one evening we said 'Let's arrange a masquerade.' . . . D'Azeglio said that, pretending to be pauper and blind, Rossini and Paganini had to act as the orchestra, strumming two guitars and dressed up as women. Rossini filled out his already abundant form with bundles of straw, looking really nonhuman! Paganini, as thin as a door, and with a face that seemed to be the neck of his violin, appeared twice as thin and loose-limbed when dressed in drag.

Rossini seemed to catch up on the carefree times that had escaped him as a youth. Nicolò Paganini loved the boyish jokes and the noisy company of his friends. He was not only a virtuoso of the violin but also a composer, a conductor and a very generous man.

Rossini left Rome while the Carnival was in full swing: bulls were unleashed on the streets with the panache of Pamplona; horse races took place in Piazza Navona; crowds went on parade, dancing and singing, oblivious to the fact that Austrian troops were crossing the Alps, reaching Naples in March and crushing the constitution and the Carbonari revolt in no time. Rossini and Paganini, travelling together, reached Naples in the wake of the troops. 'The Germans are on the Po, the Barbarians at the gate, and their masters in council . . . and, lo, the Italians dance and sing and make merry,' Byron commented bitterly.

Indeed, sick and tired of the Neapolitan political shifts, Barbaja too took advantage of the fact that he and his company had been dismissed by the short-lived Neapolitan parliament in order to negotiate his own flight from Naples. He was in touch with the Kärntnertortheater, the forerunner of the Staatsoper in Vienna. Finally, in December 1821 Barbaja signed a contract which would take the Neapolitan company to Vienna. Rossini's contract too had to be renegotiated because his agreement was not with the Bourbons but with Barbaja who was giving him back his freedom – up to a point. A new opera by Rossini would open the Vienna season, it was decreed, and that was to be *Zelmira* (for which there would be a trial run in Naples in February 1822).

La riconoscenza ('Gratitude'), Rossini's last Neapolitan cantata, was performed on 27 December 1821. Its Neoclassical mood was in striking contrast with Rossini's latest output – and with the times. Once again it featured classical entertainment with philosophers and idyllic priests in Arcadia. The great Rubini, his wife and Benedetti sang, but not Colbran who was preparing to be the lead in *Zelmira*. This cantata was not composed for the Bourbons or for a particular festive royal event but as a valedictory piece for Rossini himself. As Bruno Cagli has pointed out, this cantata was an anomaly in Rossini's output:

> On the stage of history, times were changing and so were the roles. For the first time, one might say, a solemn cantata united a composer and a king, for the first time an artist occupied a role generally destined for the mighty ones of the earth. Just like Beethoven, Rossini – in different surroundings and with different means – had won for himself a social position and function quite new for an artist and for the art of music . . . This profound change in the 'public' status of a composer should not pass unobserved.

Rossini was bidding farewell and extending thanks to a now reviled king. He had come a long way since being described as 'a certain' Rossini, as he had been on his first arrival in Naples four years earlier. 'Rossini, whose name alone is worth more than thousands of eulogies, the glory of Pesaro, the ornament of Italy, Rossini is about to leave our midst,' the same newspaper announced. Before his departure, the maestro made provisions for the city's musical welfare; he invited Mayr's promising pupil, Gaetano Donizetti, to perform *La zingara*, his new opera. Donizetti was less than happy with the experience. In a letter to Mayr he wrote:

> Signor Rossini had to edit the entire part. At the rehearsals he lazes about jesuitically with the singers who don't follow him well and then, at the orchestra rehearsals, there he is, gossiping with the prime donne instead of conducting. As for me, I don't care to watch any more of this. But Barbaja says that he will give it later in Vienna, and that there it will sound as it should.

Rossini's mind was on other things. But an anonymous music critic, writing for the *Journal des débats*, 11 March 1822, described a different Rossini at the rehearsals of *Zelmira*:

He never gets ruffled; he hardly says two or three words . . . His principle is not to upset the orchestra and, above all, not to humiliate the singers. His prodigious memory allows him to make his observations singly to each one after rehearsals. Leaving the San Carlo, I accompanied him to the house of the copyist to whom he pointed out some fifty mistakes without looking at the score! The more one observes this man at close quarters, the more one finds him a superior being.

Towards the end of November the previous year, Rossini had announced to his mother his betrothal to Isabella, 'whose heart and character have bound me in an indissoluble knot'. On 18 January 1822, just before leaving, Isabella and Goachino wrote a letter to Anna in alternate paragraphs, expressing fondness for each other and making it clear that Rossini did not marry Isabella for money. He was by now so rich that he could afford to keep his parents in two separate houses and buy a new one for himself. The style and tone of Rossini's parts of the letter are so different from his previous ones that they are worth quoting at length:

My good Mother
Time and reason that all oversee and establish, has led me to the path of reason and of happy tranquillity. Until now I looked after you, my dear parents, and while I was absorbed by these noble feelings, there was a person who prepared me for a most beautiful future. This is Colbran whose heart and character bound me by an indissoluble knot. You know how well she loved her father and this gives me comfort because I know she will love you, and I know how happy I shall be among all those things of yours for which I would happily shed my blood. She has a heart for which she seeks everybody's well-being and she is resolved not to oppose anything that would antagonize you; her heart would crave that, of two families, we would make one, but if you were not to agree, she'll suffer that you choose to live alone, on your own; I say alone only in the sense that you'll be in a seperate dwelling since in love and affection we must all form a single heart and an undivided well-being.

A lot I should write if I were to describe what I owe to this woman. I shall relate the most interesting: since I gave myself to her, I did not suffer from any disease, I changed my impetuous character into a sweeter one; I was messy in everything, now I am as tidy as my Mother

– you can see that I could not but love this woman. If you were only to hear the respect and the dedication with which she talks of you, my parents, you'd be enchanted.

Whether or not the letter was written (or at least supervised) by somebody else, a lot of work had gone into its wording; Rossini (and Isabella) are inviting Anna to live with them at Castenaso. From this letter, it is clear that Anna and Giuseppe had already met not only Isabella but also her father; it is also evident that they knew about Gioachino's disease.

Having arrived in Bologna three days earlier, Gioachino Rossini and Isabella Colbran were married on 16 March 1822 in the sanctuary of the Blessed Virgin of the Pilar, a few miles from Bologna, and blessed by Don Martino Amadori, the parish priest. The witnesses were two of their menservants. Isabella, 'daughter of the deceased Teresa from Madrid', was seven years older than her groom. She was very religious, a Spanish type of almost pagan devotion. Rossini was not at all devout. Whatever the rumour (her rich dowry, his taste for money, his cynicism), it was a love match or, rather, a conjugal union reconfirmed. The two had learnt to trust and support each other. They shared the secret of the disease and the knowledge that their marriage would be barren (she was in any case past childbearing age and Gioachino had passed his gonorrhoea on to her). Later, Rossini was to say that his mother had insisted that his illicit union should be sanctified, but the truth was that the couple had long weathered the storms of reciprocal infidelities and gossip. 'I am now Colbran's husband,' Rossini wrote to Benelli in London. 'I entered into this marriage a few days ago at Bologna in the presence of my parents. To put things briefly: I do not want to return to Naples after Vienna nor do I want my wife to return there.'

Thus a very important phase of Rossini's life ended with his marriage and the prospect of new horizons opening in Vienna, the city of Mozart and Haydn. He was going to lose his 'innocence', as Stendhal put it, his musical innocence, that is, because Rossini had never known innocence. He could not afford to. Northern Europe was going to deliver him to the world of Romanticism, which he had known intuitively and which he had appeared to develop instinctively.

ACT TWO

BEETHOVEN
AND ROMANTICISM

The figure who dominated the nineteenth century as an image is the tousled figure of Beethoven in his garret. Beethoven is a man who does what is in him. He is poor, he is ignorant, he is boorish. His manners are bad, he knows little and he is perhaps not a very interesting figure, apart from the inspiration which drives him forward. But he has not sold out. He sits in his garret and he creates. He creates in accordance with the light which is within him, and that is all that a man should do; that is what makes a man a hero.

Isaiah Berlin, *The Roots of Romanticism*

I

MAESTOSO

Vienna, the city that welcomed Rossini for the opera season of April–July 1822 with unprecedentedly feverish enthusiasm, was the capital of a vast empire. The Habsburgs had dominated European politics for several centuries by extending their territories through advantageous marriages. As a result, they had blood ties with many European royal families including the Neapolitan Bourbons. Even Napoleon was related by marriage to Emperor Franz I: Marie Louise, Bonaparte's second wife, was the emperor's sister.

Vienna had doubled in size and population in the course of the three decades before Rossini's arrival, and social divisions cut the city into three different zones. At the time of Rossini's visit the houses of the aristocracy, built in Baroque or Neoclassical style, were within the ramparts which had twice withstood the Turkish sieges. (In 1857 the Ringstrasse, a large landscaped boulevard, took the place of the demolished fortifications.) These fine buildings were centred around the cathedral of St Stephen and the imperial palace; the walled city had a population of 55,000 people. Spreading out beyond the ramparts were residential districts, the province of the liberal professions and the world of commerce, where the buildings reflected substance and respectable solidity – the kind of Vienna associated with the bourgeois life and artistic traditions of Biedermeier. The third zone of the capital, on the left bank of the Danube, was dreary. Here the proletariat that came from all parts of the Habsburg Empire existed in overcrowded accommodation with little sanitation. There were about 180,000 people crammed into this area, which the likes of Beethoven and Rossini, or Schubert for that matter, probably did not penetrate. Schubert was not often seen in Vienna's upper-class centre, while Beethoven was no longer a desired guest among the aristocracy. Instead it was Rossini whose presence was craved in the grand palaces.

Beyond the city, green slopes led to the Wienerwald with its pretty villages and open-air cafés. The artistic middle classes loved to go there, not only to promenade and collect gossip but also to spend forbidden weekends in remote hideaways. Every traveller who came to Vienna was amazed by the musicality of the city. 'Music is the Viennese pride and it can be said that it is the most important element of their education. For this lovely people a new opera by Rossini at Kärntnertortheater is a happening no less important than the opening of Parliament for the English,' wrote Charles Sealsfield in 1828. He went on to describe how there was a piano in every household and how visitors would be welcomed with biscuits and the sound of the lady of the house playing at her keyboard.

The person who presided over all this from his Schönbrunn palace was the bureaucratically minded Franz I, he who had been coolly received at the San Carlo opera house and even less graciously welcomed at La Scala. Counselled by the aristocratic Prince Metternich, Franz could not forget that his aunt had been guillotined and his empire turned upside down by an upstart Corsican. Having imposed heavy fines on the losers, the Austro-Hungarian Empire was climbing back to its feet. Under Metternich's influence the Habsburgs promoted opera as a form of entertainment. Rossini was their man, and fun-loving Vienna imbibed his music like bubbling champagne; almost every opera that Rossini had so far composed was staged by the state theatres and in countless drawing-rooms all over the empire. The Viennese couldn't have enough of him. Rossini was received in every salon, including the most select of them all, that of the imperial court, where he was asked to play and sing.

Prince Klemens Wenzel Lothar Metternich, the staunch defender of the *ancien régime* was born in the city of Koblenz in 1773. He had become Austrian foreign minister as early as 1809. The fact that Barbaja's company had been invited to Vienna was due to Metternich's love of Rossini's music. Metternich had insisted that a season featuring the Italian company should have operas by Rossini alone;

the Austrian public should be fully exposed to the new genius. This decision, with its underlying political motivation, enraged the Teutonic composers. Why should operas by Schubert, Beethoven and Weber be so seldom performed in Vienna? The main reason was that those musical voices, especially Beethoven's, were a threat to the established Metternichian order. 'Many eras witnessed tyrannical governments but what gave a special characteristic to life under Metternich was the sense of deep and widening disappointment,' wrote E. H. Gombrich.

From the day of his arrival Rossini's notes were resounding everywhere. His scores had been printed by several Viennese publishers and images of him were sold all over elegant Vienna. Those who did not have enough money to buy a box at the opera were the same people who lived in fear of Sedlnitzky, the chief of police. Following the bloody and exhausting war, the Austrians had hoped for an improved world but were instead plunged back into Metternich's restoration of the past. Rossini and his music were well suited to Metternich's design: pleasant, capable of arousing the great emotions of love, but not a sublimation of uprising, rebellion or revolts.

Arriving with Barbaja and his company, Rossini and La Colbran stayed at the imposing hotel Zum Goldenen Ochsen. 'Wherever he shows his face in the street, crowds gather and people follow him everywhere,' wrote the *Wiener Zeitung*. The couple was entertained every night – not good for Isabella's voice. There was tension between the newly married couple and Barbaja; but also Rossini, meeting many interesting people, began to be aware of Isabella's limitations. It would have never occurred to Rossini to take his ignorant wife with him should he succeed in his wish to meet Beethoven, for example. Rossini had read some of Beethoven's scores and, shortly after his arrival in Vienna, heard the Third Symphony for the first time. This was the work originally designated 'Eroica', in dedication to General Bonaparte; but when Napoleon ceased to be the liberator, when Napoleon the Titan became a mere mortal who had the *folie de grandeur* to crown himself emperor, Beethoven scrapped the dedication; and, on the symphony's publication, he described it as having been 'composed to celebrate the memory of a great man'. By now Beethoven had become even more disaffected: he felt alienated from humanity; he was angry and he wanted to shout it out, to shake the world into action. Rossini sought to meet this man but was told that Beethoven was morose and misanthropic; it would be pointless, he was assured, even to ask to visit him because he was so deaf that he could not follow any conversation. But Rossini persevered. He was determined to meet the composer whose music, angry and aggressive, seemed to break the boundaries of Neoclassicism. With *Fidelio* (1805), the opera that Vienna did not want to hear, Beethoven tried to awaken people to the need for justice. Metternich thought that this kind of music was politically dangerous. Schubert too risked being arrested for the same reasons. Rossini on the other hand, composed melodies which people hummed with delight; his music extolled love and expressed the joy of life; this was the music the Viennese establishment needed. Not something as stirring as Beethoven's *Fidelio*, as desperate as Schubert's Ninth Symphony nor as sombre as Weber's *Freischütz*. And in some of Rossini's comic music, there is a foretaste of the operetta genre which was to explode in Vienna and which also greatly influenced Offenbach.

No answer came to Rossini's first requests for an encounter with Beethoven. But Rossini, instead of sulking, tried to understand. Why was Beethoven not held in the esteem that he deserved in Vienna? The first intermediary from whom Rossini sought help in his quest was Signor Artaria, Beethoven's publisher; but this attempt was unsuccessful. Then Rossini asked Antonio Salieri, the composer who had ruled Vienna's musical scene in spite of Mozart's presence. Salieri's request was also dismissed by Beethoven. Finally it was Giuseppe Carpani, one of Haydn's earliest biographers, who was able to lead Rossini up the rickety wooden stairs of Beethoven's house in the old Schwarzspanierhaus. Beethoven barricaded himself in a filthy room festooned with dusty cobwebs. He was attended by a housekeeper who prepared a bit of food for the grumbling man and then disappeared, leaving the place in total disarray. He was unkempt, with dishevelled, oily hair. His appearance in the street caused his nephew Karl to be ashamed; he spoke loudly and was obsessed by thoughts of death. When he coughed, he spat into a handkerchief to see if there was any blood; in fact, he did have consumption, which his mother had suffered too. Among the surviving eye-witness accounts of Beethoven's daily habits is that of Dr Lorenz:

> *Beethoven rose daily at half past six and at half past seven breakfast was served. Afterwards Beethoven would go for a walk. He strode*

about the fields, shouted, waved his hands, walked slowly then very fast, and would suddenly stop to write something in a note book. At noon he would return for lunch remaining at home until three o'clock. Then he went out again into the fields until nightfall. He would write up to ten o'clock and then went to bed. Sometimes he played the piano in the drawing room.

The fact that Beethoven did not refuse to meet his apparent antithesis, Gioachino Rossini, suggests that the indomitable giant recognized the controversial Italian as an equal. Beethoven would certainly have been aware of Rossini's presence in Vienna. To Theophilus Freudenberg, a composer, who had asked him for an opinion of Rossini's music, he had written: 'It is the translation of the frivolous and sensuous spirit that characterizes our age, but Rossini is a man of talent and an exceptional melodist. He writes with such ease that he takes as many weeks for the composition of an opera as a German would take years.' So the Romantic torment of the Northerner was in comparing himself to the imaginary sunny ease of the Mediterranean which eluded him. Beethoven who was soon to write his last five string quartets which would be his crowning glory, had been groomed by those composers Rossini most admired, Haydn and Mozart. Unlike Rossini, Beethoven composed slowly, constantly re-examining his own process. He had patrons and friends – but he also had many enemies. Rossini was profoundly moved by the squalor of Beethoven's lodgings. He noticed that there were even leaks in the ceiling. The 'van' which had been foolishly added to the family name for the sake of aristocratic airs was betrayed by Beethoven's peasant-like features. But his own inner nobility was noticeable when he read the questions addressed to him by Rossini. Behind the table where Beethoven sat was his grand piano, one of the best available at the time, built for him by Conrad Graf. The instrument was now wrecked, its strings broken. On the table Rossini observed the ear-trumpets and the conversation books in which questions were written by the few visitors who bothered or dared to visit Beethoven. There were a few odd coins, several quill pens, a broken coffee cup and his brass candlestick, in the surprising shape of a Neoclassical statuette of Cupid. Rossini later described this momentous meeting to many people, including Wagner, Hiller and Hanslick:

Portraits of Beethoven give a good idea of what he looked like but no picture could express the undefinable sadness so clear in his every feature. Under the heavy brows, his eyes shone as if from the back of a cavern; they were small but they seemed to pierce. His voice was soft and rather veiled . . . As I went up the stairs leading to the poor lodgings in which the great man lived, I had some difficulty in containing my emotion. When the door was opened, I found myself in a sort of hovel, dirty and frighteningly disorderly . . . When we entered he, at first, paid no attention but continued to correct some proofs. Then suddenly, raising his head, he said in quite good Italian 'Ah, Rossini, so you are the composer of Il barbiere di Siviglia. *I congratulate you, it is an excellent* opera buffa *which I have read with pleasure. It will be played as long as Italian Opera exists. Never try to write anything else but* opera buffa; *any attempt to succeed in another style would damage your nature.*

Rossini would never forget this remark, even alluding to it long afterwards, when contemplating death: he jokingly dedicated his last work to God, but also repeated Beethoven's statement; in other words, only God and Beethoven were to know that Rossini was not destined for serious music.

Carpani had prepared Beethoven for the meeting by sending scores of several *opera serie*, including *Tancredi, Otello* and *Mosè*, and reminded him of this fact. Beethoven answered:

Yes, and I looked at them, but, believe me, opera seria *is ill-suited to the Italians. You do not possess sufficient musical knowledge to deal with real drama, and how in Italy, should you acquire it? Nobody can touch you Italians on* opera buffa, *a style ideally fitted to your language and temperament. Look at Cimarosa, how much better are the comic parts of his opera than all the rest. And the same is true of Pergolesi. You Italians have a high opinion of his religious music, and I grant that there is much feeling in the* Stabat; *but as regards form, it is deficient in variety and the effect is monotonous. Instead* La Serva Padrona . . .

Rossini recalled how he then expressed his 'profound admiration for [Beethoven's] genius and my gratitude for having been allowed to voice it in person.' How modest – and great – of Rossini not to take umbrage and instead to pay homage to the towering genius who had reluctantly agreed to receive him. (And how wrong Beethoven was about Pergolesi: his *Stabat mater* is a masterpiece, and has proved much more enduring than *La serva padrona*.) As Rossini wrote down his words of admiration – Beethoven understood Italian although Rossini might have tried his newly acquired German – the great man answered 'with a deep sigh: "Oh, un infelice!" [Oh, I am an unhappy wretch!] Carpani, Beethoven and Rossini were silent for a while. What did the great German composer think of the thirty-year-old Rossini, elegantly dressed and quite portly? Beethoven broke the silence by asking about the state of music in Italy. Were Mozart's operas performed there? If so, how often? He went on to wish Rossini well for his forthcoming *Zelmira* and then announced that the visit had lasted long enough. On leading the younger composer and Carpani to the door, he uttered his final words to Rossini: 'Remember, give us plenty of *barbiere*.'

A sense of deep sadness struck Rossini as he descended the dilapidated stairs. Having himself achieved economic security, he was sorely affected by Beethoven's destitution and found himself in tears, crying copiously and noisily. Carpani tried to console him, also pointing out that Beethoven had only himself to blame for his isolation. But Rossini could not erase from his mind the sadness expressed in the words sighed in Italian, 'un infelice'. The same evening, at a dinner given by Prince Metternich, Rossini described the experience:

> *I couldn't protect myself from an inner feeling of confusion at seeing, by comparison, myself treated with such regard by that brilliant Viennese assembly, and this made me say without discretion what I thought about the conduct of the court and the aristocracy toward the greatest genius of the era, who needed so little and was abandoned to such distress.*

He then tried to persuade some members of that glittering society to guarantee a permanent income for Beethoven; but nobody would listen. Even if Beethoven was given proper accommodation, they told Rossini, he would move from it; every six months he did so. As for his servants, he dismissed them every six weeks.

> *I demanded to know, however, if Beethoven's deafness didn't deserve the greatest pity, if it was really charitable to bring up the weakness*

with which they were reproaching him, to seek reasons for refusing to go to his assistance. I added that it would be so easy, drawing up a small subscription, to assure him an income large enough to place him beyond need for the rest of his life. That proposal didn't win the support of a single person.

At the reception after the dinner, all Viennese high society was present. 'One of Beethoven's most recently published trios figured in the programme . . . the new masterpiece was heard with religious fervour and won a splendid success,' Rossini said. How could it be, Rossini asked himself, that the world enjoyed Beethoven's music played in such luxurious surroundings while ignoring the man who had composed it and who lived in total squalor? His account continues:

I told myself sadly that perhaps at that moment the great man was completing – in the isolation of the hovel in which he lived – some work of the highest inspiration destined, like his earlier pieces, to develop into sublime beauties; the same brilliant aristocracy from which he was being excluded amid all its pleasures was not disturbed by the misery of the man who supplied it . . . I wanted to try to get together sufficient funds to buy him a place to live. But the Viennese always answered 'Beethoven is impossible'.

Goethe, whom Beethoven accused of being a poet for princes, said of the composer: 'Unfortunately he has an utterly untamed personality, not altogether in the wrong, holding the world detestable. But he does not make it any more enjoyable either for himself or for others by his attitude.' On another occasion, Goethe had written about Beethoven: 'A layman must have reverence for what is spoken by one possessed of such a demon.'

Rossini did not give up trying to raise money to help Beethoven. Some weeks later he opened another subscription list headed by his own name alongside an impressive sum of money. Again the Viennese did not want to know. Although Rossini himself did not mention it, a subsequent visit to Beethoven is documented in Anton Graeffer's autobiography.

I myself took Rossini to him when he lived at Kaiserstrasse. In spite of the fact that the public had turned to this Italian above all other composers in the world, Beethoven repeatedly embraced him and, with brotherly affection, showed that he very much appreciated his talent.

Rossini would have had to see Beethoven more than once in order to bring him the subscription funds he had collected. The welcome described by Graeffer is very different from the one that Rossini remembered when he later talked to Wagner. It is not surprising that Rossini's recollections focus on the Carpani visit as the most important, since it was his first.

There were other things for Rossini to do while in Vienna. At the Hoftheater, he attended a performance of *Der Freischütz*, a ripe fruit of German Romanticism conducted by Weber himself. Weber, emaciated, a long face behind thick spectacles, ugly beyond description, could not stand the orgy of praise that the Viennese directed at Rossini and insulted him as often and as vociferously as possible. Indeed the Viennese had gone mad: people fought to catch a glimpse of Rossini and paid good money to shake his hand. He was expected to perform in salons and even sing in the street. There were Rossini hats, cravats and walking-sticks, even restaurant dishes were named after him. There were countless receptions in his honour. He was a regular guest of the banking family Arnstein-Enkels and it was to Baroness Cecilia Enkels that he dedicated his *Addio ai viennesi*.

Despite all this bustling activity, Rossini was still haunted by the image of Beethoven. Beethoven's genius was inextricably linked to his dark temper and to the rage he felt against society; Beethoven did not compose to please or to serve other people's taste. Maybe it was after this confrontation that Rossini thought of no longer aiming to please; he realized that, having composed so much and so successfully, he had always been at the service of others. Music was now moving in a different direction, where painting and poetry had already preceded it. Music was going to disturb and provoke; that was what Beethoven was doing, that was the reason for the reprimand of labelling him an *opera buffa* composer. Yet Beethoven understood *opera buffa* as a vehicle for satire, as did the authorities. Today's audiences all too seldom detect the inflammatory criticism hidden in *opera buffa*, especially Rossini's. His *opera buffa* was inevitably critical of society, which is why it can still be so funny. *La Cenerentola* pokes fun at bureaucracy and greed, while *Il barbiere di Siviglia* derides conservative elements of society – the priesthood, notaries or the army – which were the props of the ever more fragile reactionary regimes ruling Italy at the time.

Had he been morose and angry instead of witty and worldly, had he shut himself in a hovel and written music that went against the established order, Rossini too would have been rejected by society. Rossini, like those before him but unlike Beethoven, approached composition primarily as a means of earning a living; it was a job like any other. That attitude was no longer possible in the Romantic age. The sonorous entrance of Beethoven burst open the gates of Romanticism. Romanticism existed as a word – and certainly as a concept – at the time of Rossini's visit to Beethoven, while the philosophy underlying the Romantic movement was to evolve dramatically. Even disease and poverty (Bellini's *La sonnambula*, Verdi's *La Traviata*) were to become subjects for the Romantics and yet Gioachino Rossini had already touched the mood in writing an opera about a servant girl accused of theft, a Moor destroyed by jealousy or indeed unrequited love by the Scottish lakes. The musical freedom that Beethoven had chosen brought him to destitution and that was something that Rossini did not want; the mere possibility frightened him.

II

ANDANTINO PASTOSO

After his giddy time in Vienna Rossini returned to Castenaso – now his own property as much as Isabella's – where he composed eighteen *gorgheggi*. It was the last time he was to write for his wife and these exercises might have been an effort to help Isabella to recover her voice; he was still fond of her, although the musical bond which kept them united was slackening. From now on he was to compose without Isabella in mind, producing *opere buffe* and music that needed a different vocal register. Loaded at last with his own money, he started negotiations to buy Palazzo Donzelli, a seventeenth-century building in Strada Maggiore, the main street in Bologna; he was to live there seven years later, but without Isabella. Now rich and famous, Rossini had many friends in Bologna. As he walked under the arcades of that fine city while his coach and horses waited for him at Piazza San Petronio, acquaintances would stop and shake his hand, recalling their shared past and perhaps offering him a glass of wine or a cup of coffee. By then his parents did not see each other at all; his chronically ill mother, sadly grown ugly, was with him at Castenaso, where she could receive physical comfort and good medical care.

In November 1822 Rossini received an invitation – actually a summons – from Prince Metternich. Seeing how quickly his territorial order was disintegrating, Metternich decided to call for yet another congress, this time in Verona, which was then under Austrian control. Rossini probably welcomed this opportunity. Rossini and Metternich had more than a little in common – mainly a good dose of pessimism but also a predilection for beautiful women and fine food. In fact theirs was more than a friendship, it was an intellectual exchange; Rossini looked up to Metternich and learnt from his mannerisms, his elegant turns of phrase and his cynicism. Rossini was asked to compose ceremonial cantatas for the Congress of Verona and, by his illustrious presence, entertain a group of powerful men, just as Beethoven had done at the Congress of Vienna. 'Seeing that I was the god of harmony, Metternich wrote to me, would I come to play where harmony was so badly needed?' Rossini later commented in a much-quoted aside.

Almost as soon as Isabella and Gioachino settled in the elegant apartments put at their disposal in Verona, where they were to stay for two months, Rossini received a visit from the chief of the French delegation. This was none other than the poet and diplomat Chateaubriand, a great admirer of his music, who wanted to discuss the possibility of the composer working in Paris. During the congress, Rossini was presented to Emperor Franz of Austria, to Tsar Alexander and to the Duke of Wellington (who was in Verona because the British foreign minister, Lord Castlereagh, had shot himself earlier that summer). In the evenings there were banquets and entertainments of all kinds.

The Congress of Verona gathered the most impressive collection of heads of state since the Congress of Vienna. Besides the representatives of the Holy Alliance, all the rulers of Italy except the pope were present at what turned out to be more of a social event than a political assembly. In fact Wellington immediately refused to commit Britain to help crush the revolution in Spain. 'The Holy Alliance was neither holy nor an alliance,' Rossini commented. A banquet was held in the Roman Arena (the amphitheatre that now features an annual opera festival) and Rossini participated on equal terms with all the emperors and prime ministers. Before the Napoleonic era a mere composer, a self-made man, could not sit at the same table as these mighty figures and talk to them on equal terms. Times had changed. Not many years had gone by since Louis XVI or, for that matter, Ferdinand of Naples ate alone. The entertainment in Verona included colossal ballets in the afternoons, mimes, dances and balls; also an orchestra of 128 players taken from the military bands stationed nearby which, Rossini said, played horrendously. The atmosphere of vacuous power and the delegates own self-importance made the congress little more than a frivolous theatrical experience. If Rossini was flattered to be in Verona among such a crowd, the pressure also irritated him and wore him out. A few signs of anxiety manifested themselves at this time. For example, while conducting (ironically) under the statue of Concordia, he was seized by a fearful frenzy thinking that the marble figure might fall on him at any moment. This is an early instance of Rossini's nervous fragility.

Rossini's two cantatas for the congress, *La Santa Alleanza*, and *Il vero omaggio*, are both lost. The former, commissioned by Metternich, was performed in the Arena on 24 November; the latter, written for the castrato Velluti with two tenors, bass, chorus and orchestra and played at the Teatro Filarmonico on 3 December, involved little compositional labour because it was drawn from *La riconoscenza*.

While he was in Verona, Rossini was corresponding with Benelli. Gioachino and Isabella had already decided to visit London and experience the city that was fabled as the richest in the world. And Chateaubriand had whispered in Rossini's ear to persuade the couple to stop in Paris. Not that Rossini needed much persuasion; Paris had been a potent beacon for some time. Rossini needed to save as much of his music as possible for his forthcoming travels and future commitments, hoping that it would be heard by a real audience and not just by a few grandees. This also explains why he hoped that *Il vero omaggio* would not circulate, as some ears might spot that it was almost totally based on one of his earlier compositions. But when he went to the Verona concert hall to collect his autograph scores he was barred from doing so, the commissioners alleging that they had bought all his music, lock stock and barrel. It was the first time that Rossini was to contest the subject of copyright, the right to the ownership of his own work. But establishing intellectual rights on his compositions took a very long time. He paved the way for the struggles ahead, when composers could safeguard their creations and bar theatres from using and misusing them; Verdi became involved in similar disputes.

Rossini's presence at the Congress of Verona was hard to swallow for those who had worshipped him as the composer who had alluded to *La Marseillaise* in one of his most successful operas, whose words extol Italian action against foreigners. Now liberal ears had to hear his feeble cantatas in honour of the Holy Alliance. His time with the Bourbons had been excused because Rossini had never really kowtowed to the court or conveyed messages of praise for its politics. But being a jester at Verona was unacceptable, and the continuing perception of Rossini as a man of the right dates from this phase. In retrospect, it is easier to see Rossini as the image of the modern man, the individualistic creature that the French Revolution, the Empire and now the new age of Romanticism was promoting, a self-made man, pragmatic and businesslike.

By 9 December 1822 Rossini and Isabella were in Venice for a new version of *Maometto II*, an opera which was to be reworked for the French stage. At the opening performance later that month, Colbran was not at her best and the Venetian public booed to such an extent that the opera had to be withdrawn; its substitute, *Ricciardo e Zoraide*, was not a success. The fact was that La Colbran's voice was badly damaged. Furthermore, Rossini was facing a new and disagreeable phenomenon: having become so popular, his operas began to travel; they were now 'in repertoire'. His audiences still expected new operas, but what Rossini was offering at times seemed like old hat which had already featured elsewhere. A new *opera seria* was wanted for La Fenice; the agreement specified that Rossini was to compose and supervise its production. Rossini started to work on *Semiramide* when he was back at Castenaso. It proved to be one of the few operas on which he had time to ponder, about four months. Like *Tancredi*, it was drawn from a tragedy by Voltaire. More complex than his previous *opere serie*, it displays vertiginal acrobatics in *bel canto* over which Rossini lavished great care. Gaetano Rossi, his librettist who came to Castenaso so that they could work together, described the place to Meyerbeer: 'Delicious, really, in all its agreeable surroundings; beautiful gardens, a voluptous little chapel, lake, hills, woods and a magnificent and elegant home.' Within five days of Rossi's arrival on 5 October, the shape of the opera had been worked out. Still at Castenaso at the end of the month, Rossi informed Meyerbeer that Rossini was not behind schedule. Commenting on the music, he wrote: 'What pomp! A truly imposing picture.' As Philip Gossett has pointed out, the opera's 'monumental proportions are strongly rooted in neo-classical traditions'. The overture, which is one of Rossini's best known, incorporates themes to be heard later in the opera and, unlike any of his previous works, the entire composition is symphonic in scale. The highly charged tale of love is expressed in brilliant *cavatine* and it is the high point of Rossini's *bel canto* style, soon to be outmoded because few singers could cope with its demands. Tsar Alexander and Franz II attended some of the rehearsals and evidently enjoyed what they heard. However, while the former gave Rossini a snuffbox studded with diamonds, the latter merely smiled and shook his hand (he was notoriously stingy).

Semiramide was to be sung by one of the most glittering casts of the time, including Isabella Colbran and Filippo Galli. When it was first performed, on 3 February 1823, the Venetian public found it too long – they hadn't yet experienced Wagner. As a result, Rossini cut the first act quite radically for the twenty-eight ensuing performances. But again, the trouble with the first night of *Semiramide* had been Isabella's voice; the Venetians splashed mourning posters reading '𝕽equiescat in pacem' all over the walls around La Fenice. Many Italian families still announce the deaths of their relatives with fly posters. In this case, the Venetians were cruelly announcing the artistic death of Isabella Colbran.

Leaving Venice, Rossini stopped in Treviso on 1 April 1823 to unveil a memorial bust to Antonio Canova, who had died the previous year, and conducted his *Omaggio pastorale*, a cantata for three female voices and orchestra, a fitting tribute to the Neoclassical sculptor. Rossini and Colbran then returned to Castenaso, remaining there for several months. It was a dark period in their conjugal life: Isabella was no longer in demand, but he was; she was no longer occupied with theatrical activities – reading scores and librettos, rehearsing and meeting interesting people – but he was. She had too much time on her hands, no children to occupy her and no hope of having any. Moreover, relations with her mother-in-law had deteriorated. Isabella felt socially superior to – and possibly jealous of – Anna, the person that Gioachino loved most. Maybe Isabella also resented her husband for having composed *Semiramide* for a voice which was now beyond her; her husband had thus damaged her career and reputation. The situation soon became public enough for Rossini to receive a letter referring to Isabella as 'your boring companion'. Meanwhile the composer was seeking refuge with some old 'friends' in Bologna's brothels. Perhaps hoping that a period of intense collaboration would improve their mood and relationship, Isabella and Gioachino then signed contracts for London with Benelli. In spite of their promises, neither of them ever returned to Naples; and, more importantly, it turned out that *Semiramide* was Rossini's last opera for an Italian audience and the last of his Neoclassical works. On 20 October 1823 they left for England, travelling via Milan, where the Duke of Devonshire gave them letters of introduction for use in London. They would also stop over in France which, of course, meant Paris, the centre, the glittering heart of cultural Romantic Europe.

ACT THREE

BALZAC AND THE INTELLECT

Il faut convenir que les passions sont un accident dans la vie, mais cet accident ne se rencontre que chez les âmes supérieures.
                                        Stendhal, *Le Rouge et le noir*

[It has to be agreed that passions are an accident in life, but that accidents are not to be found except amongst superior beings.]

I

ALLEGRO MOLTO

After Milan and a stop in Geneva (which they reached after a troubled but spectacular coach journey), the Rossinis arrived in Paris on 9 November 1823. For a month they were the guests of the Genoese writer Nicola Bagioli at 6 rue Rameau. The French press went wild: there were daily features reporting the sayings of Rossini, his every movement, his every host. The composer arrived in France with the advantage of being popular among the restored Bourbon monarchy. A musical party in Rossini's honour was given by the Duchess of Berry during which he accompanied himself at the piano in arias from his operas. He also sang at a soirée given by Countess Merlin and, when Mlle Mars gave a party in his honour, the great actor Telma recited and Rossini sang. The painter François-Pascal Gérard also hosted an evening where the young Honoré Balzac (not yet *de* Balzac) was introduced to him. Stendhal's *Vie de Rossini* was now available in bookshops and was rapidly becoming a best-seller.

By this time most of Rossini's operas had been performed in Paris, although in bastardized or truncated versions, which was quite common when the composer himself was not at hand. For the performance of *Il barbiere di Siviglia* two days after Rossini's arrival the composer was of course present. Under the direction of Ferdinando Paer since 1812 (Rossini had made his theatrical début in Paer's *Camilla* at Bologna back in 1805), the Théâtre-Italian had fallen into a state of disorder and mediocrity. The only way to hear new music played well was to attend a private salon. Parisians had come to the conclusion, based on fact, that their philistine administration had pursued a campaign to bar Rossini's music from their theatres. Therefore the enthusiasm with which Rossini was received had plenty to do with the restoration of the Bourbons. Contempt for the *parvenus*, who had been conducting their affairs by filling their purses rather than feeding the public's intellect, was strongly felt among the intellectual avant-garde, the Romantics. In fact the crop of people favoured by the late Napoleonic Empire had much in common with today's Thatcherite and Blairite peers, promoted for the money and adulation they gave to the political movement, but generally devoid of knowledge; like the New Labour peers, their Napoleonic equivalents were busy aping the aristocratic mannerism of the old order. The Bourbon nobility and the Parisian artistic avant-garde who were in full reaction against the Neoclassical Empire, its pomp and fake titles, were instinctively in sympathy with Rossini. They must have loved and recognized with glee the Pappataci and Kaimakan in *L'italiana* as much as Don Magnifico's distribution of favours and titles in *La Cenerentola*. In one way or another, musical Paris had heard Rossini's music, but mainly at private evenings.

So frenetic was the Rossini fever that seized Paris that a week after his arrival a grand dinner was prepared for him at the Restaurant Martin in Place du Châtelet known as 'du Veau qui tette'. On Sunday 16 November over 150 guests, the cream of intellectual Parisian society, crowded the fashionable rooms of the restaurant. Among those present were the painter Horace Vernet, the composers Auber, Boieldieu and Hérold and three top singers, Giuditta Pasta, Manuel García and Laure Cinti-Damoreau, who were at the time as famous as certain film stars are now. As the (paying) guests arrived, they were greeted by the overture from *La gazza ladra*. Everything to do with this meal, from the decoration to gastronomy, had a Rossinian connection. There were speeches and verses. A medal struck for the occasion was given to all the guests, whose departure was accompanied by 'Buona sera' from *Il barbiere* – not the best way to dispatch gentle ladies if one recalls the way in which Don Basilio is sent away: the aria ends with the stretta, 'Maledetto, andate via, presto andate via di qua' ('Bastard, get out of here, get out of here fast').

This dinner became so celebrated that a vaudeville mocking it was written and performed within a fortnight at the Théâtre du Gymnase-

Dramatique, with a text by Eugène Scribe and music by Edmond Mazères. Called *Rossini à Paris ou Le grand diner*, it effectively contained more criticism of the envy that Rossini's success had provoked than of Rossini himself. The famed composer is due to arrive in Paris any minute; everybody wants to meet him but nobody knows what he looks like. The innkeeper Biffteakini plans a grand dinner that will bring him large profits. He loves food and music and he will honour 'le grand Rossini, le divin Rossini, Apollon Rossini'. Although all Italians are rogues, Biffteakini is convinced that 'le divin' alone is good and honest. The cast of course includes a pretty young lady, Biffteakini's daughter, who after three months at the academy still cannot sing a note. But the handsome young Giraud turns up at her father's inn. Penniless, Giraud is a student from the conservatoire who has great ideas about producing French operas – a pointed mockery of the state of French music at the time. After Rossini's arrival in Paris is announced, Biffteakini gives his spectacular dinner in Rossini's honour cooking eels 'à la sauce Kreutzer' while singing 'Di tanti palpiti'.

> De Rossini, partisan fanatique
> j'aime à chanter ses airs et ses rondeaux,
> tous ses finals ont un pouvoir magique;
> leur souvenir me suit jusqu' aux fourneaux
> Maitre divin! Ah! combien tu me touches,
> humble traiteur, j'admire ton talent
> et je l'envie en un point seulement,
> c'est que ton nom remplit toutes les bouches,
> et que mon art n'en peut pas faire autant.

Mistaking the student for Rossini, Biffteakini and his dining companions realize that Giraud is not Rossini ('Rossini, Rossini pourquoi n'est-tu pas ici?'). The composer was invited to attend rehearsals and, being a witty man, he turned up and responded enthusiastically.

Before leaving Paris for London, Rossini was approached by the Marquis of Lauriston, Minister of the Royal Household, who offered Rossini an official position so that he would not leave Paris, in fact the new sense of national pride demanded higher musical standards. The composer asked for 40,000 francs per annum, offering a package of new compositions and conducting which would restore quality in the

Parisian theatres. His price was considered exorbitant. Yet Rossini was keen to explore potential opportunities in London, a city that should offer something for his neglected wife. Colbran was to sing at the King's Theatre but if they stayed in France she would have been reduced to the status of spectator. Paris was aware of her reduced vocal talent. Before leaving Paris, however, no less than the band of the Guarde Nationale followed Rossini to rue Rameau where they played Lindoro's serenade. No composer had ever been treated with such favour in Paris. He was even voted an associate member of the Académie des Beaux-Arts.

II

ANDANTE CON MOTO

Now it was England's turn to succumb to Rossini fever; everybody wanted to catch at least a glimpse of Europe's most successful contemporary opera composer. On his arrival, the influential musical magazine *Harmonicon* announced:

> *Of all living composers Rossini is the most celebrated. He has been invited to every grand theatre of Europe in succession. Last year he was to have presided at King's theatre in London but he preferred Vienna. Paris next solicits him; and if he be not exhausted by the admiration of the French, or overladen with their opulence, he will come to London, the last, loftier, and the most lavish of capitals, fed upon by men and song.*

Now thirty-one, Rossini found his first crossing of the Channel so traumatic that on his arrival in London he had to retire to bed for a week. For Rossini, travelling in a monstrosity which spat smoke and fire, a demon which looked like Cerberus, was a fearful experience. He and Isabella were used to the peaceful sailing ships which crossed the bay of Naples; the sight and sound of these new-fangled steam boats were beyond endurance. Flaubert's *L'Education sentimentale* gives us an idea of the shock of the new steam power:

> *the sailors ignored all enquiries; people bumped into one another; the pile of baggage between the two paddle-wheels grew higher and higher;*

and the din merged into the hissing of the steam, which, escaping
through some iron plates, wrapped the whole scene in a whitish mist,
while the bell in the bows went on clanging incessantly.

When Rossini eventually reached London on 13 December 1823, Prince Livens, a relation of the tsar who, as Russian ambassador, had met Rossini at the Verona Congress, came to summon him to His Majesty's presence but was rebuffed. The composer needed to be kept in solitary confinement, Prince Livens was told. It was an odd way to treat royalty, and Rossini could not afford to snub a king as powerful as George IV, but he had been terrified by the speed of the ship, by its noise, the sense of being carried out of control. Indeed Prince Livens was convinced that the composer's appalling appearance was the result of some kind of seizure, as he then reported to the king at the Royal Pavilion in Brighton.

This is the first time that we witness Rossini experiencing a deep nervous collapse, but he must have had unrecorded others. Crossing the Channel deterred him from working in England; he was never to return to London. As Simon Wessely, Professor of Psychiatry in London explained, victims of panic attacks are reduced to a state of fearful incapacity; the circumstances in which each attack occurs can never be repeated. In Rossini's case, any form of travel by steam-driven transport would leave him traumatized and lethargic, incapable of leaving his bed for days; he could neither talk nor write – nor compose. Isabella was unable to help. The couple had taken up residence at 90 Regent Street, a smart new terrace recently built by John Nash. For company there was a flamboyant parrot.

When Rossini recovered, the two of them left London for Brighton where the king, a long-standing admirer, was expecting him. They arrived on 29 December. The newly rebuilt Royal Pavilion must have been even more astonishing than it is today, and to Rossini's eyes this extravaganza, a joke out of an Ottoman opera, an oriental fairy tale, probably reminded him of the Bey Mustafa's palace in *L'italiana in Algeri*. Every room inside the pavilion echoed with music and there were good instruments and good listeners everywhere. The king loved music. But Rossini was still half stunned and was in an odd disposition, distant, apathetic. Besides his recently manifested phobia for sea travel, he was probably horrified by the wintry Brighton sea; those brown waves must have seemed a far cry from the turquoise froth of the Bay of Naples. Nevertheless, he was able to enjoy playing the magnificent pianos at the Royal Pavilion. One day, while he was doing so, King George suddenly entered the room and everybody respectfully stood. Rossini went on playing. Relieving his courtiers from total embarrassment, the king walked straight up to Rossini and said: 'It is apt that the king of music should go on playing when a mere king enters.' Having upset the courtiers through his lack of respect, Rossini made things worse by singing Desdemona's Willow Song in falsetto in order to demonstrate how a castrato voice might sound – many a noble nose wrinkled in distaste. When he sang 'Largo al factotum' in *voce baritonale*, the king joined in. Then George took Rossini by the arm and they had a private conversation – no doubt they talked about the king's late wife Caroline of Brunswick and her disorderly life in Pesaro. The king probably revelled in Rossini's recollections.

But suddenly Rossini did not seem to care about all those society figures and was judged extremely bad-mannered. The truth was that he was distancing himself from his former admiration of power; he was partly digesting the lesson that Beethoven had unwittingly given him and partly he was overtaken by a strange depression. He felt that nothing he could do or had done was worth doing. His time in Paris had changed his attitude towards the world of courtiers. He needed more depth and less pleasantry.

In London Rossini moved with ease from Apsley House to Devonshire House and apparently spent almost all his time among royals or high aristocracy. The king often accompanied him, especially at the Thursday morning musical matinées of Prince Leopold of Saxe-Coburg at Marlborough House. Rossini also befriended Sir David Solomons, the Lord Mayor and founder of the Westminster Bank, for whom he composed a fine *Duetto* for cello and double bass. There was a special concert given at the King's Theatre for which a print was struck showing the composer at the piano with the soprano Angelica Catalani, the most expensive diva of her time. Between them, Britannia herself is depicted crowning the two heads in glory while angels and cupids are spread about the stage. Elegant ladies watch the composer adoringly from the boxes. At the same concert, Clementi's fine Third Symphony had its première but Britannia does not bother to crown its composer.

Sporting a blue suit and wearing a new cravat every day, Rossini cut an elegant figure, his attitude coupling indifference with geniality –

today he would be called 'cool'. But yes, alas, he had lost his trimness and his hair was thinning. 'He looks more like a sturdy beef-eating Englishman than a sensitive fiery-spirited native of the soft climate of Italy,' the *Quarterly Musical Magazine* reported. Another writer commented that he looked like a jolly fat man but added that 'his mastery at the pianoforte is miraculous'. The capital was completely unlike any city that Rossini had visited before. Crowded and with its sky darkened by coal smoke, London in 1823 was expanding and busy; in less than a century its population had multiplied by four. An Australian traveller writing at the time, labelled it 'this modern Babylon'. Another traveller, Hippolyte Tansie, noted that London was so crowded with all types of vehicle that a whole morning was needed before one could reach the outskirts; in this respect, of course, London has hardly changed.

The aristocracy which counted for five per cent of the population lived entrenched in their country houses; the intermediate classes, including merchants and bankers, were happy to accept a subordinate position, lacking the ambition of their continental equivalents and basking in their ignorance; the masses lived in poverty. Some aristo-crats had been awakened by the Grand Tour but, on the whole, England lacked the political and social stimulus that had electrified France, Italy and Germany; in fact it was producing plenty of money but few real artists. Apart from Turner, the field of painting was foremost, the nation's musical coffers had been empty for decades and its foremost cultural expression lay in literature and in scientific research. In spite of George IV's efforts, the city lagged behind Paris in all the arts, especially music. Rossini found orchestras to be second-rate, the public ignorant and noisy, operas put together badly and at the last moment. During his seven months in England he did his best to raise standards. Even if his operatic season did not go down well, his efforts as a conductor were recognized by *The Times*:

> The orchestra of this theatre is decidedly better than last season; not that the performers, taken separately, are superior but the ensemble is more perfect; which is owing without doubt to the personal super-intendence of a man of real talent . . . The improvement of the chorus, under the short rule of Rossini, is as conspicuous as that of the orchestra.

Under the terms of his contract with Benelli, Rossini was to compose a new opera for the King's Theatre, which was in the process of being remodelled by Nash. He was also to produce several of his own operas and oversee the performance of others. The *Morning Chronicle* announced: 'The King's Theatre under the new management is to be decorated with great splendour. The whole of the interior will be newly ornamented and the boxes will have new linings and draperies.' After a spell of financial difficulties and empty seats, the theatre had been leased to Benelli, who was so lavish with money and cavalier with creditors that he ended up bankrupt. Rossini's London season of 1823–4 opened with *Zelmira*, his last Neapolitan opera. The public filled the theatre from the earliest hours of the morning. 'When he entered the orchestra he was received with loud plaudits and so eager was the audience to catch a sight of his person that every individual in the pit stood on the seats to obtain a view,' the *Chronicle* wrote. Yet the opera, which had so excited Vienna, failed to please; again, Colbran's voice was not up to the part. However, with her looks and presence she was still a fine actress, and she received £1,500, far more than anybody else, including a composer. Rossini wrote to his father that the opera 'ha fatto furore' was a resounding success. There were seven other operas by him in the season, of which *Ricciardo e Zoraide* marked the end of Isabella's singing career. Not even *Il barbiere di Siviglia* went down well with the London audience. Only *Otello* and *Semiramide*, featuring Giuditta Pasta and Manuel García, were received with enthusiasm. Rossini himself coached the beautiful Giuditta and was to collaborate with her again the following year when he summoned her to Paris.

But the new opera promised by Rossini, although begun, was not performed. While he was extravagantly rewarded for his appearances at private concerts and for giving piano lessons to the children of the rich, he was beginning to be resented. The English press started to complain that his presence was costing dear to the British coffers. And *Ugo, re d'Italia*, the London opera that was not to be, failed to materialize for financial reasons. The musicologist Andrew Porter solved the mystery in 1964. Rossini did not deliver *Ugo, re d'Italia* because he had not been fully paid for it and, in so doing, he behaved like any businessman, which the English should have appreciated. But his withholding the promised new work made him unpopular. Where

Rossini did behave deviously was in conniving with Benelli in the latter's flight from the Haymarket Theatre; the impresario having sold the theatre's costumes and scenery that were not his to sell. After Benelli was declared bankrupt, Rossini deposited the incomplete score of *Ugo, re d'Italia* and some of the money he had received for it in Ransoms bank.

The bellicose philo-hellenism which had taken Byron to his death on 19 April 1825 had been sparked off by Greek rebellion against Turkish occupation. The Turks had retaliated by hanging the Greek Patriarch of Constantinople and three bishops in their ecclesiastical vestments while as many as 30,000 Greeks were killed on the island of Chios alone. Practically the whole of Europe (even Charles X of France) sided with the Hellenistic rebels. Byron became 'Greece's noblest friend' and, when he died of fever at Missolonghi, the Romantic world wept. Rossini composed a funeral lament, *Il pianto delle muse in morte di Lord Byron*, and sang the tenor part of Apollo at its first performance on 9 June. As Richard Osborne put it: 'The music [is] made up of solemn drum rolls, sudden grieving exclamations, and broken repeated lamentations all coaxed by Rossini into a song of mourning as gracious as it is brief.' As for the unnamed author of the Neoclassical rhymes, I am tempted to attribute them to the Italo-Greek Ugo Foscolo, then a political exile in London, whose admiration for Byron was well known and who met Rossini on several occasions. The words on the manuscript (which is in the British Museum) are of course in Rossini's hand:

APOLLO
Ahi, qual destin crudel
invola al nostro core
te, prima gloria e onore
dell'Elicolio stuol.

APOLLO
Ah, what cruel destiny
robs you from our hearts
you, prime glory and honour
of those who live in Helicon.

MUSE
Piu'non sara'chi'l labbro
sciolga a quei divi accenti

MUSES
There will be no more person whose lips
give form to divine phrases

APOLLO
ch'udian sospesi i venti,
figli di patrio amor.

APOLLO
which stopped the wind,
children of love of their motherland.

MUSE	MUSES
Ah non é piú quel grande,	Ah, that great man is no longer,
taccia la cetra e il canto:	that lyre and songs stopped.

APOLLO	APOLLO
Altro sfogo che pianto	Only in tears
il nostro duol non ha.	our lament finds appeasement.

Years later Rossini was asked by his friend Felix Moscheles (a brother of the Bohemian composer) whether he had even met Byron. 'Only in a restaurant,' was the answer, 'where I was introduced to him; our acquaintance, therefore, was very slight; it seems he spoke to me but I don't know what he said.' When he gave this laconic and vacuous description, Rossini was deeply depressed, so it should not be judged as an offhand or unkind recollection.

Rossini did not disclose that he had signed a contract at the French Embassy in London as early as 27 February, negotiating terms with the Prince de Polignac for his return to Paris. Rossini needed the stimulus of his environment and in the English drawing-rooms of princes and marquises, he had found no Balzac, Hugo or Delacroix. Perhaps that crossing of the Channel had also convinced him that he was not made for England. And perhaps he hated both the food and the climate, although he did not mention either, as for Verdi, a few years later, these became prime considerations for not working in London. Probably dreading the Channel crossing, he left English shores for ever on 25 July 1824.

III

PRESTO

W hat made Paris so extraordinary at that time? Certainly what appealed to Rossini was the sense of creative ebullience. Now that the ceaseless military campaigns seemed to be over, an increasingly influential bourgeoisie crowded the city. Artistic activity was at a peak, centred on a cluster of painters of the calibre of Delacroix, Géricault, Ingres and David. And, besides his lucrative contract, there was also the challenge of rescuing and recreating an opera tradition that France had momentarily lost. The artistic interplay was equally new and typical of the age. Music and painting took inspiration from literature, with Berlioz's inspiration from Virgil and Shakespeare or Delacroix's from Shakespeare, Byron and Scott being only the most obvious examples. At the same time, literature was often inspired by music, as in Balzac's *Gambara*.

By autumn 1824, Rossini was installed in Paris at 10 Boulevard Montmartre with his wife and parrot. They were ready to re-enter the intellectually stimulating life of the cafés and salons, where novels in the making were read aloud. Victor Hugo would ask his friends – Balzac included – to listen to his latest polemical poem or play. The cafés were an extension of the salons: the Café Frascati, in rich Empire style; the Café Anglais among the most elegant. They were beautifully decorated and the service was considered as important as the quality of the china. Balzac was a frequent visitor at both cafés and was also to be seen with Rossini in such restaurants as the Rocher de Carcal and Tortoni's. The rich would host musical afternoons and evenings where

Liszt and Paganini would play. The atmosphere of such occasions can
be judged from the words of George Sand:

> *No other art [than music] can so sublimely arouse human sentiment in*
> *the innermost heart of man. No other art can point to the eyes of the*
> *soul the splendour of nature, the delights of contemplation, the char-*
> *acter of nations, the tumults of their passions and the languor of their*
> *sufferings, as music can. Regret, hope, terror, contradiction, enthu-*
> *siasm, faith, doubt, glory, tranquillity, all these and more are given to*
> *us and take form thanks and according to the best of our own.*

And the sense that what Isaiah Berlin called 'a shift in consciousness'
was taking place at all venues in Paris can be captured in the words of
Delacroix's diary entry for May 1824 (while Rossini was in London):
'*Barbiere* at the Odéon; all good. I was next to a man who had known
Voltaire, Grétry, Diderot, Rousseau etc. "I see in you," he said as he
was leaving, "a century that is starting; in me, one that ends in
Voltaire's century."' For Victor Hugo, Romanticism was 'shadow
and light, the grotesque and the sublime, the animal with the spiritual'.
The middle class was at the vanguard of the movement, being made up
of a mix of people among whom foreigners were accepted – especially
if they were as rich as the Spanish banker Aguado, who opened his
house to artists, or James de Rothschild who, before Napoleon, would
have never been able to acquire the chic that surrounds his family to
this day. The new France was based on bankers and businessmen –
what in fact became the *haute bourgeoisie*. As Eric Hobsbawm put it
in *The Age of Capital*, Paris was the city where

> *bourgeois civilisation was invented . . . Formerly kings had official*
> *mistresses; now successful stock-jobbers joined them: courtesans*
> *granted their well-paid favours to advertise the success of bankers*
> *who could afford them . . . It had become the capital of a new society;*
> *energy, shrewdness, hard work and greed had found their channel in*
> *that city.*

Isabella found a new pleasure in shopping – and Gioachino a new
dissatisfaction in paying the bills. These flooded in from the Magasin
de Nouveautés des Menus Plaisirs, from the Petite Jeanette (*tissus,*
notes de tailleur) and from James Deulniau (*chevaux*); there were bills

from Adèle Martinet (*couturier*) and Amable Normandin (*coiffeur; brodeuses, tapisseries, quittance de loges*). On 26 November 1827 there was a bill from La Reine Marguerite & Cartier *fils* (*plumes et fleurs*); in January 1828 another (*A la lampe merveilleuse, gantier parfumier*). The list was infinite. Rossini's own expenses are also recorded, with bills from Gambaro (*marchand de musique*) and Andreoli (*copiste du Théâtre-Italien*). It was of course at the Théâtre Italien that Rossini started his intense Parisian activity. He was to put it back on its feet. Meanwhile there were other distractions. In order to compose for the French and understand the Parisians, Rossini needed to explore Paris, which he did thoroughly. He began to acquire a taste for a more sophisticated *table*, and grew ever more rotund in the process. Taste, wrote Balzac, was mastered and experienced by great people alone 'among whom is the illustrious Rossini, one of those men who have most studied the laws of taste, a hero worthy of Brillat-Savarin'. And of course there were the salons where Rossini's music was discussed with an intensity as yet unfamiliar to him and where there was plenty of opportunity for conversation. Balzac, elated after a performance of *La gazza ladra*, related: 'At the end, a very pretty lady gave me her arm to lead her out. I owed this gentle gesture to the high consideration that Rossini had just showed me; he had told me some flattering words that I cannot remember but that must have been eminently fine and spiritual: his conversation is in fact equal to his music.' And it is more than likely that the Rossinis would have been invited to the salon of the painter Horace Vernet, whom they had met at the dinner at the Restaurant Martin. So, naturally, they also met Olympe Pélissier, the spectacularly beautiful courtesan who had been Vernet's mistress and who, by then, had been 'passed on' to the novelist Eugène Sue; meanwhile she had moved on to Balzac's bed – a rather crowded berth. In 1831 Balzac published a cruel portrayal of her as Foedora in *La Peau de chagrin*:

> At the theatre, Foedora displayed herself as a play within a play. Her opera glass scanned one box after another; uneasy, though superficially tranquil, she was a slave of fashion: her box, her headgear, her carriage and her personal appearance meant everything to her . . . Foedora concealed a heart of bronze beneath her frail and graceful envelope. The deadly knowledge I had gained of human psychology stripped many of her veils. If aristocracy of mind consists in forgetting oneself

for the sake of others, in maintaining a constant gentleness of voice and gesture, in pleasing others by making them pleased with themselves Foedora, in spite of her acuteness, had not eliminated every trace of her plebeian origin; her self-forgetfulness was a pretence; her manners, instead of being instinctive, had been laboriously acquired; in short, her politeness smacked of servility.

That 'heart of bronze' bewitched Rossini. Balzac's characterization rings true and others had far worse to say about Olympe. Whenever he heard others praise her, Balzac said he felt ashamed for her: 'I knew that deep down in her there dwelt the soul of a cat.' She was certainly beautiful (according to Balzac, the most beautiful of the courtesans), but Edouard Robert, one of the directors of Théâtre-Italien, called her 'Madame Rabat-joie' ('Kill-joy').

The salons of respectable or semi-respectable ladies (generally those belonging to the aristocracy) could be attended by almost anybody, generally on specified afternoons; a shunned card implied lack of welcome, in which case the doors of *maisons particulières* belonging to the grand courtesans would be opened in the evening to more or less the same people, wives excluded. As later evoked in *La traviata* (which is based on Dumas' *La Dame aux camélias*), a kept woman, with a host of admirers – some of them aristocratic – could gamble, drink, and eat deliciously, occasionally but not necessarily enjoying sex.

These sorts of people wanted to be well entertained in their leisure time and Rossini was to cater to their needs with his directorship of the Théâtre-Italien, where he ensured that the music of contemporary composers could be heard at its best. On 25 September 1825, for example, Rossini arranged the Parisian première of Meyerbeer's *Il crociato in Egitto*, which had been hugely successful in London the previous July; this work launched Meyerbeer's European reputation. Rossini also nurtured new singers, among them the legendary Maria Malibran, of whom he said: 'Ah! that marvellous creature! She surpassed all her imitators by her truly disconcerting musical genius, by the superiority of her intelligence, the variety of her knowledge and her fiery temperament, it is impossible to give an idea.' Rossini tried to hire the best singers. 'Paris is a city where they sing little but where they pay a lot in private concerts,' he wrote to his father when he was trying to engage Domenico Donzelli (Barbaja accused Rossini of 'stealing' him). It was also part of Rossini's contract to produce operas in French, specifically composed and orchestrated for the French ear. He wisely took his time before embarking on his first French opera. Writing for a French audience required music for inordinately opulent ballets and elaborate scene changes of a kind that was completely different from what was expected anywhere in Italy or Vienna.

While he was working on improving the Théâtre-Italien, there was one official duty with a fixed date: the coronation of Charles X at Rheims Cathedral on 19 June 1825. Charles was in his early thirties when the Revolution drove him into exile and nearly sixty when the Restoration of the French monarchy allowed him back. After he became king at the age of sixty-seven, the tall and handsome monarch loved to spend the day anonymously hunting rabbits in the royal forest of Fontainebleau, dressed as a commoner. He was accepted by poachers as one of them to such an extent that he was even asked to be godfather at a christening; not even the priest recognized M. Leroy as Charles, *le roi*. In the style of the cantatas that Rossini had composed for the Bourbons, where a Bourbon king was once again anointed after the shame of Napoleon's empire, *Il viaggio a Reims* was intended to poke fun at everything and everybody – first of all at the cantata form. In fact that style would never again be repeated. As Bruno Cagli observed:

> Setting to music the new 'cantata scenica' as he called it in honour of another Bourbon celebration, Rossini would tear up by the roots the cantata tradition and would insinuate into the interior of those glorious epiphanies of human royalty the worm of doubt and scepticism, implicitly prophesying the immediate downfall of his protector the King, but also exploiting all that he had learnt from recent history.

Some of the characters of *Il viaggio a Reims* were borrowed by the librettist Luigi Balocchi from *Corinne ou l'Italie* by the tiresome Madame de Staël who, having been a staunch royalist and loathed by Napoleon, was back in favour. Ironically the theme recalls the meeting between Stendhal and Rossini at Terracina in that nobody knows what really happened at the inn; similarly, despite the title, there is no *viaggio* in the plot: the story has no story. It is in fact a partial satire of Madame de Staël's autobiographical fantasy but maybe it is also a satirical form of a cantata for a royal event which deserved satire. For the première Rossini had eighteen superstars from the Théâtre-Italien to choose from, one of them being his old flame Ester Mombelli. All the witty exuberance of *Il viaggio a Reims* bypassed the monarch and the court for whom it was written. The last of only three performances was staged by command of the Duchess of Berry, for whose fateful wedding Rossini had written his very first cantata in Naples. *Il viaggio a Reims* was performed there only three times. Its entire score was lost until, reassembled, it was performed at the Rossini Opera Festival in Pesaro by an ideal cast in ideal circumstances under the conductor Claudio Abbado.

A few days after the première, Rossini was seized by yet another nervous crisis and took to his bed for three weeks unable to move. When he felt ready, he settled down to his second revision of *Maometto II*, which resulted in *Le Siège de Corinth* (Opéra, 9 October 1826), followed by a reworking of his Neapolitan *Mosè in Egitto* as *Moïse et Pharaon* (Opéra, 26 March 1827). 'But for the love of God, how can I fulfil my promises to the management of a theatre that is cursed by all the gods, that remains open only by a miracle, with a French opera that even if being rehearsed daily, will cause me to die of consumption before the public gets to hear it?' Rossini was desperate.

By transposing *Maometto II* into *Le Siège de Corinth* (the first opera that Rossini sold to a publisher; Eugène Troupenas paid 6,000 francs for the rights), Rossini was expressing his support of the Greek patriotic cause, in aid of which he had conducted a concert. At a time of restoration of monarchies, Hellenism was the only ideal that helped to reconcile liberal and conservative sentiments, becoming a source of inspiration all over Europe. Besides, the Bourbons hoped that one of their own family would occupy the Greek throne if and when it was liberated from the Sublime Porte.

Based on Byron's short story in verse, the opera closes with the total destruction of Corinth by the Ottomans. Rossini changed the setting from Negroponte (Eubea) to Corinth; the victims under siege were no longer the Venetians (as in *Maometto II*), but the Greeks. Both orchestra and chorus have more prominence in the Paris version. Among the few entirely new pieces of music is the hymn 'Divin prophète', a highly charged addition to the Act II finale. *Le Siège de Corinth* was a triumph in every way and Rossini dedicated it to his father, a sign of real affection. Charles X offered him the accolade of the Légion d'Honneur (a Napoleonic order!), which Rossini turned down – less a political gesture than out of deference to other French composers who deserved it, in fact he accepted the honour a few months later after some of his contemporaries had also received it. Among other examples of Rossini's generosity towards his colleagues, often overlooked, is that which he extended to Weber. Despite Weber's attack on Rossini the previous year Rossini regarded the German composer as 'a great genius and a true one'. In Paris Rossini had Weber's music performed at the Théâtre-Italien and gave him a letter of introduction to the British monarch George IV who 'being very gracious to the arts' would help him. Rossini knew that Weber was very ill, and tried to dissuade him from embarking on such a perilous journey; in fact Weber died before his London *Oberon*. Rossini also helped Donizetti as later he aided the young Verdi. As anybody who has studied Rossini's correspondence will vouch, he also wrote countless letters of introduction for singers and composers. Indeed the generosity of his character is all too apparent in his music; nowhere better than in *Mosè*.

Mosè in Egitto is one of the century's most beautiful operas: the quartet 'Mi manca la voce' became famous all over the world. After leading the Israelites to the Red Sea, Moses sings, 'Del mio stellato sogno', a mystical melody of great power and inspiration that leads into the Israelites' great prayer. Balzac discussed *Mosè* at length in his novel *Massimilla Doni*. The protagonist, a Venetian duchess, announces: 'Tomorrow they are staging Mosè, the most immense opera born out of the finest Italian genius.' Later, the lady explains to a French guest.

This is not an opera but an Oratorio, a work which effectively resembles one of our most magnificent buildings inside which I will happily guide you. Believe me, it will not be too much to give our great Rossini all your intelligence, because you need to be at the same time a poet and a musician to understand the breadth of such music . . . That language of music, a thousand times richer than that of words, is to the spoken language what thought is to the formulation of words; it awakens feelings but leaves them intact. That power within our own inner self is part of music's grandiosity . . . the sublime symphony with which the composer opened that vast biblical scene [deals] with the sorrow of a whole people . . . Rossini has kept the strings to express the day when it follows darkness, and thus attains one of the most powerful effects which music has known . . . that scene of sorrow, that deep night, that cry of despair, that musical painting is as beautiful as le deluge *of your great Poussin.*

Moses raises his stick, the day dawns.

in which ancient or modern opera can you hear such a great score? the most splendid joy opposed to the deepest sadness? What a cry! what notes! the oppressed soul breathes, what a delirious moment, that tremolo in that orchestra, the beautiful tutti. It is the joy of a saved people. Don't you shiver with pleasure?

While he was composing, Rossini decided to leave the all-too-distracting capital and rented a village house in Puteaux which he shared with two couples, the Gallis and the Levasseurs. Gone were the days when he could write an opera in a few days. In Puteaux he and his companions entertained many friends and dined at the same table, sharing expenses and friends. Perhaps this was also a way to be separated from Isabella whose company he no longer sought. It was a telling sign for a man who earlier could have written a masterpiece standing on his head. Now circumstances were changing, and so was he. But it is also tempting to suggest that Rossini had gone to Puteaux to be near the beautiful woman who was so attentive towards him. Unlike Isabella, Olympe Pélissier seemed to understand his moods and treasured his company. And so did he hers.

While *Moïse* was in rehearsal, Dr Gaetano Conti from Bologna came to see Rossini with the news that his mother Anna was mortally ill. However it was thought that the emotion her son's visit would cause her might prove fatal so he was advised to refrain from rushing to Bologna.

As things were in Paris – with rehearsing his new operas and his relationship with Olympe – it was more convenient for Rossini to listen to what Dr Conti said, but he was never to forgive himself for letting his mother die without him, her only precoius son, by her side.

IV

REQUIEM

Nothing could have prepared Rossini for the loss of his mother. Being celebrated in a big city was worthwhile only if, in a distant place, there was the reassurance that she was following his every step. Anna was and remained his staunchest supporter, the only person he cared to please, to reward with his 'ha fatto furore' or to comment on a failure as 'un fiasco'. Her death on 20 February 1827 at fifty-five years of age, although forewarned, was impossible for Gioachino to absorb. That he was told after the event, furthermore not even by his father, made his pain even greater. On 9 March 1827 Gioachino wrote to his father from Paris, omitting to start the letter with his normal and affectionate 'Caro Padre'. Sad but forgiving words poured from his pen:

From the moment of that wretched letter of Dr. Giorgio about my mother's state of health, I never ceased fixing my eyes on those who surrounded me in order to understand from their silence the fatal announcement that my father himself should have made to his son. Because of your age, I forgive the lack of courage that you showed at a time when there was a need for virtue and fortitude of spirit; I did not cry but turned to stone. I feel this loss, I bind myself to the anchor that remains to me; together we shall find a new source of love in honouring the memory of the wife and the mother. This is the best choice we can give ourselves. Thus I grieve because I did not share with you the sorrow and the great consolation of not giving the last comforts to my good mother, all the same, receive my feelings of sympathy and also my good wishes for your well-being and because you give me proof of love and courage. Your personal duty is now the burial of the cold corpse; later her son will do what is owed to the one who gave him life.

The flow of Rossini's wounded phrases is poignant. While the letter is full of reproach, it also shows understanding. Beneath the surface of his burning words, many things are left unsaid. Gioachino offers reconciliation and love to Vivazza who had been a poor husband and father all his life, even making excuses for his failure to inform their son of Anna's death. Six days after the death, Giuseppe wrote to Francesco Guidarini, his wife's brother: 'Gioachino . . . would have been here some time ago but he was advised not to do so because if he arrived, she would surely have died in his arms. Two years ago, when he came to Italy, just seeing him, out of happiness she remained ill in bed for more than two weeks.' Of course that was a lie. Gioachino had not gone straight to Bologna because his own father had not told him how close Anna was to death. And also because Dr Conti's advice, turned into a matter of convenience while rehearsals were in progress. On the other hand, he was not capable of taking decisions, not any more. Depression is the enemy of resolution. After his mother's death Rossini's depressive tendency grew deeper, though whenever possible he tried to hide behind a façade of bonhomie. He barely budged from Paris and pushed himself into frenetic activity. At the same time he began to harbour a kind of resentment towards his wife who had been at odds with his mother, Anna's every memory now became sacred.

And he was doubtless affected by the news of another death. Far away, in another country, a man who belonged to a different world but who had made a great impression on Gioachino, died abandoned by society in general, but admired by a few contemporaries of stature. Beethoven, who had lived in Vienna for thirty years, changing his address at least thirty-five times – often losing his manuscripts and claiming that they had been stolen – died on 27 March 1827 with just a few friends by his side. It was said that a storm broke out and that lightning flashed into the room where he lay dying. Some 20,000 people attended his funeral; Schubert carried a torch. Delacroix had called Beethoven the genius who 'really reflected the modern character of the arts'. He had expressed 'what is melancholy and what, whether correctly or not, is called

Romanticism' (*et de ce qu'à tort ou à raison, on appelle roman-tisme*).

Not understanding the sombre tone of his son's letter, Giuseppe answered: 'Don't reproach me for not having given you the news myself, my heart was too pierced.' Gioachino then begged his father to join him in Paris, a proposal that he regretted not having made to his mother. But Giuseppe was reluctant to embark on such a long journey, largely because of his age. In any case, were he to agree, would his son remain in Paris? Or would he leave him alone with a manservant for weeks on end? Eventually one of Isabella's Spanish manservants was sent to Bologna to fetch Vivazza. Giuseppe found that his son was working in spite of his mood; within six days of Giuseppe's arrival, he had finished a cantata for six solo voices and piano, written for the baptism of Aguado's son. A sympathetic man who had been a friend and the protector of Rossini's union with Olympe, Aguado was extremely rich and financially shrewd. The banker had given Rossini continous hospitality and assistance – not only medical assistance, but also invaluable financial advice. He knew about Rossini's worsening depressions and had witnessed his deteriorating relationship with Isabella as well as her gambling, which offended Rossini's unstable attitude to money. Aguado also knew that by 1830 – only two years away – Rossini wanted to forsake opera and return to Bologna; to leave music and to leave Paris would mean cutting himself off from society. But who would believe him, the most successful composer of his time leaving everything behind? Rossini might have joked that since he was born on 29 February, on a leap year, it would have taken him 120 years to reach thirty. Even a mind like his would have tired of writing melodies and seeing people.

He still owed Paris another work but this was readily available because *Il viaggio a Reims* had been heard by so few that some of it could be reused. Eugène Scribe, the co-author of *Rossini à Paris*, had become the most successful librettist of the day and Rossini asked him to supply a text (with Charles-Gaspard Delestre-Poirson) after their play *Le Comte Ory*, an erotic saga turned comedy, a melancholic vaudeville. Everything goes wrong for the protagonist: whether disguised as a hermit or as a female-pilgrim, the wily count is unable to seduce the countess; when he eventually reaches her bedroom, it is her page, not the lady herself, to whom he offers his love. The sense of failure echoes the feeling of impotence of a composer who had lost faith in himself. The count's impotence is Rossini's own, and that impotence should, I think, be understood in every sense of the word. Rossini's depression reduced if not destroyed his libido.

Although he had learnt to live with attacks of gonorrhoea, Rossini was now also suffering from a form of urethritis possibly made more acute by his increasingly excessive eating and drinking habits. Naturally, around that time, Isabella's affliction had deteriorated too; there was no cure for gonorrhoea and the medical treatments available were often worse than the actual disease. From then onwards Isabella was in the hands of unscrupulous doctors and she was not only unrelentingly reproachful but also resentful towards her husband. His own suffering, which included periods of persecution mania and phobia, did not seem to move the heart of the old diva. It is unlikely that Giuseppe, absorbed as he was by the difficulties of adjusting to Paris and to his son's wealth, noticed that his son was so ill.

Despite all this, *Le Comte Ory*, first performed at the Opéra on 20 August 1828, was a huge success. Even Berlioz, an obstinate critic of Rossini's music (and of Rossini himself), admired it. Rossini was indifferent, perhaps even a touch cynical, about this. He received 16,000 francs from Troupenas for the publication rights, and the run of sixty performances made a profit of 7,000 francs. Having been paid next to nothing for the wholly original pieces of his youth, he now began to lack his earlier self-confidence. He kept signalling to his friends that soon he would leave the world of opera.

After the second performance of *Le Comte Ory*, Rossini retired to Aguado's country house near Fontainebleau, where he arrived to fulfil his next contractual obligation. Meanwhile his father returned to Bologna together with Isabella and one manservant. This opera was to be Rossini's last, and he knew it. It was to be in the French style: Romantic, big, the prototype of what French grand opera, *le monstre*, was going to become. One feels that when he started composing *Guillaume Tell*, he had all those adjectives in mind. The libretto is based on Schiller's *Wilhelm Tell*, as adapted by Etienne de Jouy and others, including himself. The 'new' Rossini was attracted to this story (whose theme Heine described as 'the grandeur and harmony of nature and the unpredictable character of politicized man') because it contained all the Romantic themes that were likely to be well received by the contemporary fashion. Indeed the story has all the elements dear to the Romantics: a rebel who fights against the Austrians for the liberation of his fatherland; Mathilde, a Habsburg princess, who loves a commoner who happens also to be a rebel; and a quintessentially medieval setting. Like Victor Hugo (and indeed Shakespeare), Rossini was drawn to the idea that a bandit can make a better man than a ruler, that a pauper can be nobler than a nobleman.

On 15 October the composer was back in Paris and rehearsals of *Guillaume Tell* started on 1 November. Lady Morgan attended a dress rehearsal, where she found Rossini relaxed and gently encouraging the musicians with such instructions as 'Caro violoncello troppo piano' and 'Signor mio flauto, troppo forte', all in a supplicating tone of voice. The press was following every moment of the opera's development because Tell was, in effect, Rossini's first opera written specifically for the French stage. But a series of hiccups delayed the awaited première, which eventually took place at the Opéra on 3 August 1829. It was conducted by Antoine Habeneck, as Rossini himself was by then in no state to appear in front of the Parisian public. Everyone was keen to be present at the event; some had even postponed their summer departure from the hot summer city to be there. Excitement and impatience had been mounting, as Lady Morgan's journal testifies: 'For the last months of our residence in Paris nothing has been talked of in the world of musical fashion but the expected opera of William Tell.' After the first night *Le Globe* reported that a new era of music had begun.

The overture of *Guillaume Tell* is a piece that everybody knows and, a bit like the *Mona Lisa*, it is difficult to isolate it from its own fame. But it is worth noting that its four-movement form is different from anything that had been heard before. The sound of the opening solo cellos suggests 'the calm of profound solitude, the silence of nature when the elements and human passions are at rest', as Berlioz put it. Donizetti's reaction was that, while the first and third acts of *Guillaume Tell* were written by Rossini, the second was composed by God.

It is clear that for Rossini the effort of composing *Guillaume Tell* had been disabling. Giovanni Carli Ballola observed:

> To the conscience of an artist who would very soon be classified for ever, by stupid critical prejudice, and by the equally stupid stereotype for having been a purveyor of spontaneously happy and naif music, it was all too clear that the inevitable obligation to write a completely

new French opera, awaited by public opinion with ever increasing impatience, would represent by far the most traumatic and exhausting undertaking in a whirlwind career strewn with anxieties and haunted by the fear of the blank page well known at the time and attributed to chronic laziness.

Rossini himself called *Guillaume Tell* an opera 'of melancholy tint, mountains, miseries', but was still uncomfortable about the obsession with individual self-expression that marked the characters of this story. After the première, members of the orchestra and cast, gathered outside his house to repeat the rousing Act II finale.

Exhausted, on 13 August Rossini left Paris, having given up his apartment on boulevard Montmartre. He had reshaped the whole of the French opera scene and set it on its future course. It was *Guillaume Tell* which gave birth to *le monstre*, paving the way for Meyerbeer's *Robert le Diable* and *Les Huguenots*, the grandest of all grand French operas, to be followed by Berlioz and Gounod. On his way to Bologna, Rossini stopped for a few days in Milan, where he went to the Teatro della Canobbiana to see Bellini's *Il pirata*. Its young composer, in a letter to his uncle (dated 28 August 1829), described his unexpected meeting with 'the celebrated Rossini', when he 'shook all over' with excitement and appeared just as he was, in his shirt sleeves. The prospect of meeting such a great genius he told Rossini, who had been fetched from his room by a servant, had not given him time to change. Rossini answered that the way one dressed did not matter, going on to compliment Bellini on what he had heard: 'I recognize that your operas start where others end.' That remark could be taken two ways: the younger man perhaps not realizing that Rossini was talking about himself, found it immensely encouraging. Rossini heard *Il pirata* a second time and told friends that he considered Bellini's music to be that of a mature man. The two composers met again at a lunch hosted by a rich Jewish family called Cantù; this time Isabella was also among the guests. Bellini repeated his delight at having met 'un si grand'uomo'. Rossini left Milan thinking that, as he was abandoning composing altogether, he had found his heir: the handsome young man from Catania, who had studied in Naples, was promising to focus on melody, an element missing in the new composers.

V

STRINGENDO

He was retiring. Rossini now longed for the peace of the countryside at Castenaso and the familiar atmosphere of Bologna, where everybody knew him and where he hoped to help the local musical institutions. He was no longer well enough to cope with the intensity of Paris and maybe Bologna was devoid of the melancholic *mal-du-siècle*. Tired of salon life, he would try to enjoy his father's company before it was too late. He spent the rest of the summer in the villa, where the distractions of wine making and planning more extensive gardens were marred only by Isabella's extravagance with money, her gambling evenings and her noisy friends. When his house in Bologna was ready – a real palazzo in the Strada Maggiore – Rossini moved in. The Teatro Comunale prepared a special welcome for the prodigal son with a season of *Tancredi*, *Otello* and *Semiramide*, all featuring Giuditta Pasta, who by then had become a personal friend of both Gioachino's and Isabella's.

Before leaving Paris, Rossini had left behind two excellent co-directors to look after the Théâtre-Italien, Carlo Severini and Edouard Robert, who kept in touch with the maestro. Robert arrived to consult Rossini in March 1830: 'I am unable to retain the Maestro's attention for longer than a minute at any one time,' he complained. It was even more difficult to pin him down in Bologna than in Paris as 'he amuses himself too much here with these accursed Bolognese idlers.' From morning to night they were always visiting him at home. 'When I go out with him in the hope of focusing his attention for at least a short time, he ends up by slipping away behind the pillars of the arcades and, once he starts gossiping with friends, it is no longer possible to agree on anything.' It sounds as if Rossini was finding in Bologna what he had begun to miss, the simple provincial life. Indeed with the advent of spring and back at Castenaso, he started to feel better and was even ready to compose again. He asked for a new libretto: 'I cannot work without a poem,' he stressed. In June he was in Florence, where he sat for the then famous sculptor Lorenzo Bartolini. The libretto had not arrived on his return to Bologna, as Rossini complained to Severini (whom he liked a great deal more than Robert) on 7 July. Having somewhat recovered his spirits, he ambitiously set to work on his own version of Goethe's *Faust*.

Life with Isabella was going from bad to worse: he was thirty-eight and ill; she was forty-five drinking heavily and disappointed. She started giving secret piano lessons, probably more for company and to keep a foot in the musical world than for any other reason; but the gossip spread suggesting that Gioachino was a miser who was too mean to give his wife enough to live on comfortably. Confronting her made no difference. Rossini might also have been missing Olympe. Just as he started thinking of going back to Paris to see her, the echo of revolutions and firearms was enough to make him change his mind. Indeed, popular discontent in Paris was causing the whole of Europe to follow events in France. The harvest had been disastrous, there was starvation in the city, the change from rural life to the factory system had created a sub-class wallowing in unemployment, disease and starvation. Charles X's new cabinet, headed by the Prince de Polignac (who, as Louis XVIII's ambassador, had arranged Rossini's contract when in London), was made up of hard-liners: the elections which strengthened the liberal front, prompted Polignac to attempt a *coup d'état*; he called for new elections with a severely reduced electorate and silenced the press with draconian laws. As these measures were being imposed, the king left to hunt in the forest of Rambouillet. His army was totally unprepared for what happened next. Paris stormed with angry men and women building barricades and armed with anything they could find. It was then that Delacroix painted his *Liberty leading the People*, showing the bare-breasted France-Marianne taking the masses to battle, a street urchin holding her hand. 'People and poets are marching together!' wrote Charles Sainte-Beuve while Alexandre Dumas manned a barricade and Liszt roamed the streets encouraging the insurgents. Witnesses of the people's anger included painters who left sketches of streets blocked by barricades; one oil painting now in the Musée Carnavalet depicts a lonely student advancing towards a platoon of soldiers reminding us of Tianamen Square – times have not changed that much. Facing the line of muskets aimed at his body while calling for fraternity between army and people, the student was shot dead soon after this able brush succeeded in capturing his fragile shape confronting the massed uniforms of the infantry. Indeed the Royalist troops began to desert and by 29 July most of Paris was in the hands of insurgents.

Charles dismissed Polignac the next day but it was too late. The king was driven from his throne and fled abroad after the three 'glorious days' of revolution: on 27, 28 and 29 July the people of Paris – including workers, students, Carbonari and republicans – rose against Charles X's despotism. His place was taken by the constitutional monarch Louis-Philippe, the son of Philippe Egalité.

When the waters of the Seine seemed to have calmed, about two months later, Rossini set off to Paris accompanied by a manservant ostensibly to look after his interests. But his interests were not only financial, because they included Olympe Pelissier. Isabella stayed behind.

With the July Revolution the Opera ceased to be a royal establishment and the civil list from which Rossini's annuity was drawn was reduced. Rossini knew he would find a new regime which had abolished all previous contracts – his own included. Gioachino told his father that he would not stay long in Paris but in fact he was not to return to Italy for four years. The object of this journey was to settle the terms of his annuity – but in Paris he had also left behind some true friends, like Aguado and Balzac.

VI

ADAGIETTO

Rossini's concern with his annuity was a cover for returning to Olympe, the woman he loved. At a time when he needed care and affection, Rossini found in Olympe Pélissier the support he needed so badly. In spite of bitter comments, not only from Balzac, but from Giuseppina Strepponi and Verdi amongst others, Olympe was to help Rossini like nobody else could. She dedicated herself wholly to his wellbeing; and nobody could say that she had jumped on to a rich man's bandwagon since she was very rich herself; nor that she sought respectability, because many years went by before Rossini was able to marry her. She loved him for his vulnerability, his dependence on her and his gratitude. Certainly she was attracted by Rossini's fame and talent, but he also offered her pleasant and sensitive companionship. She was not going to share her life with an Adonis; the handsome Rossini of bygone days had become ugly, his face disfigured by pain and his body overweight as a result of compulsive eating brought on by depression. He was becoming a physical wreck and needed what Olympe longed to be, a formidable yet caring nurse; by the time of Rossini's return to Paris in autumn 1830, she considered herself mature, if not old – in fact, past it. Olympe was thirty-one and Rossini thirty-eight.

Olimpe [sic] Louise Alexandrine Descuilliers (Rossini's will refers to her by this surname, with which she also signed her own testament) was born in rue des Bons-Enfants, the illegitimate daughter of Marie Adelaide Descuilliers. Brought up at 12 rue Neuve de l'Abbaye, the home of her stepfather Pélissier who adopted her, she spent her childhood in destitution. Her mother could not support her for long and when Olympe was fourteen she was surrounded by 'protectors', men who kept her in exchange for sex. According to G. de Courcel's *Mémoires d'un bourgeois de Paris* (1853), she was also to be seen around the Palais Royal, 'ce bazaar picturesque', where women were on sale with 'le jeu de l'amour a tout prix'. At the age of fifteen, Olympe was sold to a young duke. He fell ill and passed her on, for a fee, to a rich Anglo-American. Because she was beautiful, intelligent, cool and wise, from mere cocotte she developed into a courtesan, a kind of western geisha who presided over a salon where sculptors, writers and painters were to be seen. She also received the aristocracy, notably the Rochefoucauld, Laurison and Girardin males. Many members of the Jockey Club frequented 23 rue de la Rochefoucauld, where she moved in 1831. Her erstwhile lover Horace Vernet painted a portrait of her as Judith, the heroine who slashed Holofernes' throat. Olympe figuratively slashed several throats when she started a pawn-broking business; she was able to provide large loans because she kept a gambling table at her salon (like Flora's in *La traviata*). Balzac wanted to marry her because she was rich and he was full of debts. He was refused, but kept in touch as he saw in Olympe a means to mix with those she entertained in her salon – this was around 1829 when he had little access to *le beau monde*.

The Romantics started a new movement, *le dandyisme*, which was not exactly about being a dandy. For the first night of Victor Hugo's *Hernani* (1830) Théophile Gautier wore a scarlet waistcoat and Verdi's large felt hat became his trademark. When the weather was cold, Rossini wore two or three wigs, one on top of the other to keep his head warm. Without knowing it, he had joined the world of the eccentrics, of the dandies. Apart from George Sand, women did not succumb to dandy dress but instead covered themselves with velvets and jewels; Olympe enjoyed covering herself with diamonds.

In 1831 Aguado, anxious for Rossini to see Spain, accompanied him to Madrid. Apart from the usual royal encounters and a perfor-mance of *Il barbiere di Siviglia*, they met Manuel Fernández Varela, an eminent churchman, the Archdeacon of Madrid, who wanted an autographed composition by Rossini exclusively for himself. Rossini was unwilling – besides he did not like Madrid nor did he care much for Spain – but Varela insisted, asking Aguado to persuade Rossini to compose a *Stabat mater*. Finally, to please Aguado to whom he owed so much, Rossini agreed but, as he had been confined to his bed because of lumbago (so he said, but in all likelihood this was another nervous collapse) he composed six movements entrusting another six to Giovanni Tadolini. As he was leaving, Rossini demanded that his *Stabat mater* should be performed only in private and for the archdeacon alone. This was to have repercussions.

In Paris, having no formal residence, Rossini went to live on the top floor of the Théâtre-Italien. It was a simple set of rooms with five flights of stairs to climb – very good for his physical health Rossini used to say. But there were more occasions when visitors climbed up to see him than when he descended. He often stayed with Olympe. He even broke his musical reticense by offering her a composition, a cantata which was thus dedicated:

> composed expressly for
> Mlle Olympe Pélissier
> by Rossini
> called Grande Scena-Giovanna d'Arco,
> Paris in 1832.

By 1832 Rossini was living as an invalid at Olympe's apartment in rue Neuve-du-Luxembourg where Balzac was a frequent visitor. Balzac's interest in medicine and exploration of arcane branches of medical science led him to believe that the *pietra mesmerica* (of *Così fan tutte* fame) might cure Rossini's bouts of depression and physical prostration. Mesmerism was 'the universal fluid preserved in every part of the universe, a force that governed celestial beings.' Several letters from Olympe to Balzac survive, most of them written in spring 1832 and addressed 'Mon cher Balzac', a mere hint of their previous intimacy; one of them more specifically says 'I count on your "ancienne affection".' In a letter of 17 November 1833 to one of his current loves, Balzac complained that Rossini 'makes me dine with his mistress, who is precisely the beautiful Judith, the former lover of Horace Vernet and of Sue, you know.' How characteristic of him to keep quiet about his own liaison! Almost a year later Balzac described a dinner party he had hosted as 'a great success. Rossini declared that he had never seen or eaten anything better when dining with sovereigns. It was also sparkling with wits. The lovely Olympe was gracious, wise and perfect.' In 1834 Olympe had a box at the Opéra and was often at the Théâtre-Italien; Balzac once went to Rossini's box, from which 'the dangerous presence of the beautiful Olympe' caused him to depart as swiftly as he could.

Money for music was scarce. The Restoration years had seen a flourishing of the arts due to a period of peace and prosperity rather than to any encouragement from the Bourbons. The fifty-seven-year-old Louis-Philippe tightened the nation's belt. The personification of constitutional monarchy, the guarantor of liberty, equality and fraternity, the Citizen King shrewdly readopted the tricolour, but was soon to make clear that he had no intention of sharing his rule with that new force, the *grande bourgeoisie*, which by then had become the bastion of the French economy. In vain the proletariat – a newly coined word – waited not only for reforms but to be given a share and a role. Under Louis-Philippe the salons were still open although few of the aristocrats seemed to be around. Rossini was now to be seen at Madame Orfila's musical salon with Olympe by his side. Madame Orfila was a small, dark Neapolitan and Madame Malibran could be found 'assise entre Mme Recamier, au moins sexagenaire' and there was also the 'new' Countess Merlin, very rich and interested in music. Fashionable young ladies were changing their appearance; fashion can stress the great reversals in society, hairstyles, less rigorously tidy than before, were hidden under wide-brimmed hats and silk ribbons trailed in the air. It was no longer shameful for a lady to be seen walking, rather than in her carriage. The crowd of prostitutes and cocottes which had made the court of the Palais Royal a place for men alone, was being dispersed. The *juste-milieu* did not like that kind of Paris.

Balzac who, as a young man had absorbed Saint-Simon's 'romantic socialism', now thundered against Louis-Philippe whose power leant on the petty middle class, *le juste-milieu*, as vividly described in *Eugène Grandet*.

Having dedicated *Le Contrat de Mariage* to Rossini (a novel not published until 1847), Balzac went on to write *Gambara* (1837), which is about a composer going mad. Everyone knew who Gambara was, but Rossini was not offended, and he remained in Balzac's eyes 'the composer who transported more passions than anybody in the art of music'. Balzac started to describe this musically silent Rossini setting his stories in foreign aristocratic houses:

Gambara is a carrier of unknown treasures, a pilgrim who sits by the door of paradise having ears to listen to angels singing and not having any longer the language to repeat it. The drama of Gambara is that when he imposes on his composition a kind of ivresse of the unconscious, he is followed but when he wants to make the music of ideas, he falls into his own imagination. In his overcharged imagination, Gambara becomes mad because others don't see.

The two men continued to meet in cafés and restaurants, normally alone. It seems that they mostly discussed music, women and nervous disease. In one of his letters Balzac asked for Rossini's autograph on behalf of a friend, also requesting some written thoughts on music. Rossini replied:

Mon cher Balzac.
Vous me demandez un autograph, et bien, le voilà. *What shall I write about? Of yourself, you who mark this century with your masterpieces? You are, my friend, too great a colossus for me to entertain and what could the help of my foreign simplicity add for you? So I only tell you that I love you with tenderness and that you, in turn, must not disdain having bewitched the man from Pesaro.*

At this time Rossini's protégé Bellini and his music were all the rage in Paris and women fell for him one after the other. On finding Olympe in the offices of the Théâtre-Italien, Bellini was 'delighted to see her' and even asked her permission 'to go and visit her at home' – a bit of a cheek since Olympe was by then Rossini's woman. When an epidemic of cholera struck Paris, most people fled the capital, while Bellini decided to stay; it was murmered that he was having an affair with the beautiful Maria Malibran. Fear seized everyone, Rossini included. 'The word "cholera" sweeps from mouth to mouth,' wrote the Duchess of Berry. Madame Récamier fled Paris 'together with Monsieur de Chateaubriand' and so did the great diarist Madame de Boigne (she who inspired Proust). Once again it was Aguado who took Rossini away to Bayonne; but even the country air failed to help the composer recover from a new depressive torpor and Rossini was bored in Bayonne in spite of Olympe's presence; he would have preferred to be in cholera-stricken Paris. The Aguados took him to Toulouse where he remained gloomy.

But Edouard Robert needed Rossini back at the Théâtre-Italien, so on 12 September 1832 he wrote telling him that the epidemic was over and back Rossini went. There were all sorts of troubles in the world of music, many of them caused by Bellini. He was jealous of everybody, especially of Donizetti, whom Rossini had invited to Paris. He need not fear because Donizetti's answer, addressed to 'Most Honoured Maestro', asked whether the invitation could be deferred as he had obligations at La Scala: 'The flattering expressions in your letter would invite me to do everything or rather I shall say to abandon everything and free myself in order to be in Paris with you . . . I have so much wanted to come to Paris.' Rossini eventually had Donizetti's *Marin Faliero* staged at the Théâtre-Italien with moderate success.

In 1834 Bellini was working on the score of *I puritani*. Rossini 'now protects me and wishes me well', he wrote to a friend. 'If his protection becomes stronger my glory will profit very much, as in Paris he is the musical oracle.' In effect Rossini's genuine affection was not repaid by the scheming young genius. To another correspondent in Naples Bellini related: 'I asked [Rossini] to advise me like a brother and begged him to love me well. "But I do love you well," he answered. "Yes, you love me well," I added, "but you must love me better." He laughed and embraced me.' At that time Rossini had rented a villa just outside Paris and enjoyed the privacy of life in the country. Most evenings his groom would ride him to Paris, where he followed rehearsals of Bellini's *I puritani* and attended the première in Olympe's box on 24 January 1835, sincerely glad about the success of his protégé.

Bellini's death eight months later, on 23 September, came as a devastating shock. Some said he had been poisoned, others that he had died of cholera. Paris paid great honour to the thirty-four-year-old composer whose romantic looks and love affairs had become almost legendary. The funeral service took place at Les Invalides, the pall-bearers including Carafa, Cherubini, Paer and Rossini, who described the procession to the Père-Lachaise cemetery. It was raining and Rossini cried all the way – some distance. Now that Bellini was gone he felt musically alone and plunged even further into depression. Later he was to explain to the contralto Mariette Alboni that the rumours that Bellini had been poisoned were false:

There was this talk, but it was not true. I loved Bellini who had been recommended to me. I was at my villa at Puteaux, close to Paris when he fell ill. His doctor, an Italian I had never met, would not let anybody visit him. Somebody wrote to me saying that the poor young man was ill; I returned to Paris and I was told that he had recovered, so I returned to my villa. On the following day I was given the news of his death. So I went back to Paris, having heard a rumour that he had died of poison given to him out of jealousy by his lady friend in whose house he lodged, I asked for his corpse to be opened by a celebrated surgeon . . . and he found that his intestine was full of disease so that he could not have lived long but that the cure of his bad doctor had in any case shortened his life. I was distraught; I sent his mother and brothers in Sicily some precious objects of that poor young man but they answered that they would have preferred money.

When his mysterious illness and nervous crisis would leave him in peace, Rossini was able to compose some occasional pieces. In 1835 Troupenas collected twelve of them and published them as *Soirées musicales*, although Rossini intended them for private use, he wanted to exclude the public. But Liszt, in the absence of copyrights, transcribed some for virtuoso piano and published them with Ricordi.

It was thought that travel would distract the composer from his increasingly depressive state, so he gratefully accepted an invitation from Lionel de Rothschild to accompany him and Olympe to Belgium and the Rhineland. It was an adventurous and interesting journey. In Frankfurt he met Mendelssohn, then twenty-seven, who played the piano for Rossini; an eye-witness remarked that Mendelssohn 'submit[ted] to Rossini's amiable demands as, sitting near the piano, he made observations and criticisms in such terms as to make one understand that the heart, and not the intellect, spoke in him.' But during the 1830s and 1840s Europe was of course awakening to the industrial conquest of speed and metals, of steam and energy; Rothschild persuaded Rossini to try the newest and fastest way of covering a long distance, the train. Remembering what he had endured crossing the channel, Rossini dreaded the prospect. The violence, the noise, the speed and the smoke were all a huge shock. It was so fast! – up to twelve or fifteen miles an hour – and there had been fatal accidents. As professor Simon Wessely explained to me, cases of train-panic were not uncommon: 'There was a general concern about the health effects of travel, not directly expressed in psychological terms, but leading to psychological problems. For example, in the 1830s and 1840s, there was a medical concern that people would not be able to breathe if trains exceeded a certain speed.' Later Rossini even wrote a piano piece, one of his *Péchés de vieillesse*, describing a train accident; he composed it with such a verve that it suggests that he wouldn't have minded if the horrible experience had ended with a bang. But that is what he wanted to convey, a nonchelence towards anything that had affected him deeply.

In November 1836 Rossini returned to Bologna, having spent several weeks in Milan beforehand. He had come to an important decision: he wanted to agree terms for a legal separation from his wife (as had been discussed with Isabella through Giuseppe), so that he could settle in Bologna with Olympe at his side. He was in constant touch with the gentle Severini in Paris, every letter mentioning Olympe in the most affectionate terms: 'I thank you for your friendliness towards Olympe. I am and always shall be obliged to you for anything you care to do for her.' 'I feel the greatest indifference for having abandoned the capital of the world . . . the only privation I feel is that of you and Olympe; but I hope that time will restore everything to me . . . Embrace Olympe.' She wrote to Rossini almost daily.

In February 1837 Rossini's negotiations with Isabella were drawn up. He would continue living in his Bologna palazzo and he bought an adjacent building for Olympe. Castenaso would remain Isabella's, for whom there were other generous financial provisions. Meanwhile Edouard Robert had sent Rossini a letter, describing how Olympe had left Paris in her 'old hovel of a carriage' with an enormous collection of cases and bundles containing table linens and bric-a-brac; how was Rossini doing in 'giving comfort to that crowd of beauties who were in despair' in Bologna? There was that wonderful brothel near Palazzo Guidotti, Robert added. What was Rossini doing in asking Olympe to join him in Bologna? 'Maestro, I admire you but I don't understand you.' There Rossini had a bore of a wife and now he asked another bore, and an even more dreadful one, to be with him. 'Have you gone mad? Are you an enemy of your own peace? Now she has left, on the last Sunday of Carnival, at one in the afternoon and she made a fine start by breaking her coach on the Pont-Neuf.' But Rossini needed Olympe the nurse, not the pretty girls in the brothel near Palazzo Guidotti. So in March 1837 Olympe was installed in Bologna. One of her letters says that Isabella 'must receive me in her homes as an accepted fact. I had to go to Mme Rossini whom I found pretty and unaffected; she was pleased with me.' In fact Isabella was pleased with Olympe only that once; thereafter she avoided contact and tried to set her friends against the new couple.

Olympe and Rossini were to live in separate houses until their marriage. 'God gave me strength a long time ago to see only a friend in Rossini. His friendship and protection will console me for some sacrifices of self-esteem which I make for his personal tranquillity. Today I have no *arrière-pensées* about Rossini who conducts himself toward me so nobly.' No matter whether they had been lovers in the past, sexual intercourse was now out of the question. Rossini was too ill for sex, and for Olympe it had never been much more than a business. Theirs was a relationship founded on mutual dependence and devotion.

Balzac called on the couple in Bologna on 29 May 1837 in the company of Countess Clara Maffei (who later had an affair with the young Verdi) and described the visit in a letter:

> *We went to see la* Sainte-Cecile *by Raphael in Bologna and also la* Sainte-Cecile *of Rossini's [i.e. Olympe] and also our great Rossini! . . . Hélas, we found no music anywhere apart from that which slept in the head of Rossini himself and which is listened to by the angels in Raphael's painting. France and England buy music at such a high price that Italy demonstrates the truth of the proverb: there is no one as badly shod than a shoe-maker.*

There were also dark moments. Although he had promised to establish her in Florence or Milan if she became unhappy in Bologna, Rossini shouted at Olympe when she did indeed threaten to leave. Nevertheless she asked her accountant to sell her apartment in Paris and to liquidate her considerable assets. In September 1837 the act of legal separation between Rossini and Isabella was signed. It did not mean much in a Catholic country: Gioachino and Olympe could not marry as long as Isabella lived.

ACT FOUR

VERDI AND REVOLUTIONS

Ici bas, rien n'est plus complet que le mal-
heur.
    Honoré de Balzac, *La Peau de chagrin*

[Down here nothing is as total as unhappi-
ness.]

I

ANDANTINO

By coincidence, in 1837 both Gioachino Rossini and Giuseppe Verdi were in Milan, the former having arrived with Olympe in the hope that she would be happier than in Bologna. Verdi, then in his mid-twenties, was sporting a Mazzini-like beard and longing to change the world, to contribute to the upheaval of the established order – and he would do that through music. He had little money, a lot of pride and many debts; he had married Margherita Barezzi, the daughter of his benefactor. Verdi lodged in a modest room in the poor district towards the Ticino Gate, while his wife stayed behind in their native town of Busseto; their daughter (born there on 26 March) was named Virginia after the tragedy written by Vittorio Alfieri, a fiery republican drama. Rossini and Olympe took rooms in Palazzo Cantù at Ponte San Damiano and were to spend almost five months in the city. 'I am in Milan, enjoying an almost brilliant existence,' Rossini wrote to Carlo Severini on 28 November 1837. 'I hold musical evenings every Friday. I have a lovely apartment where everyone is eager to be present. We have a great time, we eat well and often talk about you. I shall spend the whole winter here and go back to Bologna at the end of March.' Rossini had grown more and more attached to Severini, who not only looked after the Théâtre-Italien but was also in charge of the composer's financial interests in Paris. So fond was he of Severini that Rossini made him buy a house adjacent to his own in Bologna which he jokingly called La Severiniana. They were all longing to finish their business and live together in Bologna and in peace.

Rossini and Olympe often saw Giuditta Pasta, either at her villa on Lake Como or in Milan, where she also had rooms in Palazzo Cantù and received in style. It was at one of her salons that Stendhal ('ce grand menteur', as Rossini labelled him) exchanged a few words with the subject of his bestselling biography. Balzac too was in Milan, this time in the company of a short and hideous mistress (according to Marie d'Agoult's *Mémoires, souvenirs et journaux*) 'en travesti, à la George Sand', whom he liked to introduce as his page so that the presence of yet another woman by his side should not reach the ear of Madame Hanska, his future wife. Countess Clarina Maffei was the bluestocking of the politico-social salons and she would soon welcome Verdi into hers. Having left her husband, the poet Andrea Maffei, she was now living with Carlo Tenca, a minor left-wing poet, and had been in Balzac's arms the previous year. He wrote to her from Sèvres in October 1837

> *Merci, cara, for the page embalmed with the souvenir which reminded me with delight of your beloved salon and the evenings that I spent there and of the one you familiarly call 'la petite Maffei'; she occupies too large a space in my memory for me to allow myself to use that expression. There are days in which I dream of Milan Cathedral and of the painting by Raphael which we saw together, but mostly of a camelia whiter than the whitest marble.*

Ah, those camellias, metaphors and symbols, red or white, that the nineteenth century preferred to the equally metaphorical rose! Olympe wanted her salon to become like Clara Maffei's or the one she had left behind in Paris.

As Milan was known for its liberalism, unmarried couples were not viewed with the censoriousness characteristic of Bologna. On the other hand, several people sneered at Olympe's past, not least Liszt's mistress, Countess Marie d'Agoult. 'Rossini spent the winter in Milan with mademoiselle Pélissier whom he tried to impose on society,' she wrote. 'But no lady of high status would visit them.' Not even La Saimoyloff, on whom the countess herself turned her back. As already mentioned, Giulia Saimoyloff was a Russian beauty settled in Milan, where she enjoyed a 'suite non interrompue d'amants mediocres presque tous musiciens', as the snobbish d'Agoult put it. And yet Marie had already had one daughter by Liszt while still married to the

Count d'Agoult; she was soon to have a second, Cosima, who continued the tradition of producing bastards by bearing two children to Wagner while still married to Hans von Bülow. Liszt noted: 'Rossini, rich, idle and illustrious, has opened his house to his compatriots.' Rossini and Liszt remained friendly, but Gioachino avoided meeting the countess and did not introduce her to Olympe.

Verdi did not frequent the salons and he would have not been a welcome guest at any of them – not yet. He certainly admired Rossini to such an extent that he had learnt most of the maestro's operas by heart. 'How marvellous it must be to be Rossini!' he was to exclaim. Of course at that stage Rossini had no idea who Verdi was. 'The composer with a helmet', he was to describe him. They represented opposite poles of Italian music and Italian culture. Both were men of their times but they were also at the opposite ends of historic events. What they had in common was a sense of sorrow and despair. While Rossini came from a family of poor musicians and belonged to an urban society, his childhood had been lonely and wretched; Verdi described himself as coming from a peasant background (on both sides of his family were small landowners), and then he had been stricken by the deaths of his young wife and two infant children. Born in 1813, Verdi lived in a state ruled by the Duchess Marie Louise, daughter of the Austrian emperor and widow of Napoleon, while Rossini came from the Papal States and had already travelled the world. Verdi was a staunch republican and a fervent believer in the new Romantic concept of the nationalist cause. In contrast Rossini had gone through a phase of liberalism, but had been disappointed by everything he had seen. When both men were in Milan, Rossini's main disappointment was with himself.

Divided into many reactionary states, the Italians had followed events in Paris with increasing curiosity. In 1831 Giuseppe Mazzini, then living on French soil, had founded the Giovane Italia, a clandestine organization aimed at unifying Italy. In the same year came the revolution. Modena, Bologna and Parma, together with the northern part of the Papal States, ousted their governments but the rebel forces, formed mainly by Carbonari, were soon overcome by the Austrian army. Ciro Menotti, the leader of the rebellion, was executed. (Garibaldi was to call one of his sons Menotti.) Born in Genoa in 1805, Mazzini was an advocate of nationalism but although he had a large following, he was not an effective politician. A prolific writer in favour of Romanticism, he forsook a legal career to join the Carbonari in 1829; he was imprisoned the following year. According to his *Filosofia della musica* (1870), Mazzini saw Rossini as 'the Titan of power and audacity, the Napoleon of a musical era who has achieved in music what romantics achieved in literature.'

Thanks to its many divisions, its multiple customs barriers and obstacles to communications, Italy remained a peasant society. 'Italy's steam is nowhere to be seen,' commented an English visitor. Indeed the railways that were beginning to link all of Northern Europe had not yet been contemplated in Italy; the Austrians actually regarded them as a threat to security. On the economic front, France and especially Britain were booming. In 1837 the young princess Victoria was crowned queen of a country which, with its flourishing trade, advanced technology and command of the seas, was the envy of Europe. The British upper classes travelled and brought their fashions with them; no Milanese gentleman would be seen entering a salon if not wearing a top hat and tails, as the English did. Male waists were tightened by ferocious corsets. The 'dandy' was at his peak. Britain also enjoyed a liberty that could not be found in Italy, where censorship imposed by the Austrians was severe. As Heinrich Heine observed:

> *Speech is forbidden to the poor Italian slave, so it is through music alone that he can express the emotions of his heart. All his hatred of foreign domination, his longing for freedom, his rage at his impotence, his sorrow on remembering his former lordly greatness, all this is embodied in those melodies. This is the esoteric meaning of opera buffa.*

In Milan Rossini was feeling relatively well and cheerful, believing that he could finally settle down. But his serenity was shattered when he read in a newspaper that on the night of 14 January 1838, after a performance of *Don Giovanni*, the Théâtre-Italien had been gutted by fire; it was as if the infernal flames that consume Don Juan were to spread wider to burn the world. Everything was destroyed: costumes, Rossini's papers (including scores), scenery, everything. But what was even more devastating for him was the loss of his friend Carlo Severini who died while trying to escape the fire. The co-director Edouard Robert had been severely burnt but survived. Thus ended Rossini's long and formidably successful collaboration with the Théâtre-Italien.

Rossini and Olympe then had to leave Milan and go back to Bologna because Giuseppe was clamouring for their return. The old man had been left alone to cope with the embittered and increasingly hostile Isabella and wrote to say that he was ill and needed his son by his side. Rossini's own health declined in Bologna, and he led the life of a recluse. Once his father had recovered, Rossini forced himself to return to Milan for a grand musical soirée given by Metternich, whose resemblance to Stendhal's Count Mosca in the current literary success, *La Chartreuse de Parme*, was remarked by Balzac. But of course Metternich had summoned rather than invitated Rossini; there was no possibility of turning him down, although by now the composer had little time or inclination for society. The death of Severini, the destruction of his beloved theatre and with it the burning of many of his papers depressed him profoundly. And his chronic physical symptoms were also getting worse: he was now suffering from haemorrhoids as well, and his urethritis had developed into a condition known as Reiter's syndrome, provoking terrible arthritic pains. Following any panic attack, whether it involved travel by train or steamboat, Rossini would never contemplate returning to the scene of irrational terror. Another emotional attack occurred when he heard Paganini – who had the fame of being devilish – perform one of his virtuoso pieces; he would never again risk listening to his old friend play the violin.

Despite his ill-health, in January 1839 Rossini accepted an honorary position at the Bologna Liceo Musicale; he did not take this task lightly, trying (albeit unsuccessfully) to attract to the Liceo such composers as Saverio Mercadante, Antonio Pacini and also Donizetti. He would have liked Donizetti to do for Bologna what he himself had achieved in Paris.

Then the news of yet another friend's death plunged Rossini into despair: the French tenor Alfred Nourrit, a handsome but depressive man whom he had trained for many of his scores, committed suicide in Naples on 8 March 1839. Rossini's world was crumbling among too many deaths and too many modern engines, and he felt like disappearing from an environment which was too mechanized and foreign for him, which he felt hostile, alien. While Rossini was in this abyss, on 29 April 1839 his father died. 'I have lost everything on earth that was most precious to me, without illusions, without a future, imagine how I spend the days!' he wrote to an unknown correspondent. He walked around the house touching those objects that had belonged to old Vivazza and bursting into tears. He would weep for hours. Doctors wanted him to change cures and to go to Naples in order to distract him from the gloom into which he had plunged and take the mud baths. 'I spent such a terrible winter that I must make up my mind to do this journey.' A change of environment was recommended, and Olympe succeeded in persuading Rossini to spend the summer in Naples; this should have recalled sweet memories of youth, he could revisit the beautiful bay and see his old friends, 'but in the despair in which I live at present, it will be a matter of total indifference to me.'

In fact the thermal cure Rossini was offered did nothing to change his state of body or mind. 'Might I at least be cured of my glandular troubles and the painful joints which have transfixed me throughout most of the winter?' Olympe and Rossini were Barbaja's guests at the same villa in Posillipo where Gioachino's love for Isabella had first blossomed. Olympe and Barbaja were not made to like each other: he, the flamboyant and ignorant buccaneer, almost a character from the *commedia dell'arte*, certainly a splendid opera impresario, must have loathed on sight the rather prim former courtesan pretending to be a *grande dame*, although Olympe's glowing complexion and jet black eyes doubtless made an impression on him. But what did Barbaja make of the once handsome and energetic composer from whom he had parted in Vienna? To see Rossini in a state of physical and psychical dejection must have saddened the man from whom even kings borrowed money, the great collector of paintings and of women.

Both in Naples and on his return journey, in Rome, Rossini was feted and honoured but he hardly noticed. Back in Bologna, and in spite of his lethargy, he involved himself with the Liceo, attending examinations and conducting the orchestra. But his physical and mental condition continued to deteriorate. Olympe seemed to understand her husband and his depression better than any of the many doctors who were consulted. A series of letters she wrote to her friend and financial adviser Hector Couvert, a solicitor, shed light on this dark period. Her descriptions of life in Bologna and of herself are introspective, frank and, at times, even witty. She reports, for example, that neither she nor Rossini was well because the only thing that they were intent on doing was eating. 'The Maestro and I live for food . . . I am a fat woman, occupied from morning to night with digestion.'

Music evidently mattered little to Rossini at this time. When the Teatro Comunale transformed *Guillaume Tell* into *Rodolfo di Sterling* (the opera was even to appear as *William Wallace*) he did not protest. The word '*Liberté*' which closes the original opera in heavenly spasms was eradicated from the text, just as the concept had been eradicated from public life. The Austrians would not have accepted Tell, a hero who had fought them and won.

Visiting Venice in February 1841 should have been a pleasure; that was the city of Rossini's triumphant premières of *Tancredi*, his first wonderfully inventive *farse*. The Venetian public, the Venetian ladies hidden behind their pretty masks and dominoes, the sleek gondolas and the melodious barcaroles, as well as seeing old friends, should have brought a glimmer of hope to Rossini's darkened universe. Instead he suffered from terrible stomachache and diarrhoea, possibly psychosomatic, which seemed to sharpen the distressing physical symptoms of his urethritis and his acute anxiety. He was not even capable of enjoying Olympe's amazed reaction to the lace-like marbles of the Palazzo Ducale, the reflections of the Gothic shapes, the gold trembling in the lagoon. He felt awful. How could he recover just by remembering what had been good in life? Bologna and his past had not helped him either. When a famous doctor from Dresden descended on Bologna, Olympe decided to consult him and convinced Rossini to try the new medical science from the North. But the cures that this doctor prescribed would be enough to send anyone straight to the grave (flower of sulphur mixed with cream of tartar, application of leeches to the haemorrhoids and so on). The fashionable thermal waters of Marienbad were also prescribed; Rossini and Olympe went instead to the nearby thermal spa of Porretta but to no avail. He lost weight through persistent diarrhoea. One of Olympe's letters to Couvert stresses that Rossini's changes of mood worried her more than his physical weakness.

During the summer of 1841 Rossini was visited by the Belgian musicologist François-Joseph Fétis, whose eight-volume *Biographie universelle des musiciens* (1835–44) remains a standard (if often eccentric) source. Fétis who wrote down his impressions of the conversations he had with Rossini was trying to encourage the composer to shake off his lethargy and return to composing possibly a religious work. 'Thank God I no longer occupy myself with music,' was Rossini's answer. The urge to compose would soon return, Fétis insisted, also noting that Rossini's apparent indifference made him seem selfish and remote, which he was not. Indeed Simon Wessely, who has studied Rossini's medical papers, stresses that apparent indifference and self-deprecation are classic hallmarks of depression. According to Fétis, it was the composer's own fault that he was badly misrepresented by the public: he had always concealed his true character. One day the world would see what a great man Rossini really was, he continued, and to what lengths he had gone to diminish his own stature. But Fétis, however inadvertently, was right that Rossini would return to compose church music.

II

RONDÓ

What prompted Rossini into action was the news that a French publisher had acquired the *Stabat mater* that he had reluctantly written for (and given to) Archdeacon Varela in Madrid in 1831. This was distressing because he had to confess that he had delegated half of this work to Giovanni Tadolini; but of course at the time anything was distressing for Rossini. Nevertheless, the information served to shake him from his torpor. In fact Varela's heirs had sold the autograph manuscript to Antoine Aulagnier, who intended to print it and market it – by then anything composed by the reclusive but famous composer was hot property. Rossini wanted to prevent the publication of a score that he had originally given – not sold – though he had admittedly received a box studded with diamonds as a gesture of appreciation. So he set to work on the *Stabat mater*, replacing the six pieces originally composed by Tadolini with his own music and sold the result to his own French publisher, Troupenas. A quarrel between publishers was inevitable.

This was an ideal time for Rossini to take on a *Stabat mater*. He had been devastated not only by the recent deaths of both his parents and two close friends, but the tragedy of his theatre burning down and now the death of his own self-respect – such losses would draw him to compose tender music for a text concerning a mother who sees her son die by slow torture and of the mental torment she herself was enduring. Rossini's revised version was premièred on 7 January 1842 at the newly restored Théâtre-Italien, all the seats having been sold within an hour. At the final rehearsals, the chorus and orchestra stood up after the last notes of the splendid fugue which leads to the finale. Spontaneously everyone present invoked the name of Rossini in a heart-felt ovation to the absent composer. His name was suddenly once again on everybody's lips.

There were of course many people who castigated Rossini's *Stabat mater* for its operatic feel. Protestant and Puritan protests were followed by those of Mendelssohn, a Jewish convert, whose comments were among the most vehement. Heine, another converted Jew, disagreed: 'The Stabat by the great Maestro was the outstanding musical event of the year . . . holy . . . and fashionable tears flowed . . . In France Herr Mendelssohn has always been a failure.' It is interesting that the 'holiest' parts of the *Stabat* are written for either tenor or bass, as if Rossini were channelling his suffering through them. The splendid quartet 'Sancta mater, istud agas, crucifixi fige plagas cordi meo valide' ('Holy mother do this for me: stamp the wounds of thy crucified Son firmly in my heart') provoked Heine to declare after the première that the Théâtre-Italien 'seemed like the vestibule of Heaven'. And Rossini must have had the fire in mind when he set the following aria for soprano and chorus:

Inflammatus et accensus	So fired and ablaze
per te virgo sim defensus	may I be protected by thee, Virgin,
in die judicii.	on the day of judgement.
Fac me cruce custodiri	Let me be guarded by the Cross
Morte Christi praemuniri	Strengthened by the death of Christ,
confonderi gratia!	sheltered by his grace!

The flames flare up with violins and cellos describing vividly the threatening blaze. The work was repeated in Bologna on 18, 19 and 20 March, for Rossini Bologna had become more important than the Paris première; it was performed by an amateur chorus and dilettanti soloists (but what dilettanti!) under the baton of his friend Donizetti. He was the only musician who could do justice to his music, Rossini pleaded. Donizzeti responded by rushing from Milan in a diligence crossing three states, bringing with him the Russian tenor Nicholas Ivanoff, one of the soloists. During the third and last performance, Rossini fell victim to a new panic attack. Shivering and dripping with sweat, he was taken to a room from which he could follow the rest of the performance without being observed. His friends tried to humour him and they all had a good giggle until Rossini was seized by trembling fits all over again. Rossini recovered in time to join Donizetti on the stage and embrace him, his eyes full of tears. When Donizetti left Bologna, Rossini gave him four diamond studs. 'If you could have seen how he wept when we parted!' Donizetti later told a friend.

While in Bologna in autumn 1842, the twenty-nine-year-old Verdi visited Rossini. By now the ailing maestro had heard many reports of *Nabucco* – from Donizetti and others. No record of the conversation between Verdi and Rossini survives, but in all likelihood they spoke about each other's music. Verdi would never have dared ask Rossini why he had stopped composing but he might have commented on the *Stabat mater*. The visit was evidently a happy one, as Verdi wrote to Countess Emilia Morosini (with whom he enjoyed a playfully amorous relationship): 'I have been in Bologna for 5 or 6 days. I went to see Rossini who greeted me very politely and the welcome seemed to me sincere. However that may be, I was very pleased. When I think about Rossini and his reputation all over the world, I could kill myself, and with me all the imbeciles.' In their subsequent letters (several remain at Verdi's country house of Sant'Agata), the two described each other's work. For example, Verdi on Rossini: 'In a word, melody, harmony, declamation, *canto fissato*, orchestral effects, local colour, are nothing but ways of approach . . . in the *Barbiere* the sentence "*Signor giudizio, per carita*", this is neither melody or harmony, it is the declaimed word, apposite, genuine and it is music.'

But medical concerns remained uppermost. In December 1841 Olympe had written to the celebrated surgeon and urologist Jean Civiale in Paris, asking for an appointment. On 2 February 1842 she sent him a description of Rossini's symptoms over the past five years; and over a year later decided to risk the long journey in the hope that the Parisian doctors would be more successful than the ones in Bologna and Milan. Four days after their departure, the couple stopped in Parma where, on 18 May 1843, they were visited by Verdi. He was in Marie-Louise's capital to rehearse *Nabucco*. 'I have seen here the Supreme Maestro,' Verdi wrote, without irony, to his friend Isidoro Cambiasi. The letter goes on to suggest that Verdi and Rossini had decided to meet again in Milan on Rossini's way back, though that was not to be. Rossini's journey to Paris took thirteen days, and who knows how many papers and letters were required to cross the various frontiers; Rossini and Olympe arrived in Paris on 27 May. They settled in lodgings at 6 Place de la Madeleine where a persistent line of friends and admirers queued to catch a glimpse of him, or exchange a word. Rossini and Olympe were to spend four months in Paris but for three whole months Rossini was kept in total isolation. 'I am progressing slowly in my cure,' he wrote on 20 June. 'I live by privations.' But things began to improve, probably due more to Olympe's loving attention than to medicine. 'At the end of September I'll be back in Bologna,' he announced.

The new director of the Opéra, Léon Pillet, was now begging for a new opera from Rossini, who told him to use *La donna del lago*. It had not yet been staged in Paris because there was no tenor in France who could sing it, Rossini explained. So Pillet came out with *Robert Bruce*, a rough adaptation of *La donna del lago* scored to the requirements of French grand opera. Giuseppina Strepponi saw it and wrote to Verdi that, in spite of the lamentable pastiche and gross translation of both language and style, Rossini was still the greatest of all composers. Once back in Bologna, Rossini squeezed out a choral triptych for piano and a dozen female voices to attach to *Edipo a Colono*, a version of Sophocles for which he had provided incidental music before 1817.

While in Milan preparing for La Scala's première of *Giovanna d'Arco*, Verdi received a letter from Rossini, 28 January 1845:

Most Esteemed Maestro and Friend.
What will you ever say of my long silence? A boil or nail-in-the-flesh spread over my legs and arms and, without telling you the pain that I have suffered, I will tell you in justification that it has been impossible for me to write to you before today to thank you so much for what you have done for my friend Ivanoff who feels blessed to have one of your lovely compositions, which has earned him a great success in Parma. Enclosed you will find a draft for 1,500 Austrian lire which you will accept not as payment for your effort, which deserves much more, but as a simple gesture of thanks on the part of Ivanoff, there resting on me alone the obligation to you whom I esteem and love.
    I due Foscari *made a furore in Florence, the same will happen with* Giovanna d'Arco. *That is what is desired for you with all his heart by the one who is completely your affectionate and admiring Rossini.*

At last he was enjoying some serenity and sleeping less badly than usual; but when he heard that Isabella was desperately ill, his dark mood returned to obsess him. On 7 September 1845, with Olympe, he went to Castenaso. This was his first – and last – visit since the irrevocable rift with Isabella. Alone, Rossini entered the bedroom where his wife and companion of so many good and bad times lay dying. His face was drenched in tears when he re-emerged from her room, half an hour later. Exactly a month passed before Isabella died with his name on her lips.

III

MOLTO AGITATO

On 16 August 1846 Olympe and Gioachino were married in Bologna. Rossini was fifty-four and his bride forty-nine. A respectable eleven months had elapsed since Isabella's death. They had both changed enormously since their first meeting in Paris when, according to Balzac, Olympe was 'la plus belle courtesan de Paris' and Rossini the most celebrated composer of the day. They had both become fat and depressed and looked older than they were, yet they were confident in their true companionship. Olympe wasted time playing cards with scroungers but mostly dedicated herself to improving her husband's deteriorating condition. In exchange she had his total gratitude (as well as ours) and respect. Given the state of apathy into which Rossini had sunk, it is amazing that he could summon the energy to organize a wedding.

The couple hardly ever quarrelled and maybe seldom talked. With Isabella, passion had flared up like Mount Vesuvius and had lasted as long as the short spasm of an eruption – after that, habit and boredom had set in; too many things had changed their lives. How did Olympe and Rossini become aware that they needed each other? What was it, for Rossini, that he saw in Olympe, something he had never obtained, neither from Isabella nor from his mother? Perhaps their sexless union drove Olympe to love Gioachino with a motherly attitude, loving him like the child she never had and dedicating pure affection towards him. All forms of sex were probably odious to her because of her past, a past which had deprived her of the joy and the understanding of sex as an exchange of love, as the communication of complete intimacy. Patiently Olympe put up with a man who seemed to be incurably stricken not only by physical illness but also by a mysterious disease for which every cure seemed to fail. She showed a practical side, writing to doctors and searching for possible medicines. Nurse-like, she offered consolation to her husband in the loss of many close friends during the recent painful years. Even Aguado, the Spanish friend who had always helped him with financial advice and with his admiring companionship, had died in April 1842.

Olympe and Rossini conversed in French; Gioachino's letters at this time are flowing in style. Olympe, who had been educated between the sheets, never achieved good Italian. Less than two years were spent in Bologna, sheltering behind dark shutters and taking occasional trips into the countryside in their pretty carriage, towards the Apennines when the hazy heat of the summer invaded the plain; but to Pesaro, which was so near and so full of recollections, they did not go. When she strolled, Olympe was covered in diamonds, but in Bologna – or indeed in the countryside around it – there was hardly anybody worth showing them to.

Under pressure, Rossini managed to put together – compose would not be the appropriate verb- a cantata in honour of the new pope. In a letter to Giuseppe Strada dated 1846, Rossini underlined: 'I have been and still am unwell . . . as far as composing a cantata, it should be remembered that I laid down my lyre in 1828 and it will be impossible for me to take it up again.' The election of the mildly liberal Pius IX was seen as a break with the past and therefore Rossini was among those who signed a petition asking for musical reforms within the Papal State where, it must be stressed, he lived and acted. So now he reluctantly fulfilled demand by sketching a composition with new verses to fit old music, not even reorchestrated. Gaetano Gasbarri, who was part of Bologna's council, wrote to a friend that the work was 'una vera inerzia, ed indegna percio' del grande autore' ('a real nonsense and unworthy of such a great composer').

Less than two years had passed since Olympe and Gioachino's wedding when all of Europe again exploded. To quote from the opening of Eric Hobsbawm's outstanding *The Age of Capital*:

Early in 1848 the eminent French political thinker Alexis de Tocqueville rose in the Chamber of Deputies to express sentiments which most

Europeans shared . . . We are sleeping on a volcano . . . Do you not see that the earth trembles anew? A wind of revolution blows, the storm is on the horizon.

In 1848, the year in which Marx and Engels had their Communist Manifesto published, the revolution burst its banks like a mighty river. A wave of uprisings spread through Italy, beginning in Sicily, until the whole of Europe was up in arms. Europe was shaken for a short time, but to its very foundations. Increasingly rapid means of communication were perceived as being among the main causes of social upheaval. So was education; the schools that Napoleon had opened to all had transformed many young peasants into students, into thinking human beings. And then there was another great culprit: music. The spread of music as a political weapon had seriously alarmed the rulers. Music – operas, not cantatas! – were no longer just a pastime for the rich; music had become a tool for political destabilization. Music stirred thinking youths; opera plots with a political message inflamed the imagination so much that theatres like La Scala were watched by the secret police. La Scala was boycotted by Italians when the Austrian ballerina Fanny Elssler (mistress of the hated Field-Marshal Radetzky) was dancing. To his daughter, who enquired about the behaviour of the Milanese nobility, Radetzky answered that Casa Litta, one of the most aristocratic Milanese houses, 'is openly against us'. Constitutional monarchies appeared to be failing the needs of a new class which was not entitled to vote and whose only wealth lay in their children, in Latin *proles*, hence the new word proletariat. A republic, the *res pubblica* – public ownership – was what people clamoured for. In addition, by 1848 the new word 'socialism' was in current use.

In France a republic was proclaimed on 24 February; in March there were rebellions in south-west Germany and Bavaria; Berlin followed and when a popular insurrection broke out in Vienna (13 March), Metternich fled and the emperor had to concede the constitution. Hungary joined the revolution which now reached Milan.

The previous November all the Milanese had stopped smoking in order to deprive the Austrian treasury of the taxes levied on tobacco. The Austrians sneered back and, on 2 January 1848, an Austrian captain had his cigar knocked from his mouth. Radetzky issued all ranks with cigars and sent his white-liveried soldiers around Milan to puff out scented smoke on any Milanese they could find. It was like the plot of a Rossini opera. The cigar-puffing officers were hissed, jeered and also assaulted in street-fights that became more and more violent.

The initial uprising in Sicily was fanned by the usual mix of mafia and separatism but also by an unlikely romantic nationalistic sentiment; conical hats and black cloaks worn by the bandit freedom-fighters became the fashion among European students and featured in operas of the time, such as Verdi's *I masnadieri* and *Ernani* (both based on fashionable texts, by Schiller and Victor Hugo respectively). Music had set the pace. In March 1848 Verdi was writing from the cauldron of Paris: 'You will have heard about everything that has happened in Paris; and I can only say that, after the 24th, the only sign of insurrection is the funeral procession of last Saturday that accompanied the dead from the Madeleine to the Bastille. It was a stupendous, sublime spectacle!' For a born revolutionary like Verdi, being in Paris then was the consummation of his ideals. 'I would blame myself if I were to abandon Paris now, after having been a witness to all, or almost all.' He also wrote of 'these marvellous barricades' to his friend and librettist Piave, who had joined the National Guard of liberated Venice, Piave had himself behaved heroically in the fight for the Republic of Venice. 'Honour to all of Italy which is now truly great! The hour of her liberation has come, be sure of that. The people want it and, when the people want it, there is no absolute power that can resist' (words that sound like a Verdi cabaletta). 'Yes, yes a few years more, perhaps a few months and Italy will be free, united and republican. What else should she be?' Many years were to pass before Verdi's dream of a republic would come true.

On 27 April 1848 a group of military volunteers about to fight the Austrians gathered outside Rossini's house. As the maestro appeared on the balcony to acknowledge their cheers, the mood turned and his audience became aggressive and offensive. Those who were well-off – including Rossini – had been asked, if not compelled, to donate to the cause of independence. Rossini had offered 500 scudi and two horses, a donation considered mean coming from such a rich man. Voices were raised against him. There were jeers and shouts of 'Down with rich reactionaries!' Panic-stricken, Rossini packed his luggage and the following day left for Florence with Olympe. Rossini was no nationalist; the struggle for Italian independence left him cold and his mental state made him unable to feel passionate about anything. Yet in his

Mosè, written as long ago as 1818, Rossini had gratified the concepts of Italian unification and nationalism.

Rossini had probably already considered leaving Bologna, always a hotbed of revolt. There had been arbitrary killings both outside and inside the city and now uncomfortably close to his home. On 18 August 1848 he wrote to the conductor Angelo Mariani: 'I am dejected! may the Lord protect my beloved Bologna!' Only sixty-five miles away, across the Apennines, the landscape, the climate and the architecture were very different. Tuscan vines gave way to dark cypresses and silver-grey olive trees. Besides, social life in the capital of the Grand Duchy of Tuscany was far more interesting and cosmopolitan than life in Bologna. Olympe could finally show off her diamonds. She immediately felt happy in Florence, even though at the start they had no house or furniture and hardly any personal belongings. Florence was a quiet city; in Tuscany people had not complained or revolted while almost every other city was simmering with revolutionary discontent. Meanwhile Bologna tried to recover its most prominent citizen. Speeches, letters, pleas were all sent in vain; Rossini answered that he could not return because his wife was ill, but in truth it was he himself who was sick with a new and grave anxiety attack of anxiety. He found the political atmosphere threatening, and continued his descent from bad to worse.

Could Verdi's patriotic élan be more different from Rossini's apathetic fears? The two composers stood at opposite poles of politics, philosophy and spirituality. The former was full of hope, the latter of bitterness. One was young and in love, the other was ill, ageing, diseased and felt no love – only empathy. While Verdi was in Paris, Milan had covered herself with glory during the famous *Cinque Giornate*, the Five Days. As a result of Austrian soldiers firing on a group of protesters, the barricades went up and violence broke out. Verdi was so intoxicated by the news that he decided to return. When he reached the city on 5 April, he was greeted as a victorious revolutionary. The triumvirate that represented revolutionary Italy – Garibaldi the general, Cavour the politician and Mazzini the visionary – now had Verdi as its musical prophet.

'Viva l'Italia!' Verdi chose these patriotic words to open his *La battaglia di Legnano*, composed in that fateful year of European revolutions; the opera's first performance took place in republican Rome on 27 January 1849. Although it is set in the twelfth century, when the Lombard League united to defeat Frederick Barbarossa against the

Germans (call it a hint!), no audience could fail to notice the analogy with the Milanese revolt. Part of the audience and the chorus cried: 'Let our cities be ours, and free!' Verdi's *Macbeth*, premièred at Florence in 1847, had also stirred the Florentine public with its choruses of rebellion. After seeing the opera, Rossini told his friend Dupré: 'You see, Verdi is a maestro whose character is melancholically serious.' He had a high opinion of Verdi but doubted that he would ever write a *semiseria* opera – in short he considered that Verdi took himself too seriously.

While some musicians stood on melodic barricades, Rossini was too absorbed in his own affliction to know and follow the tragedy of his loyal friend Donizetti: during the mid-1840s, Donizetti became increasingly paralysed as a result of syphilis. Childless and a widower, Donizetti fell victim to his nephew Andrea, who put him in the lunatic asylum of Ivry-sur-Seine, even though the composer was in good mental health. Eventually Donizetti was allowed to return to his native Bergamo where he died on 8 April 1848; by then he was totally paralysed and his mind had indeed gone. Europe was too rapt in its own revolutionary spasms to take much notice of his sad end. Not even Verdi, who was currently triumphant, and to whom Donizetti had been loyal in his praise, cared to write a word or a piece of music in Donizetti's memory. Now a Tribune of the Milanese people, Verdi was bursting with joy. 'Imagine: there are no Germans here! You know what kind of feelings I had for them!'

Towards the end of May and after a short visit to Busseto Verdi returned to Paris, sparing himself the humiliation of seeing the Austrians returning to Milan. Many Milanese fled, others were imprisoned or exiled. The king of Piedmont, who had become the spearhead for Italy's unification, was defeated by the Austrians in a series of bloody battles. France too was torn by internal political struggles and the Second Republic was under attack from rioting workers. The defeat of the Italian uprisings culminated in July 1849: the Roman Republic collapsed under the fire of French artillery which the pope had seditiously summoned to his aid. Garibaldi fled, after losing most of his men. Tailed by the Austrian army, he was to witness the death of his wife Anita whose body he had to abandon on the sands near Venice. Rossini was as remote from these stirring events as if he were on the moon. Indeed, the four years Rossini spent in Florence were those of his worst depressive cycles.

IV

PIANO MOLTO

The impact of the events in Bologna, incidents magnified in his mind by anxiety, affected Rossini's health throughout his time in Florence. He was frightened. The news that even Metternich had fled before an overwhelming mob caused him sleepless nights. He could not bear solitude and Olympe had to be in attendance at all times. Politically stable, Florence seemed the only place where they could settle. As Rossini wrote to Domenico Donzelli, a tenor who had been one of Rossini's favourite interpreters, on 11 September 1848: 'I shall spend the winter in Florence, I am entering into an agreement for an apartment so that we don't go on living like gypsies.'

Several other letters, asking for all sorts of items to be sent from Bologna, suggest occasional bouts of energy, but these four years were a Calvary for the composer who had barred even so much as a keyboard instrument from his sight. Those who came to see him found a man who was losing weight, his face showing signs of a melancholia that was digging large dark rings around his eyes. He could be observed walking in the narrow streets on the hills above Florence, where nature and graceful architecture entwine: Rossini would stop and talk about his ailments with people he hardly knew – an aspect of hypochondriasis secondary to depression, (I am indebted to Simon Wessely for this insight). Normally a secretive man, Rossini would pour his heart out to almost anybody. He would complain of his lack of sleep and, as months turned into years, he started talking about the misery of a life without promise, with no future, of the distress of being the person he was. Such was his depression that on the few occasions in which he had the strength to rise from his bed in the morning, he was unable to dress. He would also say that he had attempted suicide but that he was too much of a coward to succeed.

Olympe, on the other hand, loved Florence where life was 'almost like Paris'. Written in French, in Italian and in Olympese, Mme Rossini's letters to their good family friend Antonio Zoboli (around August 1848) suggest that Rossini was getting better. He dreamt once again of retiring to Bologna but, at the same time, he couldn't face going back as he imagined enemies and dangers everywhere. Not only had his physical pain apparently decreased, but he seemed to be finding his condition less tormenting. Interspersed with times in which he felt well enough to receive such friends as Prince Poniatowski, an excellent baritone, there were days and nights during which he suffered from persecutory delusions, another sign of severe depression. In downward spirals of gloom, Rossini abandoned himself to the dark disease, without having either the will or the strength to fight it. Socially determined depressions seemed to be punctuated by panic attacks and a tendency to imagine problems. In a now familiar pattern, a particular incident would precipitate the next decline. Shuffling between one room and another, he experienced longer periods of near-suicidal despair. It was a strain on his marriage but it was also its strength. Rossini and Olympe had a tacit understanding: theirs was a patient-nurse relationship. In his inarticulacy, Rossini became more and more anxiously dependent on his wife who looked after his every need; she nurtured his dependency. He had become the famous man to keep in a glass case, all hers to look after.

After a month of insomnia, a new attack hit Rossini. On 2 December 1848 Olympe wrote to a friend:

> *A month-long nervous alteration has exercised my husband's nervous system to such a point that he has fallen into a state of moral prostration which worries me, which fills me with despair . . . since his disease is of a mental nature, all depends on God who alone can give Rossini the courage to bear the exile to which he sees no end; after the fatal demonstration in Bologna, Rossini is no longer himself.*

Being distanced from Bologna was like a punishment for Rossini, exacerbated because he imposed it on himself. 'Rossini has suffered from such a misfortune that he is subject to the unhappy influence of memories that upset his morale.' Yet, in 1850, he gave some signs of life when, in gratitude for the gift of a painting, he wrote a Hymn to Peace. Lack of energy caused him to ask his friend Pacini, by no means a bad composer, to orchestrate it for him; it's not that he couldn't be bothered, as has often been written, it was a question of depression.

Towards the end of their years in Florence, on 30 October 1852, Olympe wrote to Donzelli, begging him to help them sell their furniture in Bologna. Rossini described his own state to Donzelli as 'being not bad; so far as my morale is concerned there is little good to tell you; mankind is too wicked for me to spend my time happily in these last days of my life for which I would need constant peace.' Aware of his own anxiety, in this letter Rossini blames it on the nastiness of humanity. The catcalls at Bologna had grown in his mind to unimaginable proportions; his fears were ever present. Any sudden noise startled him; every insomniac night was an inferno He felt destined never to return to Bologna as he remembered the baying cries of the mob, a Goya-like vision of the Cyclops eating flesh, his flesh. Donzelli asked Rossini for a new piece of music for his daughter to sing in Venice. Rossini replied: 'Have you forgotten, my good friend, the state of growing mental impotence which I am experiencing?' Here Rossini is candid about his lethargy and also about his feelings of alarm. The letter to Donzelli is important because Rossini expresses judgements about himself and others, a rare thing for him. Maybe Donzelli needed letters of introduction for his daughter addressed to the Austrian authorities, Rossini added. Events in Bologna had turned him into a reactionary or, rather, he preferred to ignore what was happening around him. 'I don't know whether the Venetians are fraternizing with the Austrians or are still at war.' Verdi would have disapproved of this sentence; whether there was an uprising or not was a matter of indifference to Rossini. And yet Venice had fought for its brief moment of liberty. The more Rossini thought about how much he had done for Bologna and of his work for the Liceo Musicale, the more he convinced himself of the ingratitude of its people. But he also longed to return to the only city where he imagined he might recover his stability, even his peace of mind.

Meanwhile, even in Tuscany the revolution had gathered momentum. In 1849 the Grand Duke Leopold II had fled Florence and a democratic triumvirate proclaimed the republic of Tuscany. But, in

July, helped by the Austrians, Leopold was back on his throne. Naturally the short-lived revolution upset Rossini. Was he not to trust the Tuscans? Was Florence going to treat him as Bologna had done?

But in the interim, Rossini's old friend Balzac lay dying in Paris. It was the formidable pen of Victor Hugo which was to describe the great man on his death bed: 'On 18 August 1850 my wife came back from calling on Madame Balzac to tell me that Monsieur de Balzac was dying. I rushed round. He had suffered for 18 months from heart trouble.' So Victor Hugo wrote in *Choses vues*. 'After the Revolution in February he had gone to Russia and married. A few days before his departure I saw him on the boulevard; he was already suffering and breathing heavily. In May 1850 he was back in France married, rich and dying. On arrival he had swollen legs and four doctors examined him. One of them told me on 6 July he had not six months to live.' A few days later Victor Hugo arrived at Balzac's house in Passy:

I rang the bell. It was a moonlit night with some clouds. The street was deserted and nobody came to answer. I rang again and the door opened. A servant appeared before me with a candle. She said: 'What do you wish, Sir?' crying the while. I gave her my name and she bade me enter the drawing-room on the ground floor, where I saw on a bracket opposite the chimney piece the colossal bust of Balzac, in marble, . . . Another woman came, also weeping. She said: 'He is dying. Madame has returned home and the doctors have given him up since yesterday.' The maid told Victor Hugo: 'Well, last month when going to bed, monsieur banged himself on a piece of furniture, and his skin broke and all the water he had inside him poured out.' The doctors said, 'Well, fancy that', and were surprised and since then they have pricked him. They said 'let's imitate nature'.

Then they operated but the sore 'was all red and on fire'. So they said: 'He's finished.' And never came back. We went to get four or five other doctors but to no avail. They all said: 'There is nothing to be done.' Last night was a bad night and today at nine o'clock, Monsieur couldn't speak any more. Madame went to get a priest who gave him extreme unction, and Monsieur gave a sign that he understood. An hour later he shook hands with his sister, since 11 o'clock he has been rattling and sees nothing. He won't get through the night . . . The woman left me and I waited for a few minutes. The candles hardly shed any light on the splendid drawing-room furniture and the magnificent Porbus and Holbein paintings on the walls. The marble bust stood out in the shadow like the ghost of the man who was dying, the smell of a corpse filled the house . . . We crossed a corridor, went up a staircase laid with a red carpet and cluttered with objects d'art, vases, statues, paintings and credence tables covered with enamel objects, then along another corridor and I saw an open door. I heard a sinister rattle, and I found myself in Balzac's room. In the centre was a bed of mahogany with, from top to bottom, a whole series of cross pieces and straps suggesting an appliance for moving the patient. In this bed lay Balzac, his head on a stack of pillows and red damask cushions taken from the sofa in the room. His face was purple, almost black, tilted to the right, unshaven, hair grey and short. He had a fixed stare. I first saw him in profile and he looked like an emperor . . . An old man, a nurse and a servant stood beside the bed, and a candle burned on a table, another on a chest of drawers next to the door. A silver vase stood on the night table. The man and woman were silent and with a kind of terror, listened to the dying man's noisy rattle.

The bedside candle near the chimney illuminated the portrait of a man who was young, red-faced and smiling. An unbearable smell rose from the bed as I raised the covers to take Balzac's hands which were covered in sweat. He did not respond to the pressure . . .

This was the same bedroom where I had come to see him a month earlier. Then he had been gay, full of spirits, and in no doubt that he would get well, showing off his swelling with a laugh. We had chatted and argued about politics at length, he reproaching me for my demagogy; he was a legitimist . . . The nurse declared: 'He'll be dead at daybreak.' I went down again with the image of that livid face impressed in my mind. As I crossed the drawing-room I saw again the immobile bust, inscrutable, haughty and vaguely radiant, and I compared death with immortality.

Eighteen years later Rossini was similarly butchered by doctors. The image of that 'inscrutable' marble bust might make anybody ponder death and immortality. In Balzac's case, his enduring monument is the *Comédie Humaine*; in Rossini's it is his music but both men were stained by lurid deaths.

A marble path to immortality may have made Rossini, too, ponder death and immortality. Lorenzo Bartolini, after all, had sculpted his bust which, according to Rossini, made him look like 'a fat Bacchus'. In 1850 Rossini was well enough to appear before the Florentine public as one of the sculptor Bartolini's pallbearers.

After Bellini's death and Donizetti's, the only Italian composer to articulate the new Romantic age was Giuseppe Verdi. Rossini was scared of the aggressive and popular language of the Romantic movement. It could hardly be said that Verdi's music was the continuation of Rossini's, although Verdi had taken more from Rossini than he cared to acknowledge. Verdi did not consider himself to be anyone's heir and that was probably due to the fact that he did not owe his parents, who were no musicians, anything; he felt that he sprang from nobody, that he was the new man of the new people.

Of course Verdi was wrong, everybody comes from somewhere. 'Nothing will come of nothing,' as Shakespeare made King Lear say. But Verdi as much as Rossini expressed the culture of his time and culture is about earlier achievements, about conveying thought and furthering it. Culture is continuation.

When Rossini felt strong enough to return to Bologna, he would not do so without a police escort. Back in his palazzo, a place that he had made beautiful with superb furniture and paintings, he once again felt happy on seeing the familiar faces of old friends who flocked to via Maggiore to welcome him home. He found the Bolognese dialect more reassuring than the Tuscan – incidentally, Rossini had an extraordinary ear for accents and dialects and could mimic them most convincingly. Despite the outward appearance of a return to the good old days, however, the haven of his imagination was not giving him the tranquillity for which he had hoped and sleep eluded him. He kept open house and Olympe received with a smile. Naturally all the notables flocked to pay their homage to the great Rossini who, it was murmured, was on his way to recovery. When Count Nobili, the Austrian governor of Bologna, called on him and found him surrounded by friends, he endured what every Austrian official was experiencing at the time. All of Rossini's friends, the whole company, rose as one and left the room. Rossini considered this an act of hostility against himself, an affront. In May 1851 he made his final departure from Bologna, from his childhood dreams, his past and his nightmares. He never set foot in the city again.

Florence was certainly less riotous, the city had never endured papal power and its excesses of bureaucratic corruption. On the other hand, those were years of rage which found expression all over Italy in upheavals, arrests and assassinations. The Carbonari were more and more popular with students and intellectuals, while in Florence, the Grand Duchy encountered less opposition. In Rossini's view, there was no wish for unification in Tuscany and independence was not even discussed. Olympe eventually found a palazzetto which suited them; there was a music room and space for receiving. While Rossini paced up and down the dining-room, Olympe played cards. Two young *maestri di musica* began attacking Verdi's *I vespri siciliani* which, they said, had been a flop in Paris. Rossini interrupted them. 'Let them criticize Verdi, but they make me laugh. Only people who can write as well or better than Verdi can criticize him constructively and they have yet to be born.'

Most of Europe was now returning to absolute monarchy with the exception of France and Piedmont where King Vittorio Emanuele of Savoy had maintained a constitutional parliament. The return to the pre-1848 order was achieved with violence; after bombarding Vienna and crushing the rebellion, the Austrian emperor had recalled Metternich. Lombardy-Veneto remained in Austrian hands with Naples under the Bourbons and Rome suffocated by the papacy, the Papal States stretching as far north as Bologna and as far south as Terracina. Humiliated by political events and ostracized by his native Busseto, Verdi had touched people's hearts by setting great choral pieces which evoked the lament of the Babylonians and the Lombards. But now Verdi was composing operas describing emotions which he himself was experiencing: *La traviata* and *Rigoletto* are in effect autobiographical. Verdi's friends had either fled, were in exile or locked in Austrian prisons. In London, the exiled Mazzini set up a National Liberation Committee rather like the one that de Gaulle was to form a century later – and just as weak. Garibaldi had been arrested and fled to New York. For Rossini, the world had returned to some kind of norm; for Verdi, it was the end of a sublime dream.

V

LARGO

During the winter of 1850–1 Rossini supervised the packing of his effects and sold Isabella's villa at Castenaso. His suspicion of Bologna developed into hatred. 'You live in a city,' he wrote to the tenor Nicholas Ivanoff, 'the sons of which, great and small, survive by their wit, by fraud and lies. I still feel remorse for having induced you and the good Donzelli to live in that sewer.' In Bologna, he went on, 'more than a thousand were listed for execution', implying that he himself would have been among the condemned. He also called Bologna a place of mortadelle (the cheapest and nastiest form of salami), which seems really unfair on one of the world's centres of gastronomy. In order to make him feel comfortable, rich, and sought after, Olympe bought three adjacent Medici palaces in the centre of Florence. As it turned out, they never lived in any of them. In order to furnish the grand rooms, Rossini developed a taste for antiques and collected majolica pieces, but unlike Balzac, who had filled his houses with artefacts and his accounts with debts, he could afford to buy anything he fancied. Aguado had done wonders with his investments, Olympe was rich and money kept coming in.

At times the couple enjoyed the company of an interesting Florentine circle of painters and political exiles. But in a period when the painter, the poet, the musician had become symbols of the artist identifying with the people's ideals, Rossini once again appeared to be going the opposite way. As a result, his peers avoided him or looked at him with suspicion mixed with disdain. He was considered a reactionary. This is the memory that unfortunately has been left of him. He rarely played music himself, when he did lights had to be dimmed so that he could sob unobserved; he remembered every single note and could still improvise. Such was his wretchedness that he thought everything had passed him by. Besides his worsening mental and physical afflictions, he was also diagnosed as suffering from 'extreme neurasthenia', a condition that is now commonly known as nervous exhaustion. The study of neurasthenia was then in its infancy. By 1900, the condition was more fashionably categorized under such headings as anxiety and depression. So, in Rossini's case, neurasthenia could well have been synonymous with depression and anxiety: 'It was a very broad church,' observed Simon Wessely. In the mid-nineteenth century little medical attention was paid to nervous conditions. Rossini, however, attracted interest because he was a famous and rich man. In our times there is a lot of care and still little knowledge, the brain being a temple which human science has been loath to visit until recently. Christian ethics left the nervous system to the realm of God; no wonder that most of the study of the brain (sleep, memory, nervous system) has been in Jewish secular circles.

Rossini's musical taste was now becoming more and more conservative in that he intellectually refused Romanticism. More than a refusal, his was a state of frightened denial; maybe he felt his own impotence as he listened to music by Liszt, Berlioz – and Verdi. It was Bach, Palestrina, Mozart and Haydn that he played in Florence. He thought that the new contemporary music overemphasized the emotions; for him there were too many lavish outpourings, too many gory finales, not enough ambiguity. For one whose operas delight in cross-sex musical exchanges, where love is either suppressed or exchanged by glances and sighs alone, Verdi's blood-baths and Wagner's *coitus interruptus* came as a distasteful musical awakening.

Motivated by a similar anger against the Romantics, a group of English painters – Dante Gabriel Rossetti, William Holman Hunt among others, all equally bad and sex-obsessed, formed the Pre-Raphaelite Brotherhood, a refusal of the future and a denial of a movement which Turner for one had enormously enriched. Refusing the steam which invaded his country, William Morris abhorred mechanization and tried to impose the figure of the artisan; that kind of England was running after the past, composing cantatas rather than symphonies; the largely unmechanized Italy did not need to attack the future. But such

Rossini's meeting with Beethoven took place in Vienna and happened when the great Romantic was about to write the Ninth Symphony.

Disorders on the Bridge of the Archbishop by P. Chaperon in pre-Haussman Paris. The July 1829 revolution brought to an end the reign of Charles X for whose coronation Rossini had written a mocking opera-cantata (*il Viaggio a Reims*).

Horace Vernet, a lover of Olympe Pélissier, Rossini's second wife, portrayed the beautiful courtesan as Judith. Balzac thought that Olympe had turned a great deal of heads, not just Olopherne's.

Right: The house at Chaussée d'Antin, where Gioachino and Olympe lived on the first and second floors. From Delacroix, Lamartine to Victor Hugo, everybody flocked to their soirées.

Below: Gioachino and Olympe built their ideal country house at Passy, then an idyllic wooded spot where Balzac and later Giuseppe Verdi were to live.

LA VILLA DE ROSSINI, A PASSY. (Voir l'article à la page précédente.)

The salon of Mme Irisson by P. Lafange. In spite of the many political upheavals, salon life flourished in Paris (and Milan and Rome) throughout the nineteenth century but changed style with the shifting fortunes of the social classes.

Giuseppe Verdi's stunning success with *Nabucco* took Italy – and Rossini – by storm. Music became the voice of revolution. On his way to conduct Rossini's *Stabat Mater* in Bologna, Donizetti went to see *Nabucco* at La Scala.

In 1860 the young Richard Wagner went to see 'le vieux rococo' as Rossini called himself, in Paris, two years before the elderly composer's death.

The protagonists of Parisian salons listen to Liszt on the piano. From left, Dumas Pere, Victor Hugo, Georges Sand (sitting), Paganini and Rossini in a friendly embrace. At Liszt's feet, Countess Marie d'Agoult mother of Cosima Liszt, who was to became Wagner's wife. Byron looks on from a portrait and the bust of Beethoven blesses the company. Painting by Josef Danhauser (1840).

Not many of Rossini's doodles and sketches have survived, but he was an able draughtsman and marked the kind of sets he wanted as much as he constructed his own librettos.

Rossini dedicated his last work to God. *La Petite Messe* was W. H. Auden's favourite piece of music.

industrialization as had taken place meant that the post was now very swift and Rossini cultivated several correspondences.

One was with Ivanoff, whom he had almost adopted as a son. Ivanoff had been approached to appear in *Rigoletto*, which was to open in Venice on 11 March 1851. (It was an opera that Rossini grew to love; he played it on the piano and even sang all four voices of the great quartet from the last act.)

> *Before you accept the engagement to sing this opera, I should like you to consult Verdi so that he can tell you, with the frankness that is natural to his proven goodwill towards you, if you can discharge this obligation comfortably or whether, to this end, he would be willing to open the box of his happy inspiration to compose something specially for you to assure your success.*

Clearly Rossini was trying to tell his protégé, in the kindest possible way, that his voice was unsuitable for the part of the Duke of Mantua. The letter continues: 'When writing to him or calling on him, give him my best wishes and tell him that, for what they are worth, I add my own to your prayers that he should keep the Ivanoffian ship on its course.' But Verdi belonged to the generation of composers who could not tolerate singers to demand special arias. Indeed, when the tenor Antonio Borsi asked Verdi to insert a new aria for his wife in *Rigoletto*, Verdi answered with one of his wittiest letters:

> *Were you not convinced that my talent could improve on what I did for* Rigoletto, *you would have not asked for yet another aria. But if* Rigoletto *is to remain as it is, where do you suggest that I should insert the new piece? Where to find a place? . . . There would be one, but God forbid! We would be cursed. We should show Gilda with the Duke in his bedroom!! Do you understand, his bedroom? In any case it would be a duet. A magnificent duet!!! But priests, friars, the hypocrites would scream out against the scandal.*

Needless to say Rossini hardly composed during these painful Florentine years; there is a canzone dated 5 April 1852 based on Metastasio's lines *Mi lagnerò tacendo* ('I will lament in silence'), words that fitted his painful state so well that Rossini was drawn to set this poem numerous times, mostly as album leaves. There is also a bolero dated summer 1852 and a revised version of *Giovanna d'Arco*. But, while there was little outlet for his musical imagination, he revealed his inner thoughts in letters or conversations, something he had rarely done in his saner days. There are flashes of Shakespearean truth in these, the blind man who sees, the madman understands, the incapacitated is able – the last he finds in himself. 'I don't mind dying, what can one do in this sad world? But I mind pain. At least cholera kills in a few hours,' he wrote. And 'Death would be preferable to my present existence, all illusions of life have left me. I always held human glory in little esteem knowing how easy it is to tumble from the summit to the bottom.' He could also discuss music with great feeling. In a letter to his friend Ferrucci, who had asked him why contraltos no longer figured as protagonists, he replied: 'The contralto is the norm to which voices and instruments would be subordinated in a fully harmonized musical composition.' Rossini saw all too clearly how music belonged to the age it expressed, but of course he did not like the times in which he lived. 'This art that has its sole basis in idealism and sentiment cannot separate itself from the times in which we live; idealism and sentiment have been exclusively directed in these days to steam, to rapine and barricades.' Even when he was outwardly confused, his words were often lucid, full of originality and imagery. He cared about the direction in which music was moving and did not like what he saw:

> *With the extreme strings one loses as much in grace as one gains in force. From abuse they tend toward paralysis of the throat, turning as an expedient to declaimed – that is, forced and toneless – singing. This fosters a need born to give more body to the instrumentation, to cover the excess of the voices, to the detriment of the musical colouring. That is the way it is done now, and it will be worse after me. The head will conquer the heart: science will lead to the ruin of art; and under a deluge of notes, what is called instrumental will be the tomb of the voice and of feeling.*

Filippo Mordani, who saw Rossini between May 1854 and April of the following year, understood Rossini's nervous conditions: not only was he himself a depressive, but he was also a doctor. He kept a diary in which he noted his impressions of Rossini:

This is the first time that I have spoken with this very famous – but, oh, so unhappy a man! And of what use is his great fame to him? The light of his high intelligence seems on the verge of darkening . . . some of those who frequent his house have told me how he gives vent to heavy laments and sighs, unexpectedly breaks into violent sobbing and often, looking into a mirror, accuses himself of cowardice and says: 'What have I become, and what do I mean to this world? And what will people say when they see me reduced to being led about by a woman, like a small boy?'

Indeed, the sick man could not do without Olympe whose every moment was now occupied in comforting him. Rossini's friends resented her, feeling that she was like a ferocious guard dog. He looked weird in his different wigs, some of which were as curly and dark as a youth's. Despite his confession to Mordani that food had become an addictive comfort, perhaps his only consolation – he had lost a lot of weight. It was also to Mordani that he said: I haven't slept for three and a half months. I am in a dreadful state, believe me, I am in a dreadful state. You see how much weight I'm losing. Doctors don't know how to cure me. They would like me to take opium in order to sleep, I don't want to because I fear it might harm me.'

In summer 1854, when Rossini was sixty-two, Olympe tried to see if Bagni di Lucca, a lovely spa town in the mountains north of Lucca, beloved by Shelley and Vittoria Colonna, might help his physical if not mental condition. They also tried Montecatini, in the Arno valley, rendered famous by Fellini's *Otto e mezzo*. But Rossini showed no sign of improvement and there were even rumours that he was becoming insane. Olympe had to write a letter denying them and get it published in the *Revue et gazette musicale* (23 October 1854). He took no interest in anything and Olympe, who had always believed that there was light at the end of the tunnel, also began to fear for his sanity and hers. Once again he started talking about suicide. Despairing of doctors who seemed incapable of curing his condition, Rossini again tried magnetism. He confided his belief in the merits of Mesmer's 'animal magnetism' to the young Filippo Mordani, who in his diary, ridiculed Rossini's credulity. That Rossini should have turned to mesmerism underlines his desperate state. Franz Anton Mesmer, a man of the Enlightenment, was by then well out of favour. Rossini ignored the more conventional Italian cures – he did not visit the various shrines to the Madonna at Loreto, Lourdes or Pompeii, for example, nor did he send offerings to any other holy protector. He was probably agnostic. What remained of his Catholicism had gone into his *Stabat mater*, a prayer to his own mother rather than to the Virgin Mary.

Early in January 1855, having met Mordani while strolling in the Piazza del Duomo under the shadow of the grand Neptune fountain and the tower of Palazzo Vecchio, Rossini explained that he envied those who had no feelings, especially animals. Lately he had slept only in snatches of five minutes and the nights had been desperate. 'Death is better than living in this way. All illusions about life have left me.' He could never keep still, not even at home: 'Nobody knows what our nervous disease brings, look! I can't raise my arms more than that.' But even when he was seized by paralysis, his intelligence did not dim. 'Oh no, that never happens!' he uttered wishfully.

Now that Bologna was anathema, that Florence had failed to cure him and that France had returned to calm, Olympe began to whisper the sweet word 'Paris' in Rossini's ear. On 20 April 1855, a beautiful day in Florence, Rossini told Mordani:

> As I see that this nervous disease has no remedy and doctors know nothing, I thought of trying the hydropathic cure. I shall first go to Nice; I want to travel by post-chaise with my young doctor, short days, with all comforts; as we are talking about health, money should not be a consideration. When I reach Paris if I see that the journey has been beneficial, I want to go at once to a place nearby and start the hydropathic cure.

Later that month he and Olympe set off on the long journey across Europe to Paris accompanied by two servants, Tonino and Marietta, and by a young doctor. They spent several days in Nice and stopped frequently. Remembering his experience, Rossini refused to take the train, and their journey took over a month.

ACT FIVE

WAGNER AND DEATH

Va, que la mort soit ton refuge!
A l'example du Redempteur,
Ose à la fois être le juge,
la victime et l'exécuteur.
Qu'importe si des fanatiques
interdisent les saints portiques
a ton cadavre abandonné?
Qu'importe si, de mille outrages,
par l'éloquence des faux sages,
ton nom vulgaire est couronné?

Sous la tombe muette oh! comme on dort tranquille!
sans changer de posture, on peut, dans cet asile,
des replis du linceul débarassant sa main
l'unir aux doits poudreux du squelette voisin.
Il est doux de sentir des racines vivaces
coudre à ses ossements leurs noeuds et leurs rosaces,
d'entendre les hurrahs du vent qui coubre et rompt
les arbustes plantes au-dessus de son front.
C'est un ravissement quand la rosée amie,
diamantant le sein de la côte endormie,

à travers le velours d'un gazon jeune et doux,
bien umide et bien froide arrive jusqu'à vous.
Là, silence complet; farniente sans borne.
Plus de rages d'amour! le coeur stagnant et morne
ne se sent pas broyé sous la dent du remords
– Certes, l'on est heureux dans les villas des morts!

Philothée O'Neddy,
'Nuit Quatrième', *Necropolis*

Go, May Death be your shelter!
following the Redeemer's example
dare at the same time be judge
victim and executioner.
What does it matter if some fanatics
negate the sacred doors
to your abandoned corpse?
What does it matter if your name
is crowned by insults
by the eloquence of fake savants?

Beneath the mute tombstones, oh! how comfortably one sleeps!
without changing posture you can, in that refuge
discard from the hand the creases of your shroud

and join them to the dusty bones of your neighbour's fingers
It's sweet to feel the lively roots
stitch their knots and twigs to your bones
and listen to the noise of the wind which cuts and breaks
the shrubs planted above your head.
It is marvellous when the friendly rose
bejewelling the breast of the sleeping hill
through the velvet of the sweetly damp and shining
young meadow reach down to you.
There where you are, total silence; eternal nothingness.
Rage of passion no more! the heart, still and quiet
is no longer chewed by the teeth of guilt
Yes, one is happy in the city of the dead!

Previous Page: Gioachino Rossini on his deathbed, 1868
Etching by Gustave Doré

I

MODERATO

T he Rossinis arrived in Paris on 25 May 1855. Immense changes had taken place in the city. On 2 December 1852 the President of the republic Louis Napoleon Bonaparte had proclaimed himself emperor. Always appealing to plebiscites and personal suffrage, he tried to substitute his lack of achievement with splendid public ceremonies. Napoleon III was a flamboyant version of Tony Blair; much promise and little result (Rossini would have said *Molto fumo e poco arrosto*, 'a lot of smoke and little roast beef'), but that kind of regime suited Rossini. Napoleon III had glamour and personal charm. His beautiful wife Eugénie del Castillo watched her husband's many infidelities with sadness and prayed; she involved herself in politics and was fundamental in France's defence of the pope after the sad demise of the Roman Republic which was crushed by French military might.

Even in his apathetic state, Rossini could not have helped noticing the immense changes that had occurred in Paris. The little neighbour-hoods were disappearing, swept away by Georges Haussmann, the architect. The task which Haussmann, who was also Prefect of Police for the Department of the Seine, had been assigned, would take seventeen years to complete. Reconstructing the entire city offered the advantage of open spaces, making room for roads wide enough for an army to advance and deploy artillery against any popular uprising. Haussmann's new urban system installed the rich middle class in the heart of the city, evicting *les Misérables* in the process; the narrow

alleys and old houses were demolished. On either side of the boule-
vards rose tall buildings with apartments designed for the wealthy
juste-milieu: political architecture was being melded with military
architecture and Haussmann's city became a model for other European capitals – Vienna, for one – destroying the old urban fabric and
dividing social classes.

A new opulence was reflected in ladies' fashions, all swirling skirts
with lace, bows and frills. In contrast with the classic folds of the
previous Empire, ladies at court looked like clouds from a painting by
Francisco Hayez; their crinolines now occupied vast areas of the opera
foyer. As usual fashion mirrored the mood of the time, the triumph of
money over taste. The glittering and gilded vulgarity of Napoleon's
Palais des Tuileries was deplored by other sovereigns, but many
people enjoyed the liveliness of the Bouffes-Parisiennes and music
was to be heard everywhere. Offenbach was the rage. Rossini made a
constructive point in calling him 'le Mozart des Cafés-chantants'.
Offenbach's music has a lot of Rossinian qualities and Rossini did not
intend his remark to be pejorative; indeed, Mozart remained his great
musical hero (in 1856 he made an unsuccessful attempt to buy the
original score of *Die Zauberflöte*).

Soon after his arrival, Rossini's friends, among them the composers
Auber and Carafa, called on him in the temporary accommodation
that Olympe had found in Montmartre, 32 rue Basse-du-Rampart,
and were appalled by what they saw. Rossini's face was emaciated, his
pallid and flaccid features a mirror of his ill-health; he seemed to eat
without appetite and was always exhausted. He no longer tried to hide
the fact that his descent into depression was now precipitous and
likely to be permanent. His pessimism, undecisiveness, even his
tearfulness, came as a shock to his Parisian friends who remembered
the assertive and buoyant man of the past. On meeting Verdi, Rossini
confided: 'You can't imagine in what a prison I've been in!'

Paris not only welcomed Rossini but also made him feel as if it had
been yearning for his return. When Napoleon III paid Rossini a call
and found him apologetic since he was wearing a dressing-gown, he
reassured him: 'Among us sovereigns these things don't matter!'
Rossini began to go out and about and, when strolling in the Tuileries
gardens, he was amazed and annoyed to find that people would
recognize him and stare. The signs were that the veils of his gloom
were lifting. Because he was known to have given up composing

altogether, Rossini – who now labelled himself 'un vieux rococo' – took on the aura of a grand old man, the genius whose opinions were heard, respected and repeated in newsprint. Invented comments attributed to him circulated among friend and foe and appeared regularly in the gossip columns. Already a famous figure because portraits of him were so widely reproduced, Rossini now became the subject of the new and accurate science of photography. In Paris he sat for the most famous photographers, including the great Nadar who succeeded in capturing the despair in his ironic eyes – those images did not gain Rossini's approval. (He also sat for Carjat, Erwin Frères and Blanc.) His first photographic session occurred when he was lured into the studio of Mayer. The camera stole his image, while he was looking at a photograph of Bologna. 'Oh, Lord!' he exclaimed after inspecting it, 'You have played a bad joke on me.' He was sixty-three at the time and the photograph shows his toupee in disarray.

After looking around Haussmann's Paris, Olympe found an ideal apartment with two spacious floors in rue de la Chaussée d'Antin, on a corner between the Chaussée and boulevard des Italiens (so named because it was near the Théâtre-Italien); this was Rossini's winter residence until his death. Olympe had chosen well: their home was in the heart of the 'new Athens', the bohemian-chic district which became the centre of artistic Paris, it provided well-lit accommodation on the second floor, with several bedrooms and corners for privacy, and an ideal space for Olympe's future salon on the floor below. She had every intention of opening such a glittering salon that it would be beyond the envy of those snooty princesses who had refused her in the past. And she would keep them all out! In any case Countess d'Agoult had been abandoned by Liszt, Princess Cristina Belgiojoso had been reduced to a wreck by opium and the *ancien régime* was generally in disgrace. Only those who pleased Olympe would be allowed to climb the stairs and pass through the Orphean doors of music. They all flocked, not only musicians but people like Delacroix, Doré and Alexandre Dumas *père*. Among the composers to visit were Gounod, Saint-Saëns, Arrigo Boito, Liszt, Meyerbeer and 'a taciturn Verdi'. People came to make and hear music, not only Rossini's but new compositions as well. Thalberg, Liszt and Saint-Saëns occasionally performed virtuoso piano pieces, while Joseph Joachim and Pablo de Sarasate were equally dazzling as violinists. They all found it stimulating to play in such an intellectually charged ambience – besides,

Rossini paid good money. The most famous singers thought it a privilege to be included among Rossini's guests. The pretty soprano Adelina Patti, with her trim figure and the face of a sexy Courbet (she was soon to seduce Verdi) first displayed her wonderful coloratura singing 'Una voce poco fa' from *Il barbiere*. 'Very nice, Signorina,' Rossini commented after hearing her vocal fireworks. 'But who wrote this piece?' Apparently Patti left in tears, but she was clever enough to return to the Chaussée d'Antin and learn to sing the notes as Rossini had written them, accompanied by the maestro himself.

On Saturdays, before the 'crowd' of guests arrived, dinner was served to an inner circle of about sixteen to twenty friends. The menu was always prepared by Rossini, who often wrote it down for the guests, for example: 'Macheroni [sic], Salumi di Magro, Modena, Zampone, Pesce, Filetto (with Bordo [sic]), Funghi (vino: del Reno), Tachina-Champagne, Dolce, Formaggio (à *l'anglaise*).' One day he went all the way from Chaussée d'Antin to the Marais to find a shop that sold Neapolitan pasta. When it was produced, Rossini took a look at it and pronounced it to be Genoese – probably tagliolini – and not Neapolitan. The shopkeeper commented that if that man knew as much about music as he did about pasta, he surely was a great composer. Rossini had largely recovered his good spirits. But he re-emerged as a different man, one who accepted and was pleased to accept that by now he was outmoded, that the Romantic age had overtaken him and his music. What he wanted to do now was to compose pieces for himself, not for opera houses, bankers or kings. In 1857 he began filling volumes with *canzonette* and musical thoughts which he called *Péchés de vieillesse* ('Sins of old age'). Rossini added to this collection until a matter of months before his death; it comprises some 150 pieces – including *Un Petit Train de plaisir*, a satire on his nightmare train journey – but the most substantial is the *Petite Messe solennelle*.

It seemed a miracle that Rossini's nervous disease had disappeared. During the day he would receive in his bedroom, which was forbiddingly tidy. His head was wrapped in a huge coloured scarf, while his collection of wigs dangled on a hanger, looking rather like dishevelled crows. Mozart's marble bust topped a clock and among several ancient and beautiful musical instruments there was also a well-loved harmonium. The white walls were hung with Japanese watercolours on rice paper. To a friend who commented on the orderliness of his bedroom, Rossini laughed: 'Eh, my friend. Order is wealth!' But order was also music and the composer's once disorderly mind was ready again for orderly composition. Musicians and mathematicians are supposed to need order, although Einstein apparently lived surrounded by mess and muddle.

Rossini now returned to his favourite Metastasio text, 'Mi lagnerò tacendo', this time setting six songs. On 14 April 1857 he dedicated this collection, which he called *Musique anodine*, to Olympe on her saint's day: 'I offer these modest songs to my dear wife Olympe as a simple testimonial of gratitude for the affectionate, intelligent care with which she was prodigal during my overlong and terrible illness.' 'I shall lament in silence' had been his maxim, the philosophy of his life, for decades; he never admitted the sorrow he endured after the flop of *Il barbiere* in Rome, except in a private letter to his mother. He never protested against the abuse he had received from the Neapolitan and then the French press by which he had been lampooned with such names as Trombonini and worse. He never reacted when his music was bastardized; he never showed his tears.

In December 1857 Rossini wrote one of his letters to the librettist Felice Romani, recommending a young composer aged nineteen who was on his way to Rome:

> *Signor Bizet, first prize in composition at the Imperial Conservatory in Paris, will bring this letter to you. He is travelling to complete his practical musical education. He has done very well in his studies; he has enjoyed great success with an operetta performed here. He is a good pianist and an excellent person, deserving both your and my solicitude. I recommend him to you.*

Not many (certainly not Verdi!) would have written such a letter to help the future composer of *Carmen* who, having won the Prix de Rome, was on his way to spend three years at the French Academy of Villa Medici.

Rossini started paying daily visits – sometimes leaving as early as 7 a.m. to Passy, a village beside the Seine where the couple had rented a villa in the past. He was looking for a suitable plot of land and, in September 1858, he bought a vacant site not too far from Balzac's delightful and by then empty house. In May 1859 the building of Beau Séjour began, and Olympe planted a rose bush where their bedroom would be.

On 11 June 1859 Metternich wrote to Rossini, having heard that he had started to compose again. He was happy, he said, that 'la lyre que vous tenez sous clef, cachée' was playing again; but when Metternich died two weeks later, for Rossini another long-standing friend had gone for ever. Metternich had truly loved music:

> *Nothing has such a strong influence on me as music. It agitates and placates me at the same time. Music moves me to sweet tears, opens my heart which then welcomes my past, present and future all together, and everything is awakened in me, sorrow and happiness that are buried in the past, sorrow and happiness which I await to feel and desire in the future.*

In Paris Rossini found a contentment that involved those simple things which he had been unable to enjoy for decades. Recognized as a gourmet, a wise and grand old man of music, Rossini was finally respected and loved, even by his colleagues who once had been unable to bear his success. Politicians, musicians and composers longed to be introduced to him, just as he had laboured to meet Beethoven. Now it was Richard Wagner, the most controversial composer of the century, the man whose Romanticism encapsulated the disease and the torment of the age, who was waiting to climb the stairs of the apartment in Chaussée d'Antin.

II

MAESTOSO

In March 1860 two great musicians met and initial suspicion soon developed into mutual respect. The conversation that took place between Rossini and Wagner was not just an exchange between two composers but also the confrontation between two movements, Enlightenment and Romanticism, acceptance and revolution. Two men of genius together in the same room knew full well that they were each in the presence of greatness. Rossini listened with an ironic smile to Wagner's attacks on the old school to which he belonged. And Wagner also asked questions, wanting to know about the maestro's meetings with Mendelssohn, Weber and Beethoven. The tactful restraint of Rossini's maturity was matched by the Teutonic boldness of a Wagner – who, ultimately, understood Rossini better than anyone else, with the possible exception of Balzac. The very essence of the Romantic attitude, Wagner was the self-immolating artist who believed in the cause of art. As Isaiah Berlin observed in *The Power of Ideas*: 'Hence the worship of the artist . . . as the highest manifestation of the ever-active spirit, and the popular image of the artist in his garret, wild-eyed, wild-haired, poor, solitary, mocked-at; but independent, free, spiritually superior to his philistine tormentors.' And with great perception, he continued:

> *This attitude has a darker side too: worship not merely of the painter or the composer, or the poet, but of that more sinister artist whose materials are men – the destroyer of old societies, and the creator of*

new ones – no matter at what human cost: the superhuman leader who
tortures and destroys in order to build on new foundations . . . It is this
embodiment of the romantic ideal that took more and more hysterical
forms and in its extreme ended in violent irrationalism and Fascism.

Luckily there was a third man present when Rossini and Wagner found themselves in the same room; and it was fortunate that this man, who accompanied Wagner in order to record their conversation, should have been a musician. That was Edmond Michotte, whose account of these meetings was first published in 1906. What follows is a slightly edited and at times paraphrased version. In essence the meeting between the two men was as moving as the one between Rossini and Beethoven, and Michotte has enabled us to hide and eavesdrop in a corner of the apartment in the Chaussée d'Antin.

Wagner was in Paris trying to arrange a performance of *Tannhäuser* at the Opéra in 1861; he had given three concerts of his music in the Salle Ventadour of the Théâtre-Italien in late January and early February 1860. Berlioz wrote enthusiastically of the excerpts from *Der fliegende Holländer*, *Tannhäuser* and *Lohengrin*. Baudelaire and Gautier were also deeply moved by the new music; but the French press, which had not been invited to review the concerts, was negative if not abusive. Wagner was now labouring on the translation of *Tannhäuser* into French. All of Parisian society was talking about the short, determined and humourless German who marched single-mindedly towards his goal, never taking no for an answer. Convinced of his musical mission, Wagner had a messianic quality and was the personification of the individual that Romanticism had asserted. That was the main difference between him and Rossini, whose ironic disposition drove him to take nothing seriously, least of all himself. Wisecracks at Wagner's expense were circulating all over Paris, some ascribed to Rossini. According to Michotte, these were 'as dubious as they were apocryphal'. Actually, in spite of the denials, I don't think for a moment that they were all apocryphal. 'Monsieur Wagner a des beaux moments, mais des mauvais quarts d'heure' sounds too Rossinian not to be Rossini's. On the other hand Wagner had cruelly dismissed Rossini's music in writing and they were both aware of each other's comments.

Wagner was curious but apprehensive before meeting the *vieu rococo*, the lazy gourmet; Rossini was, after all, still influential and

Wagner would have thought it advantageous to ingratiate himself with the old composer. In the event Wagner, who had just finished writing *Tristan und Isolde*, was amazed by how different Rossini was in real life from the figure invented by popular imagination. Rossini too was impressed by Wagner's seriousness and self-belief.

It was proper that, in 1818, the venue of the meeting between Rossini and Beethoven should have been in Vienna, while it was equally apt that the encounter of 1860, with Rossini reaching the end of his career and Wagner in his prime, should take place in Paris. On the day of the meeting Wagner wrote a letter from rue Newton, his residence in Paris, to remind Michotte of their appointment that afternoon. Wagner was anxious to be punctual and, as the two climbed the stairs to Rossini's apartment, Michotte told him: 'If Rossini is in a good mood, you will be charmed by his conversation.' Rossini had secluded himself in the part of his bedroom which overlooked the boulevard des Italiens, where he spent most of the time. His bed was near his writing-desk at the end of the room, with a piano close to the window. While waiting downstairs, Wagner looked at the portrait of Rossini by Vincenzo Camuccini, which remains as well known today as it was at the time.

'That intelligent physiognomy,' he remarked, 'that ironic mouth – it could only be the composer of *Il barbiere*, this portrait must date from the period when that opera was composed.'

Michotte answered: 'Four years later. It was painted in Naples in 1820. He was a good-looking youth and in that land of Vesuvius where women are easily ignited, he must have broken many hearts.' Had Rossini been served by Leporello, he might have surpassed the 'mille e tre' total, he added.

'Oh how you exaggerate!' answered Wagner in an embarrassingly teutonic crack: ' "*Mille*" I agree but . . . "*tre*" – that's too many.' Wagner himself went for just '*tre*' but he had a tendency to fall in love with women who belonged to his best friends' households, the sense of the forbidden being for him an essential erotic propeller.

When the two visitors entered his bedroom, Rossini issued a warm greeting, in French. 'Ah! Monsieur Wagner, like a new Orpheus, you don't fear to enter this redoubtable precinct . . . I know that they have thoroughly blackened me in your eyes.' Rossini was fluent in French and Wagner spoke it well enough (he had been to Paris before) but was in difficulties when he wanted to express complicated concepts, which he tended to over-embellish with flowery words. Rossini immediately told Wagner that 'they' had bombarded him with derogatory remarks at the latter's expense. While he did not pretend to be wise, 'I do hold to being polite and refrain from insulting a musician who, like you, is trying to extend the limits of our art . . . As for slighting your music, I should have to be familiar with it first; to know it, I should hear it in the theatre and not just read the score; it is not possible to judge music intended for the stage. The only composition of yours which I know is the March from *Tannhäuser*. I heard it often at Kissingen when I was taking the cure three years ago. It had a great impact on me and – I assure you sincerely – I thought it very beautiful.' Sitting on his easy chair, Rossini was probably enjoying the meeting more than the younger man. 'Now that – I hope – all misunderstanding between us has disappeared, tell me how you are finding your stay in Paris. I know that you are discussing staging your *Tannhäuser*.'

'Allow me, illustrious *maître*, to thank you for these kind words. They touch me deeply. They show me how much your character displays nobility and greatness. Believe me that even if you criticize me, I shall not take offence. I know that my writings are of a sort that give rise to misinterpretation. Faced with the emergence of a huge range of new ideas, the best-intentioned judges can mistake their significance. That is because in my operas, I am unable at the moment to make a logical and complete demonstration of my ideas.'

'That is fair,' Rossini observed, 'for deeds are worth more than words.' Wagner had played the whole of *Tannhäuser* to the director of the Théâtre-Italien, he told Rossini, and there was hope that it might be staged. 'Unhappily the ill-will that has raged against me in the press threatens to take the form of a real cabal.'

As he heard the word 'cabal', Rossini, who had himself been the victim of many intrigues, interjected, reminding Wagner that countless composers, from Gluck onwards, had also suffered. 'I was not spared myself. On the evening of the première of *Il barbiere* when, as was customary then in Italy, I played the harpsichord in the orchestra to accompany the recitatives, I had to protect myself from the riotous behaviour of the audience. I thought that they were going to assassinate me. Here in Paris when I first came, I was greeted by all sorts of ugly nicknames. It was no different in Vienna when I was there in 1822 to stage my operas. Weber himself pursued me relentlessly after my operas were performed at the Italian court theatre.'

To which Wagner rejoined: 'Weber, oh! I know he was extremely intolerant. He became intractable above all when it was a question of defending German art . . . A great genius, and he died so prematurely!'

'A great genius certainly . . .'

It will be remembered that Rossini had met Weber in Paris when the latter was on his way to London. Previously, when Rossini had been the triumphant composer in Vienna, Weber had been more than hostile to the Italian composer. 'Not having expected his visit, I must admit that I was moved . . . as soon as he saw me the poor fellow thought it necessary to tell me – while embracing me and with difficulty in finding French words, because he had been so hard on me in his critical articles . . . but I didn't let him finish.' He had not read those reviews, Rossini told him; in any case, he could not read German.

'He was already suffering, I know, from the consumption that was to kill him a short time later,' said Wagner.

'It pained me to see him. He came back a few days later to ask for some introductions in London. I was appalled by the idea of seeing him undertake such a journey . . . With a broken heart I embraced that great genius for the last time knowing that I would never see him again. That was all too true. Povero Weber!'

On the topic of cabals, Rossini added: 'one can do nothing except fight them with silence and inertia; that is more effective, believe me, than retaliation and anger. Ill-will is immense . . . I spat on such attacks, the more they buffeted me the more I responded by laughing at them . . . Believe me, the fact that you see me wearing a wig does not mean that those bastards succeeded in making me lose a single hair from my scalp.' Here again is the thinking behind *Mi lagnerò tacendo*. But did it work? Wagner, who certainly did lament and never in silence, managed to draw attention and respect to himself. He was feared even when he was unsuccessful while Rossini, who pretended to take nothing seriously, was not feared.

Wagner laughed at Rossini's plain speaking. 'Thanks be to that inertia which you mention, maestro, that was really a strength which the public recognized.'

Wagner then wanted to hear about Salieri.

'In Vienna, where he lived for a long time, he had become fashionable because of several successful operas; he saw Beethoven at times but warned me of Beethoven's distrustful character. By the way, Salieri had enjoyed good relations with Mozart. After the latter died, people said that Salieri had killed him with poison because of professional jealousy.'

'That rumour was still around when I was in Vienna,' Wagner remarked.

'One day I said to Salieri as a joke: "It's lucky for Beethoven that he avoided dining with you, because of self-preservation; you might send him to the other world as you did with Mozart." "Do I look like a poisoner?" Salieri replied. He was hurt for having been attacked by the German press and, for a time, the matter of Mozart's death obsessed him.'

Rossini told Wagner what Beethoven had said to him about Italian opera and *opera buffa* in particular.

'That blow from the lion,' interjected Wagner. 'Wouldn't Salieri have been happier if you had been attacked?'

'No . . . he bit his lips, without hurting himself too much for . . . he was timorous to the point that the king of Hell, in order not to blush over the job of roasting such a coward, would have sent him to be smoked elsewhere!'

Clearly Rossini did not like Salieri.

Then Wagner and Rossini talked about other aspects of music. 'I preferred to deal with comic rather than serious subjects,' said Rossini. 'But I never had much choice in librettos, which were imposed on me by the impresarios. I can't tell you how many times it happened that at first I received only part of the scenario, one act at a time for which I had to compose the music without knowing what was to follow . . . The things I had to do to earn a living for my father, my mother and my grandmother! Going from town to town like a nomad . . . I wrote 3 or 4 operas a year. And don't think that all that earned me the means to act as *le grand seigneur*. I was paid only 1,200 francs for *Il barbiere* plus a hazel-coloured suit which my impresario gave me so that I could look good in the orchestra. That suit may have been worth 100 francs. Total: 1,300 francs. It had taken me only thirteen days to write the score. Taking everything into account, that came to a hundred francs a day. You see, despite everything, I earned a big salary! I was very boastful to my father, who had earned only two francs fifty per day when he had the job of trumpet player at Pesaro!'

'Thirteen days! This is unique. But maestro, how could you write those pages of *Otello*, *Mosè* in such circumstances? Superb pages that bear the mark, not of improvisation, but of hard-thought effort after the concentration of all your mental forces?'

'Oh, I had facility and a lot of instinct. Having to get along without a really proper musical education – and where could I have acquired it in Italy at my time? – I learnt the little that I know from German scores. An amateur at Bologna had some of them: *Die Schöpfung, Le nozze di Figaro, Die Zauberflöte . . .* He lent them to me and, because at the age of 15 I didn't have the means to import them from Germany, I copied them out. Initially I used to transcribe the solo vocal part without looking at the orchestral accompaniment.' Next, Rossini added he would imagine and write down his own accompaniment and then compare it with that of the great masters. 'That system taught me more than all the courses at the Liceo. Had I been able to tackle my studies in your country I feel that I could have produced something better.'

'Surely not, to cite only the *Scènes des ténèbres* in your *Moïse*, the conspiracy in *Guillaume Tell* or, of another kind, *Corpus morietur . . .*'

'You have mentioned some happy moments in my career! But what is all this compared with Mozart's work, with Haydn's? I cannot emphasize strongly enough how much I admire those masters for that subtle science, that certainty which is so natural to their art of composition.'

There were the two men talking, totally engrossed in each other, Wagner crouching in his chair, listening, surprised by the flow of Rossini's recollections, while Rossini himself enjoyed playing the role of the old guru.

III

ALLEGRO RUBATO

U nlike Rossini, Wagner came from a comfortable background and had never experienced the need to earn in order to keep both parents and a grandmother. Although he was in debt when he visited Chaussée d'Antin, he was the sort of man who expected money to come to him, typical of somebody born into a wealthy milieu. Dressed à la Modigliani, Wagner would be seen walking his dog, a generous silk cravat under his trim beard. A huge head carried a thin mouth, and he wore his straight hair combed back.

The meeting between the two composers continued with Rossini expressing his admiration for German music; Bach was an over-whelming genius, he said. 'If Beethoven is a prodigy of humanity, Bach is a miracle of God! I subscribed to the great publication of his works. Look, you'll see it there, on my table, the last volume to appear. How I should like to hear a complete performance of his *Matthew Passion* before leaving this world! But that's an impossible dream in France!'

'It was Mendelssohn who first allowed the Germans to know the *Passion*, through the superb performance that he himself conducted in Berlin,' Wagner remarked. It must have been hard for him to see how Rossini, who by then composed little, enjoyed the adoration of Parisian society. In fact Rossini's reputation was at its zenith. The French version of *Semiramide* was to be staged at the Opéra (9 July 1860), running for thirty performances; meanwhile Wagner was having difficulty in staging just a single opera.

'Mendelssohn!' said Rossini dreamily. 'What a sympathetic nature! I recall with pleasure the good hours that I spent in his company at Frankfurt in 1836. I found myself in that city for a Rothschild wedding.' Mendelssohn had played for him some of his own music as well as pieces by Weber and also Bach. 'At first Mendelssohn seemed stupefied by my request. "How does it happen that you, an Italian, so love German music?" he asked. "I don't love any other kind." . . . I heard from Hiller that, after we parted, Mendelssohn said to him "This Rossini, is he really serious? In any case, he's a very odd fish."'

Wagner laughed and said: 'Maestro, I can understand Mendelssohn's surprise.'

'Let's talk about the Future since in any discussion which is raised about you, it seems to be inseparable from this concept. Are you planning to stay in Paris? As for your *Tannhäuser*, I'm sure that you will succeed in having it staged. There has been too much talk about it for the Parisians to stifle their curiosity. Is the translation finished?'

The translation of *Tannhäuser* into French was not completed, Wagner told Rossini. 'I am working on it feverishly with a collaborator who is very able and, above all, extremely patient. For perfect understanding of the musical expression each French word had to be identified with the corresponding German word and under the same notation. It is hard work and difficult to accomplish.'

'But why don't you start by writing an opera with every number adapted to a French libretto as Gluck, Spontini and Meyerbeer did?'

This remark of Rossini's must have made Wagner shudder; it was the old formula, which Salieri had expressed with 'Prima la musica poile parole' and which Rossini himself had always attempted to follow. Besides, Wagner deplored the concept of 'numbers opera; his music drama was to have no arias and recitative, no cabaletta, no formally separable numbers. Though, in fact, what but a 'number' can one call the duet between Sieglinde and Siegmund, the solo of the dying Tristan or Isolde's prolonged longing? In a way, only *Parsifal* – his last opera – achieves Wagner's musical dream, insofar as it has no arias and no set pieces.

Rossini continued on his dangerous path: 'Wouldn't you then be better if you took into consideration the prevailing French taste?'

But that was the trouble. Wagner would not court fashion in any way; he was going to make musical history. He would bend the French taste, not vice versa. Rossini was instead suggesting that he should seek an elusive success at the cost of his own integrity. But at the time Wagner was wallowing in his own Romantic agony. Having fled Dresden in the aftermath of the revolutions of 1848–9, narrowingly avoiding arrest, he reached safety in Switzerland via Weimar. He was to be an exile in Switzerland, the guest of Mathilde Wesendonck, for whom he conceived a passion which resulted in *Tristan und Isolde*. While composing it in 1857, Cosima – who was to be his second wife – and Hans von Bülow stayed with him, on their honeymoon. Wagner's love life was disorderly and well publicized: Michotte knew all about Mathilde Wesendonck, 'that beautiful woman'.

Wagner's answer to Rossini was: 'In my case, maestro, I don't think it could be done. After *Tannhäuser*, I wrote *Lohengrin*, then *Tristan und Isolde*. These three operas, from both the literary and the musical point of view, represent a logical development in my conception of the definitive and absolute form of lyric drama. My style has gone through the inevitable effect of that transition. And if it is true that I feel capable of writing other works in the style of *Tristan*, I swear that I am incapable of taking up my *Tannhäuser* manner again. If I were in a position to compose an opera for Paris on a French text, I could not and should not follow any other road than the one that has led me to the composition of *Tristan*.'

Not only that, but a work of this kind, involving disturbance of the traditional forms, would not be understood and would have no chance of being accepted by the French.

'What has been the point of departure for your reforms?'

'It did not develop all at once. My doubts go back to my first attempts which did not satisfy me; and it was in their poetic conception that these reforms entered my mind. My first works had, above all, a literary objective. Later I wanted to enlarge the impact by adding musical expression, I deplored the way in which my thought was moving into the visionary realm, weakened by the demands imposed by routine in musical drama . . . Those bravura arias, those insipid duets fatally based on the same model, and how many other *hors d'oeuvres* that interrupt stage action without reason!'

He was treading on a minefield because Wagner was describing Rossini – or at least what his detractors were finding in him. 'And the septets!' he continued, 'for in every respectable opera it was necessary to have a solemn septet in which the characters of the drama, setting the meaning of their roles aside, formed a line across the front of the stage – all reconciled! and supplying the public with one of those stale banalities.' *Don Giovanni* finishes with a septet and there is nothing wrong with that.

'And do you know what we called that in Italy at the time?' Rossini interrupted. 'The row of artichokes. I was perfectly aware of the silliness of the thing; it gave me the impression of a line of porters who had come to ask for a tip. It was a custom – a concession that one had to make to the public who otherwise would have thrown sliced potatoes at us . . . or even potatoes that hadn't been sliced!'

By then Wagner was almost talking to himself. He was the composer who had banished trivia and who made huge demands on his listeners and interpreters. The goal of his heroes' lives was love, but this goal led to death and destruction. Love, physical love, for Wagner became a morbid and ambiguous act that drew out the body and exhausted the soul – the male's soul in particular. The act of appeased but sinful love turned into suppressed mysticism. That was surely a world which excluded women (and Rossini). Indeed the Wagnerian woman causes disasters with her love and self-sacrifice; only Sieglinde seems to be free from guilt; her incendiary love for her brother is depicted as innocent and unavoidable. What could Rossini, a man who 'had all women's diseases but for the uterus' make of all this?

'As for the orchestra,' Wagner continued, 'those routine accompaniments . . . repeating the same formulae without taking into account the diversity of the characters and situations – music that so often obstructs the most famous operas in many places . . . all that seems to me incompatible with the high objective of an art which is noble and worthy of that name.'

'You referred to the *bravura* arias? That was my nightmare. To satisfy at the same time the prima donna, the first tenor, the first bass.' The singers would count the notes of one aria and then they would 'come to me and declare that they would not sing because another of their colleagues had an aria containing a larger number of trills or ornaments.'

Rossini seemed to vent the frustration of his past on the new man of opera. One feels that it was liberating for him to recognize in those conventions a ridiculous chain that had fettered him. But had they? There is more liberty in the music of *L'italiana in Algeri*, *La donna del lago* or *Il barbiere di Siviglia* than in the whole *Ring*.

'But let's go on with your reasoning. In effect it seems to me to deal with the rational, rapid and regular development of the dramatic action. How to maintain that independence of literary concepts together with a musical form which is nothing but convention? For, if one must follow logic, it goes without saying that a man when speaking does not sing; an angry man, a conspirator, a jealous man does not sing . . . Opera is convention, from beginning to end. And what about the instrumentation itself? Who, when the orchestra is unleashed, could pinpoint the difference in the description of a storm, a riot or a fire? . . . it's always convention!'

'Clearly, and to a huge extent, convention is imposed upon one; otherwise one would have to do away completely with the lyric drama and even theatre in music. It is none the less indisputable that this convention must avoid those excesses which lead to the absurd, the ridiculous.'

Having said that he had been accused of repudiating all existing music except for Gluck and Weber, Wagner continued: 'In my view it is the musician's mission to compose an opera, to have as its aim the formation of an organism in which are concentrated the perfect union of all the arts; poetic, musical, decorative and plastic. This desire to confine the musician to being the simple instrumental illustrator of just any libretto, imposing upon him a summary number of arias, duets, scenes and ensembles . . . of pieces which he must translate into notes is like a colourist filling in outlines printed in black . . . There are certainly examples of composers inspired by a dramatic situation who have written immortal pages. But how many others are diminished following this system.'

It is interesting to note that not a word was exchanged on politics. Wagner was still a revolutionary while Rossini had become a conservative, but they must both have been moved – or maybe even infuriated – by the Italian unification which was now under way. Wagner, a nationalist, the composer of *Rienzi*, his opera of 1842 based on the populist rebel Cola di Rienzo, would have been enthusiastic about the process of Italian unification. Rossini, being uninterested in the concept of nationalism, would have been indifferent towards a united Italy, especially after what had happened to him in Bologna. But France was playing a major role in Italian affairs in the person of Napoleon III.

After Napoleon III's declaration that, if the Austrians attacked

Piedmont, he would support his Italian ally with French arms, it was left to Cavour to find an excuse for war. The Austrians fell into the trap and the bloody battles of Solferino and Magenta (the Red Cross was born out of this carnage) resulted in the Piedmontese annexation of Lombardy and Milan. Following a secret treaty, Nice and Savoy were ceded to France. Napoleon then reneged on his side of the agreement and left the Veneto and Venice to the Austrians. Cavour, Savoy's prime minister, resigned in protest. Yet Palmerston, Britain's prime minister, was intent on solving the question of Italian independence; hardly a year had passed before part of the Papal States and three separate duchies opted for Piedmontese rule and chased the Austrians out; thus the new state, ruled by the Savoy king of Piedmont, doubled in size.

By now it was clear that there would be no Mazzinian republic, nor would Verdi's dream of a socialist Italy materialize, because the Piedmontese king had Europe's backing to unite the whole peninsula under his aegis. With Garibaldi's military talent and Cavour's political genius, Italian unification was one step away, despite having an odious king of an inept dynasty at its head. It was a calamity that unification should have been achieved under the auspices of the House of Savoy, but that is another story.

No cantata, no hymn was composed by Rossini to celebrate such a moment – by then he was distant from these events and almost a stranger to Italy. He lived in order to die in tranquillity and among people who loved and stimulated him. He romanticized the past, memories of Pesaro, of his mother Anna, of his youth. Thoughts of operas and librettos were merely passing considerations.

Rossini pondered on what Wagner had just told him. 'If I understand you correctly, in order to realize your ideal, the composer must be his own librettist. That seems to me to be an insurmountable condition.'

'Why? Why shouldn't composers who learn counterpoint and study literature, also study history and mythology? There have been few dramatic composers who have not displayed literary and poetic talent. Not to go further afield, you yourself, maestro – let us take for example the scene of the oath-swearing in *Guillaume Tell* – would you say that you observed word for word the text you were given? I don't believe it. It is not difficult to notice the differences of delivery and scale which have such an effect on musicality (if I may say it that way) and spontaneous inspiration that I refuse to attribute their genesis to the intervention of a planned text.'

'What you say is true. That scene in fact was modified a great deal to my specifications but not without difficulty.'

'There, maestro, you have made an implicit confession that confirms what I have been saying . . . It is inevitable that there will be music of the future but the future of music is drama.'

'In short,' Rossini replied, 'it is a radical revolution! And do you think that the singers accustomed to displaying their talent by virtuosity will submit to changes so destructive to their reputations?'

'It will be a slow education. As for the public, does it influence the composers or do composers shape the public?'

'From the point of view of pure art, those are unquestionably long views, seductive perspectives.'

'I want melody free, independent, unfettered. A melody of very precise form that can extend itself, contract itself, prolong itself . . .'

'*Les mélodies de combat*,' Rossini whispered.

Wagner evidently did not hear, continuing: 'As for that sort of melody you stereotyped a sublime specimen in that scene in *Guillaume Tell*. 'Sois immobile', where the very freedom of the singing line accentuating every single word and sustained by the breathing strokes of the violoncellos reached the highest summit of lyric expression.'

'So I made music of the future without knowing it?'

'You made music for all time, and that is the best . . . if you had not laid down your pen after *Guillaume Tell* at 37 – a crime! – you yourself have no idea of what you might have extracted from your mind!'

'Having worked and composed 40 operas in 15 years, I felt a need to rest. Also the condition of Italian theatres was then in full decay.'

Rossini lied. That was not the real reason why he had stopped composing. Maybe he was aware of having shown his true self to Wagner – and Michotte – and too much of it, for once: Wagner and he had exchanged thoughts, truths. Rossini opted to shelter behind his curtain of mist. Rising from his chair and taking Wagner's hand, he said: 'My dear Monsieur Wagner, I don't know how to thank you for your call and particularly for exposing your ideas. I no longer compose, being at an age in which one is inclined to decompose. I am too old to look towards new horizons. But your ideas are of the sort which make the young reflect. Of all the arts, music, because of its ideal essence, is the one most exposed to changes. They are without limit. After Mozart could one have foreseen Beethoven? After Gluck,

Weber? . . . I belonged to my time. To others, in particular to you, whom I see vigorous and endowed with such masterly capacity, falls the creation of what is new and comes next – and that is something I wish you with all my heart.'

They parted as friends: Wagner found Rossini simple and natural, a genius led astray by his Latin upbringing from which he did not understand that art is a religion.

'But I must declare this,' Wagner told Michotte as they left Rossini's apartment. 'Of all the musicians I have met in Paris, he alone is truly great.'

The same evening Rossini, teasing a group of 'enemies', said that he had met that '*monstre*, their *bête noire* . . . ! This Wagner seems to me to be endowed with first-class faculties. His entire physique – his chin most of all – reveals an iron-willed temperament. It's a great thing to know how to will.' Rossini thought that Wagner 'lacked sun'. But he admired him and they both recognized each others eminence.

IV

Moderato cantabile

On their famous Saturday evenings, Olympe and Gioachino would entertain almost separately. Olympe presided over her social sector, leaving Gioachino to his musical world. A dozen or so select guests were invited to dinner and the soirées would start later, around 8.30 p.m, with the 'fashionable hordes [left] to pick their way through unappetizing tit-bits'.

Ultimately 'everybody' who was anybody attended the Saturday soirées at the Chaussée d'Antin. From December 1858, when they began, until Rossini's death in 1868, these evenings were a focal point of Parisian intellectual and musical society. Rossini himself would be found at the end of one of the drawing-rooms with a few friends. When the chatter became so loud that it masked the music, Rossini accompanied the singers himself and then everybody stayed silent – they knew how irritated babbling voices could make him. The apartment at Chaussée d'Antin became a cross between a private theatre and a rather exclusive club, a laboratory of music engaged in preserving the quality of the voice and the simplicity of the scores against the complications of the 'new' music.

Unlike other Parisian salons, conversation was secondary to music and the most outstanding pianists and some of the finest voices in Europe could be heard. Rossini commissioned pieces from his friends and people whom he admired, insisting that people should listen rather than chat. On one occasion, when the Act III trio from Verdi's *Attila* was to be played, Rossini added a few initial bars to catch people's attention; he then signed them 'Rossini, without Verdi's permission'. There would be arias from Mozart's operas and music by Palestrina, Pergolesi and Gounod and Rossini most of all, played as the written score dictated. The general public was unlikely to hear accurate versions elsewhere since amazing liberties were taken by singers and impresarios alike: operas were cut, reshaped and set to new librettos without the knowledge of the composer and certain arias became unrecognizable when altered to suit a capricious voice. At times, avoiding the salon and, semi-hidden in the dining-room, Rossini would listen without having to mix with the crowd, even though it consisted of friends. Olympe's dream had come true, she had the most impressive and sought-after salon in the whole of Paris. Invitations were distributed by special messengers and replied to at once, thus guaranteeing the exclusion of unwanted visitors. At times so many guests arrived that the music publisher Giulio Ricordi was once found sitting on the stairs with his French counterparts, the gossipy and malevolent Escudier Brothers. Even Count and Countess Frederick Pillet-Will and Baron Rothschild had to take pot-luck, but Verdi and Liszt were welcomed in the inner sanctum of Rossini's room.

Giulio Ricordi described one of these Saturday evenings:

> *My father and I wormed our way through the crowd . . . fortunately we were escorted by la Signora Rossini who, with exquisite courtesy, cut a path and led us into the music room. What a spectacle! Rossini was surrounded by le tous Paris. I no longer recall the names of all the Marquises, the Baronesses, the ministers and ambassadors who were paying court to the celebrated Maestro. In one corner of the room, standing surrounded by many people was the Pope's cardinal legate in a great violet tunic.*

The Salon Rossini was much discussed in the Parisian press. Not only did the public follow the kind of music which was played there and by whom, but some of the most piercing witticisms and ironic observations percolated through the six large shutters of the salon to the printing presses. But the soirées were designed for a private audience, music that was privately composed and privately executed, not exposed to the judgement of that public which Rossini had dismissed only once – at the time of the fiasco of *Il barbiere di Siviglia*, but which he probably had damned mentally many times.

During those last years Rossini continued to write his *Péchés de vieillesse*, not all of them slight, not all of them 'sins'. Besides piano pieces, the most notable include a witty *Choeur de châsseurs démocrates* for male chorus, tam-tam and two drums, written to commemorate Napoleon III's visit to the Rothschilds at the Château de Ferrières in 1862. The masterpiece of his late years, however, was the *Petite Messe solennelle*, written in 1863–4 in a novel and ironic style. It is scored for twelve voices, two pianos and harmonium, the instrumental colours being crucial to the disturbing nature of the music, eerie and unreligious. The pianos sketch out an asymmetrical shape and sound as if they want to go in different directions when the voices come in, while the harmonium keeps the tension high throughout. The whole is a delightful compilation of moments of angst, triumph and calm meditation. *Allegro cristiano* is the tempo indication to the Credo and he specified that the voices in the score be: 'twelve singers (the Apostles) and three sexes: men, women and eunuchs.' The work was, he wrote in a characteristic prefatory note, to be 'the last sin of my old age'.

> *Dear God.*
> *Here it is finished, this poor little Mass. Is this sacred music that I have written or is it wicked music? (Est-ce bien de la musique sacrée que je viens de faire ou bien de la sacrée musique?) I was bred for opera buffa as you know all too well. A little science, a little heart, that's all. Be blessed, then, and admit me to Paradise.*
> *G. Rossini   Passy 1863*

Here is Rossini mocking his Maker because he does not believe in him – and it should be noted that the composer sends God his blessings – not vice versa. In this dedication, Rossini repeats the same burning phrase that Beethoven had uttered so many years earlier. All he – Rossini – was good for, was *opera buffa*, words that still ached because they were as unfair and unjust then as they remain today. He knew that such works as *La donna del lago*, the versions of *Mosè*, *Maometto II*, *Guillaume Tell*, to mention only a few of his *opere serie*, are masterpieces; Balzac, Delacroix, Wagner and Verdi could not all be wrong. The allusion to needing 'a little science, a little heart, that's all' is strangely sarcastic. Just how much heart, knowledge, labour and genius went into Rossini's works from *La Cenerentola* to *Il barbiere*, from *Armida* to *Otello*, those who listen will appreciate.

The *Petite Messe solennelle* was first heard on 14 March 1864 at a private ceremony to dedicate the chapel of the Pillet-Will family. The audience was small and included the terminally ill Meyerbeer who was in tears and insisted on returning for a second performance. A year before his death Rossini orchestrated it to prevent anyone else from doing so. He wanted his *Petite Messe* heard by a private audience, in a church or in a home, but not in a public hall by the public at large. At the same time he approached Pope Pius IX himself through that new clergyman, the Abbé Liszt who had just taken his vows in Rome, to lift the ban on women singers in church. By its very nature the *Petite Messe* excluded a larger public. It was, as Bruno Cagli wrote, 'an extremely private piece destined for a select group of friends with the absolute exclusion of any outside use whether in published form or public performance.'

According to Robert Craft, W. H. Auden used to sing it when drunk (which, it must be observed, was often) – and counted amongst his favourite pieces of music.

Rossini's correspondence continued to find new and dear recipients; he became very fond of Michael Costa, a composer who established himself in London and who was to make a brillant career as an impresario. He called Costa 'my dear son' and signed his letters 'your affectionate father'. More successful than his compositions were the gifts that Costa sent to Chaussée d'Antin: 'The cheese . . . would be worthy of a Bach, a Handel, a Cimarosa, let alone the old man of Pesaro! For three consecutive days I tasted and moistened it with the best wines in my cellar.' What made Rossini so enthusiastic was a soft, green, delicious Stilton and a mature Cheddar (delightfully spelt 'Chedor Chiese', followed by the comment 'cursed be the Britannic Spelling!').

While Paris changed around him, Rossini knew that what is modern today is old tomorrow; indeed, his own music had once been avant-garde and by then was considered old-fashioned. He watched opera swelling like ladies' gowns: indeed the new Opéra, built by the architect Garnier, took thirteen years to complete and was as ornate as a wedding cake. There was much more space for the ladies to show off their *toilettes* in the foyer than there were seats inside the theatre to hear the music. But Meyerbeer, for whose grand operas this sort of extravaganza was ideally suited, died on 2 May 1864. More and more of Rossini's friends were dying: Delacroix, the last of the dandies, handsome and heroic, who had become an habitué of the salon and had written beautifully about Rossini's music, had also died the previous year. Rossini wrote *Quelques mesures de chant funèbre: à mon pauvre ami Meyerbeer*, a work for four-part male chorus accompanied by Pianissimo. It is a deeply felt dedication to a man who had been a friend and a fellow composer for fifty years. Verdi, who was no gossip, recounted how Meyerbeer's nephew had himself written a funeral march for his uncle's funeral. 'Excellent,' said Rossini, looking at the score, 'but wouldn't it have been better if your uncle had written the march and you had died?' That was how Rossini could kill, was Verdi's comment.

The villa at Passy was finished, its ceilings frescoed with portraits of Mozart, Beethoven, Cimarosa, Haydn and even Padre Martini who had brought the Bologna Liceo to prominence. Beau Séjour looked over a large square on which a very French fountain spouted water and glory; there was also a gardener's cottage and an orangerie. Rossini was a skilled draughtsman; he had designed most of it and had planned the house to suit his last days. At times he spent his day making silhouettes of various people who had been important in his life, for example his father Giuseppe, Isabella Colbran, Haydn. He also sketched caricatures reminiscent of Edward Lear's drawings and painted landscapes.

Beau Séjour became legendary for reasons different from those that drew crowds to the Chaussée d'Antin. Meals became a rite: Crema alla Rossini, frittata alla Rossini, Tournedos Rossini, they were all preparations which generally involved the use of truffles and fois gras, menus prepared by Rossini himself. Even when he was low – which was still the case from time to time – he was careful to match the finest wine with the appropriate food. After a visit to Passy the young Giulio Ricordi described Rossini:

> The Maestro appeared to me to be a man of average height but with powerful shoulders and a large, robust chest; the hands, very beautiful, white, aristocratic; the face broad, grandiose; so imposing as to inspire genuine respect and admiration; the physiognomy highly pleasant, smiling with a sensuous mouth; the eyes mobile, very vivacious with a perpetual smile reflected in them. His neck was full and fat . . . his cranium very large and completely bald. The light beating down upon it

picked out a luminous point to which my glance turned often. Rossini noticed it and, turning towards my father, said: 'Your son admires my baldness . . . what do you Milanese call it? crapa pelata dai cento capelli, tutta la notte ci cantano i grilli' *['hairless skull with one hundred hairs, during the night crickets sing on it']. Then to me 'That's my headgear.'*

He reached out with his hand and plucked from the table an object that I had taken for a handkerchief and . . . panf! planted it on his head. It was a wig and thus Rossini appeared to me as he normally was seen in the outside world.

If Rossini's strict routine was disturbed, his anger could explode. Once, when a caller interrupted his sacred afternoon nap, Rossini shouted at him: 'Allez-vous-en! ma celebrité m'embête!' He suffered a stroke in December 1866 but, by February 1867 he was well again and, for his seventy-fifth birthday he was overwhelmed with gifts, honours and speeches. Napoleon would have liked to be sublimated by music, by a specially composed hymn and there was a 'certain' insistence for Rossini to compose it. But he turned it into a joke, saying he intended the imperial music to be played in his Passy gardens. Of course it was performed, very publicly instead, by an orchestra of 800 musicians – and certainly not in Rossini's gardens. He tried to keep away from Paris, the Exposition Universale having turned the capital into 'a real Babylon', as he put it. Verdi was in Paris as his *Don Carlos* was part of the Exposition; but that opera was not to be a success with the French – strange because its sombre notes are amongst Verdi's finest. These were extraordinary times in Paris: Manet was showing his scandalous paintings; Berlioz published the vocal score of *Les Troyens*; great works of architecture were going up using new materials (the church of Les Augustins, for example, was mainly built of iron, an amazing innovation). What was happening in architecture and painting had happened in music. Manet (and before him Turner, Courbet and Delacroix) had dispensed with convention. There were no longer rules for composition or perspective. It would have been impossible for true believers in the Romantic revolution – Wagner and Verdi, for example – to digest some of Rossini's attitudes. When Rossini became president of a twelve-man commission to establish a standard musical pitch, for instance, Verdi told Rossini that he did not agree with what had been decided (Auber, Halévy, Meyerbeer and

Berlioz were members of the commission). Rossini answered that, since he had not attended a single meeting, he had no idea of what Verdi was talking about. That of course annoyed Verdi enormously.

On 10 February 1868 the Paris Opéra celebrated what it claimed to be the 500th performance of *Guillaume Tell*.

Although his health deteriorated a little in the winter, Rossini was well enough to object when Torribio Calzado, the Cuban-born director of the Théâtre-Italien, announced a novelty advertised as Rossini's *Un curioso accidente*. This turned out to be a pastiche of several operas, and Rossini insisted that the posters should state the truth. If not, he would take legal action. On 14 March 1868 he wrote from Passy to his Italian lawyer that, despite having been 'in the clutch of a nervous perturbation' for four months he was again answering letters. In fact Rossini was sinking towards death.

V

FINALE

The description of a death generally omits detailing the act itself. The same can be said of birth, but both are bloody and grossly physical – a humiliation to an aesthetic life. With the exception of romanticized versions, death does not fit greatness. Death is more acceptable if it acts with speed and a sudden gesture, but some die in painful and prolonged agony.

When it sought out the prince of Romanticism at Missolonghi, death came in the guise of a fever, without laurels or rhyming verse. It was probably a death accompanied by vomit and stench, it would have soiled linen and it would have been legible in the faces of the people who gathered around him.

Rossini died a death he did not deserve: ugly, humiliating and undignified. Apart from his wife, he was surrounded by people he did not care for, people straining to catch his last breath in order to be able to say 'I was there'. The last rites were administered, a charade which he – an agnostic if not an atheist – could have done without. Because of a lung infection he had been too fragile to engage fully in the last of the *samedi soirs* on 8 September 1868; in October his health deteriorated further. By then Rossini had returned to Passy and was visited by his personal physician, Dr Vito Bonato, who found him 'extremely nervous and in low spirits'. Rossini developed cancer of the rectum (it was called rectal fistula) and another doctor, Auguste Nelaton, decided to operate at once, there and then, at Passy. That first operation took place on 3 November and lasted five minutes; Dr

Nelaton removed as much as he could of the cancerous spread. Only Olympe was allowed to dress the wound. Two days later, seeing the devastation that the infection was causing, Dr Nelaton decided on a second operation. Rossini was in excruciating pain and could hardly speak. Every morning four huge young men would come to move his body from one bed to another; as soon as he saw them, he became panic-stricken. He would call on death, *la comare*, asking her to come and visit him instead of the four men. When a younger doctor, in over-cheerful tones, asked the maestro how he felt, he answered: 'Open the window and throw me in the garden, then I won't suffer any more.' Discreet as usual, Rossini tried to hide the horror of his suffering from Olympe in particular; possibly only his doctors knew. In effect they themselves were the main torturers. Dr Nelaton had forbidden him to suck ice or drink water in spite of the terrible thirst that was consuming him.

While Rossini was undergoing this agony, telegrams and letters arrived from all over the world. When Cardinal Chigi called on him to administer the last sacraments, he said: 'Dear Maestro, every man, however great, must sometimes think of dying.' Rossini sent him on his way. He had been thinking of death for a quarter of a century and was deeply offended that the cardinal failed to grasp that behind the mask there was another Rossini. He did not want to die in the hands of the Roman Catholic Church. But the Abbé Gallet from St Roch, the church of artists, finally took his confession and Rossini accepted extreme unction from him. When it was clear that death was fast approaching, friends called on Passy as if at a *samedi soir* to watch him die. Rossini's death become like a *levée* in the eighteenth century, or a royal birth in the sixteenth; it had to be witnessed.

On 13 November Rossini lapsed into a semi-coma and was heard murmuring his mother's name – Anna. Later he called for his beloved Olympe and before midnight Dr d'Ancona whispered to Olympe: 'Madame, Rossini has stopped suffering.' As though this humorous man had willed it, death came on a Friday 13th. Still not liberated from the public gaze, his body was sketched the very next day. Drawings and engravings by Gustave Doré based on those sketches show the dead man with a crucifix in his hands, his face collapsed around his nose. His corpse was embalmed and taken to La Madeleine.

The funeral itself, which Rossini had wanted to be modest, was a grandiose event. It took place in the vast church of La Trinité, close to the Chaussée d'Antin, and was paid for by Napoleon III. The eighty-six-year-old Daniel Auber organized the music and 4,000 people attended. Afterwards the coffin was taken to Père-Lachaise cemetery to be buried alongside Chopin, Bellini and Cherubini.

VI

RECITATIVO SECCO

B y the time of Rossini's death, his music had largely predeceased him. Only *Guillaume Tell* and *Semiramide* were still performed quite regularly, the former 'attended but not loved' and generally cut, the latter impossible to perform properly because there were no longer any adequate voices to interpret it. As for his late compositions, Rossini had seen to it that they would not be performed: the public had to be kept at bay.

Rossini the composer died as misunderstood as Rossini the man. He had become a caricature not only as a man but also as a musician. In part, he had himself to blame because he did not believe in voicing his lament. *Mi lagnerò tacendo* was his maxim and his silence was generally misunderstood. In part, misunderstandings have also arisen due to ignorance of his music and to its erratic dispersal. But the last factor makes it an exciting challenge to write his biography. Rossini had suffered desperately. Part of his condition had been brought on by a physical illness which was not only humiliating and painful but exhausting. He also had to struggle with the grave psychological disturbance which made him lose his zest for life and therefore the capacity to express himself.

When writing a biography of a great man, one often has to deal with his Vestals (some writers refer to Cerberus), those protective people who think that they alone should guard the sacred flame. I think that families are to be feared even more than scholars. There is an understandable sense of possession on the part of both families and Vestals, and they can become convinced that the only guardians of the truth are themselves and that no outsiders should cross the line. I often have crossed the stormy river, oblivious that Dante's 'Lasciate ogni speranza o voi che entrate' was written on every bank. On the other hand, the circles of hell I went through were of varying danger, some just tiresome and others even pleasurable.

Apart from his wife, Rossini had no surviving family and his guardians are people of learning, scholars who are more dedicated to spreading the truth than to jealously guarding it. Their object is to make Rossini's music better known and understood. This is a great advantage to any biographer but particularly for a writer who steps into Rossini's life and finds that the tale can be excitingly new. There is a great deal to tell about Gioachino Rossini's life that has been unknown or ignored: about his terrible diseases, his arguably illegitimate birth, his parents' separation, his unhappy childhood – generally described as being carefree. And of course there is the amazing legacy of his music, some of it still little known. But although I can give some indication of the greatness of much of Rossini's work, I have tried to describe Rossini the man, his life and times and therefore I must leave it to musicologists and musicians to continue to explore the wealth of Rossini's creativity.

Four days after Rossini's death, Verdi began to plan a Requiem to be written in Rossini's memory by thirteen composers – all Italian. Although Verdi himself was rather half-hearted about the project, *La Messa per Rossini* became part of a nationalist movement to establish Rossini as a totally Italian composer. Apart from Verdi's own contribution, the music is rather slight and the resulting Requiem was not given its first performance in Bologna as planned; it was long forgotten and is now available in a recorded version. Rossini's own music, however, was performed at memorial concerts worldwide. Those in Bologna and Pesaro were conducted by Angelo Mariani, whom Rossini had called 'Anzulett', 'Little Angel'. Verdi who, by then had become Mariani's rival in love, exaggerated Mariani's role and the fact that the Requiem for Rossini had not been performed became his excuse to split with Anzulett and take his woman as well.

Shortly after Rossini's death, Richard Wagner published *Eine Erinnerung an Rossini*, 1868; a tribute saying how important it was to recognize Rossini as the product of his times. As already emphasized, by the time of Rossini's death most of his music had been forgotten and much of it was lost. Rossini was as important to his era as Bach and Mozart had been to theirs. Rossini's achievements, Wagner stressed, would not be undersood until the events of the early nineteenth century had been fully comprehended. This is nothing new, but it certainly remains true. Rossini's circumstances influenced his creativity to such an extent that it is important to understand the events of his life in the context of the historical events he experienced. 'Of all the arts music, because of its ideal essence, is the one most exposed to change,' he had told Wagner. 'After Mozart could one have foreseen Beethoven? . . . I belonged to my time.' And after Rossini, could one have foreseen not only Bellini, but Verdi? How about Puccini or Berg?

To his eternal credit and glory, Rossini left almost his entire fortune to the Comune di Pesaro, which could therefore endow the Conservatorio di Musica, the Accademia Musicale (formerly the Liceo Musicale) and, in 1940, the Fondazione Rossini (perhaps the only good thing to happen in Italy during that appalling year). There is a tendency to overlook the fact that the Museo di Pesaro's wonderful Hercolani Collection, with paintings by such masters as Vitale da Bologna, Giovanni Bellini, Domenico Beccafumi, Guido Reni, Francesco Maffei and Tintoretto were left to the city by the composer. His legacy to Paris resulted in the Maison de Retraite Rossini, a home for the disabled operatie performers, which still houses about twenty-five people.

The Rossini Opera Festival, established in Pesaro in 1980 in order to stage the works that the Fondazione had been assembling, was also made possible by the composer's endowment. The Fondazione and Casa Ricordi are jointly aiming to publish and perform the whole of Rossini's canon. This is not as easy as it sounds because it involves recovering lost scores and restoring dismembered or drastically altered ones. In his will Rossini pointed out that the score of his *Otello* had disappeared, asking that, if possible, it should be traced. This the Fondazione succeeded in doing. Among other rediscovered works is *Il viaggio a Reims*, which had vanished in 1825 after only three performances. As mentioned, it was revived for the festival of 1984, conducted by Claudio Abbado with an ideal cast, including Ruggero Raimondi, Katia Ricciarelli, Lucia Valentini Terrani, Samuel Ramey, Cecilia Gasdia, Enzo Dara and Leo Nucci.

In 1993 the Italian parliament approved a law by which the Fondazione Rossini and the Rossini Opera Festival, being part of the national cultural wealth, would be directly endowed by the Ministry of Culture. In effect, together with Bayreuth, this is the only European opera festival whose activities extend beyond mere performance. The journey of exploration has ensured that such operas as *Tancredi*, *L'italiana in Algeri*, *La Cenerentola*, *Semiramide* and *Guillaume Tell* have all been performed at Pesaro in their authentic form for the first time in possibly 150 years; as a result, they entered the repertoire. Furthermore, such long-forgotten masterpieces as *Edipo a Colono*, *Armida*, *Mosè in Egitto*, *La donna del lago*, *Ermione*, *Bianca e Falliero* and *Maometto II*, have not only been revived at the festival, but the music is widely available through recordings. The festival is also responsible for concerts of chamber, religious and orchestral music by Rossini and his circle – it is the only place where one can hear *farse*, so fashionable at the beginning of the nineteenth century and so important to the development of Rossini's *opere buffe*. Among the great artists who have made their mark at Pesaro are the conductors Claudio Abbado and Riccardo Chailly (Maurizio Pollini has also made a single and sublime appearance as a conductor), the directors and stage designers Pier Luigi Pizzi and Jean-Pierre Ponnelle and the singers Teresa Berganza, Sesto Bruscantini, Cecilia Gasdia, Michele Pertusi, Ruggero Raimondi and Claudio Desderi.

The Accademia Rossiniana, established in 1882 as the Liceo Musicale in Pesaro with an endowment from Rossini's bequest, is an institute of study which has re-established the Rossini vocal tradition. Its early directors have included Pietro Mascagni, Amilcare Zanella, the violinist Gioconda de Vito and the composer Riccardo Zandonai. The *bel canto* singers Juan Diego Flórez and Daniela Barcellona have been alumni.

Olympe Pélissier Rossini, to whom Souvrintendente Gianfranco Mariotti hopes to dedicate a street in Pesaro, behaved in the most honourable way. She suffered greatly during the events of the Paris Commune in 1870, only two years after Rossini's death. After her own death on 22 March 1878, the terms of Rossini's will were put into effect. Olympe wanted to be buried next to her husband at Père-Lachaise and therefore rejected requests for his exhumed remains from both Pesaro and Florence. In a couple of letters which I prefer not to quote, Verdi was abusive towards Olympe about this. Eventually she agreed to the Italian demands that Rossini should be reinterred in Florence, at the church of Santa Croce. In her will she therefore wrote:

I desire that my body be deposited finally and for ever in the Cimetière de l'Est (Père-Lachaise) in the tomb in which at present are the mortal remains of my venerated husband. After their removal to Florence, I shall remain there alone; I make this sacrifice in all humility, I have been glorified enough by the name that I bear. My faith, my religious feelings, give me hope of a reunion that escapes the earth.

At the ceremony for Rossini's reburial at Santa Croce, a massive chorus sang 'Dal tuo stellato soglio' from *Mosè in Egitto* and his *Stabat mater* was performed at Palazzo Vecchio. But the monumental and ugly marble mausoleum which can be seen today, so out of tune with Rossini's music and personality, had to wait until 1902 to be completed. In February 1968 – the centenary of Rossini's death – the only bunch of flowers laid at the foot of the composer's tomb was, I am afraid to say, mine.

Verdi persisted in failing to honour the debt he owed Rossini. Asked to be honorary president of a committee to deliver Rossini's corpse to Italy, Verdi declined. On two other occasions intended as tributes to Rossini, Verdi again failed to appear. Yet he evidently understood the man whom he had begun to denigrate:

> *on that famous night during which Rossini, leaving his friends, went home and started writing the first chorus of* Barbiere, *the opera was already all there . . . who can figure out the secret fantasy of the Maestro while he looked as if otherwise occupied? who can describe the notes that were forming inside his head while he walked, while visiting some pretty singer or eating a delicious lunch or a merry dinner?*

Maybe Verdi was really speaking about himself. When, after the first night at La Scala, on 9 February 1893, his *Falstaff* was hailed as the best *opera buffa*, Verdi said, 'No, the best is *Il barbiere di Siviglia*.'

In his *Eine Erinnerung an Rossini* Wagner, who had never been overwhelmingly generous about Rossini's music, recalled how Rossini published a letter stating that the adverse comments attributed to him against Wagner were apocryphal: 'At the beginning of 1860 I gave concert performances of some fragments of my operas [and] the majority of the press was hostile to me,' but not Rossini. Wagner continued:

*Rossini cannot be properly judged until there is an effort to place him in
an intelligent way within the history of our century from its beginning.
Then and only then Rossini will be evaluated in his proper worth; what
he lacked in perfect nobility will not be put against him, within his
talent or artistic conscience, but will be attributed to his century, that
was the reason for his decline.*

It was not just the tempest of history that damaged Rossini's inventiveness but also the tornado of his disease which denied him the self
assurance that he needed to express himself artistically. For Wagner,
Rossini's main sin was his alienation from Romanticim. Although
Rossini wrote some music which was proto-Romantic and often chose
to set Romantic subjects and poets, he refused to enter that second
phase of Romanticism which made a religion out of nationalism and
individualism. Symptomatic of the Romantic attitude was the worship
of the artist, especially as the destroyer of the social order. When the
individual achieved paramount importance – very much Wagner's
message – Rossini turned away in disgust. While, for the late Romantics, the individual could destroy everything around him but still
remain pivotal to his surroundings, for Rossini the individual was part
of society and should obey the rules. That Rossini philosophy was
neither accepted by nor acceptable to the likes of Verdi or Wagner or
their acolytes in any of the arts. In recognizing the individual as the
centre of his own world, Sigmund Freud was a Romantic, and his was
an era that moved dangerously and morbidly towards Fascism and
Nazism, both of which were frustrated expressions of the self. I have
no shame in seeing the current tendency for artists to depict unmade
beds and chopped beef as a post-modern expression of Romanticism,
of the right of the individual to express himself by whatever means,
destruction being part of the Romantic creative motivation.

Many of these concepts were hovering in the letters Rossini wrote
from Chaussée d'Antin and one should see his late years as those of a
man who did not like the age in which he lived and the turmoil in
nineteenth-century Europe could hardly have been more radical and
dramatic. While Rossini's musical silence was mostly caused by a
prolonged and cruel disease, it was also due to his refusal to accept his
era; social upheaval and rebellions were not for him. He was incapable
of confronting the vast transformation of ideas, attitudes and human
behaviour towards which others in the arts were reacting. That is why

he stayed behind. Wagner was right in insisting that Rossini should be judged within the historical framework of his times. The events which took place in France and then Italy and finally all over Europe from 1789 onwards destroyed the established 'neo-classic' philosophy and civic order that Metternich tried so hard to prolong. Napoleon's short-lived rule was a catalyst to Italy and the Italian arts, more so than has been fully appreciated or debated. By the 1850s, every accepted tenet, every credo was questioned, ranging from the omnipotence of ruling monarchs to Darwin's hugely controversial theory of evolution, which brought religion into doubt. Science opened the doors to reason and, with the Romantic age, belief in reason clashed with orthodox faith. For the Romantics, truth was not an objective reality but it was created; the answers to the great questions are not to be discovered (as Enlightenment thinkers would have wanted) but invented. The unique expression of an individual took shape in the form of defiance. Music was a very important part of this process – and Rossini could not or would not understand that the 'ugly' could be a valid form of self-expression. He still thought along the Neoclassical line that only beauty had the right to be used as the language of art. In the dark years of the last century we lost our way in the forest of Romanticism. Wonderful as it is to lose one's way, we are now at Hercules' cross-roads and it is unlikely that we will choose the right direction. When faced with his own crossroads, Rossini made the right choice for him: to step aside and evade his century.

BIBLIOGRAPHICAL NOTE

I have aimed to write a story, not an academic book, the story of Rossini's life entwined with the story of his time. Much has been written about Rossini and the themes on which I touch, ranging from Neoclassicism to Romanticism and all the revolutionary upheavals of nineteenth-century Europe. The titles included here are not necessarily the best on the subject but simply those that I have consulted. Some of them are excellent and indeed the best available, others are mediocre or even objectionable, but they all contain something that I have found useful.

My greatest piece of luck was the sudden emergence of a batch of letters in the Sotheby's sale of books and manuscripts in London on 7 December 2001 (lot 175); they are described in the catalogue as a 'highly important, almost completely unpublished, series of about 250 autograph letters to his parents Anna and Giuseppe Rossini in Bologna including over 230 by Rossini, fourteen by his wife Isabella Colbran and a few jointly written, including his earliest surviving letters covering almost his entire operatic career'. For this reason alone a new biography of Rossini was needed but I must confess that my work had already started; the fact is that the 'revolutionary' context of those letters underlined what I had perceived. I thank Sotheby's European Chairman Henry Wyndham and Dr Stephen Roe, Head of Sotheby's Printed Books and Manuscripts, Europe, for letting me study them (they were bought by the Italian State for Pesaro and Naples). Many of the letters I quote in Act One are drawn from this collection and have not been published before (but for the cagalogue). *Lettere e documenti: G. Rossini*, ed. Bruno Cagli and Sergio Ragni, 3 vols (Pesaro, 1992) clarifies dates and situations and is an essential – and mammoth – work. Several other volumes are in preparation, including an Appendix with the letters from the Sotheby's sale. N. Till's *Rossini: His Life and Time* (London, 1983) is full of information and intelligent observations.

The best biography of the composer, I think, is Richard Osborne's *Rossini* (London, 1986); Osborne also wrote the entries on Rossini's works for *The New Grove Dictionary of Opera*, ed. Stanley Sadie, 4 vols (London, 1992). I have also found *Rossini* by Henri De Curzon (Paris, 1920), *The Great Musicians: Rossini and his School* by H. Sutherland Edwards (London, 1881) and *Rossini: A Study in Tragi-comedy* by Francis Toye (London, 2/ 1954) useful. And it would be impossible to do without Stendhal's *Vie de Rossini* (Paris, 1824) even though Rossini called his finest biographer 'ce grand menteur'; the excellent translation by Richard N. Coe (London, 1956) includes notes 'correcting Stendhal's many minor errors of fact'. But I often use my own translations.

Besides Osborne, I have relied on Giuseppe Radiciotti's indispensable *Gioachino Rossini: Vita documentata, opere ed influenze sull'arte*, 3 vols (Tivoli, 1927–9) and Alan Kendall's *Gioachino Rossini: The Reluctant Hero* (London, 1992). Unless given in full below, my quotations from contemporary magazines and diaries are drawn from these texts.

Isaiah Berlin's *The Power of Ideas*, ed. Henry Hardy (London, 2000) and *The Roots of Romanticism*, ed. Henry Hardy (Princeton, NJ, 1999) are basic to the whole of this work. E. J. Hobsbawm's *The Age of Revolution* (London, 1975) and *The Age of Capital* (London, 1975) are wonderful works to which I am equally indebted. Similarly, Hugh Honour's *Neoclassicism* (London, 1968) and *Romanticism* (London, 1978) were both musts.

ACT ONE
STENDHAL AND THE NEOCLASSICAL

Some of the extracts from contemporary magazines are from Radiciotti and from Herbert Weinstock's *Rossini* (New York, 1968). Stendhal is a central figure in this act; and so is, in the background, his *Chartreuse de Parme*, of which the easiest available English translation is that by Margaret R. B. Shaw (Harmondsworth, 1958).

Stendhal's *Rome, Naples et Florence* (Paris, 1826) provided me with the detail of the initial encounter between its author and Rossini. Alexander Herzen travelled to Italy and was at Terracina, in the same post house where a few years earlier Stendhal had met Rossini; his *Memoirs*, ed. Isaiah Berlin (London, 1968), make fascinating reading. I have also drawn on *Stendhal e Rossini* (Pesaro, 1999) by Stephane Dado and Philippe Vendrix. My account of *La Cenerentola* is indebted to its librettist Jacopo Ferretti, who was a real 'grand menteur' but produced the delightful *Un poeta melodrammatico* (Milan, 1898), and to Bruno Cagli's brilliant programme notes for the production at the Rossini Opera Festival of 1998; the same adjective applies to Giovanni Carli Ballola's notes for *La donna del lago* (Pesaro, 2001; trans. Michael Aspinall).

Massimo d'Azeglio, who was to become prime minister of Italy, described his evenings with Rossini and Donizetti in *I miei ricordi* (1867). Sergio Ragni tells important information about Rossini's wife in 'Isabella Colbran: Appunti per una biografia' in the *Bollettino del Centro rossiniano*, XXXVIII (1998). *Modern Europe* (London, 1997) by Asa Briggs and Patricia Clavin describes the incoming cataclysm of the Romantic age. Germaine de Staël's *De l'Allemagne*, suppressed by Napoleon in 1810 but published in London in 1813, once again made me sympathize with Napoleon's opinion of her: 'Elle est Suisse!'

In Naples Rossini flourished: *Protagonisti nella storia di Napoli G. Rossini* (Naples, 1994) was put together by the Istituto per gli Studi Filosofici (Soprintendenza per i Beni Artistici e Storici). *I poeti romantici inglesi e l'Italia* (exh. cat., Rome, Palazzo Braschi, 1980) was as useful as *Il mondo delle farse* (Rossini Opera Festival, 2001). I consulted *Tutti i libretti di Rossini* (Milan, 1991) for this and the next two acts. Giuseppe Barigazzi's *La Scala racconta* (Milan, 1991), Alessandro Baricco's *Il genio in fuga* (Turin, 1997), Alfredo Casella's *Rossiniana* (Bologna, 1942) and Raffaello Monterosso's *La musica nel Risorgimento* (Milan, 1948) include material and observations to which I am indebted. Harold Acton's *The Bourbons of Naples 1734–1825* (London, 1957) has a partiality for the Neapolitan Bourbons that I cannot share; nor can I follow his interpretation of the political events in Naples (see the Pepe-Carbonari rebellion), but his prose is a delight. Lady Morgan's *Italy*, 3 vols (London, 1821) provided me with many vignettes.

Bosdari's *La vita musicale a Bologna nel periodo napoleonico* (Bologna, 1914) should be looked at by French musicologists. I quote from Giuseppe Carpani's *Lettera all'anonimo autore dell'articolo sul Tancredi* (Milan, 1818). Other quoted correspondence includes *Byron's Letters and Journals*, ed. Leslie A. Marchand (London, 1976), *Giacomo Meyerbeer: Briefwechseu und Tagebucher*, ed. Heinz Becker (Berlin, 1960) *I salotti della cultura nell'Italia dell'800* by Maria Iolanda Palazzolo (Monza, 1985) has information which I use also in the next act.

ACT TWO
BEETHOVEN AND ROMANTICISM

The edition of Rossini's letters by Giuseppi Mazzatinti (Imola, 1890, 3/1902 was reprinted with a preface by Massimo Mila (Florence, 1965), on which I have relied for this chapter. I drew from '*Il viaggio a Vienna*' by L. M. Kaufer and R. John, *Bollettino del Centro rossiniano*, (1992) and E. H. Gombrich's Lecture *Franz Schubert e la Vienna del suo tempo* (Florence, 1978), the text of which was kindly given to me by the author. *Rossini nella raccolta Piancastelli di Forlí*, ed. Paolo Fabbri (Lucca, 2001), the Countess of Bassanville's *Les Salons d'autrefois* (Paris, 1862) and the Countess of Boigne's *Mémoires* (Paris, 1986) were avidly consulted. *The Nineteenth Century*, ed. Asa Briggs (London, 1985), includes essays by John Roberts, James Joll, F. Bedarida, John Rohl and Asa Briggs himself. I also want to thank Asa Briggs for our conversations on the nineteenth century and my theories on the Romantic age.

Anton Graeffer's manuscript *Autobiographie* of 1830 (Stadtbibliothek Wien, ms je 138011) was written under the pseudonym Pellegrino. I have also drawn on *Rossini 1792–1992*, ed. Mauro Buccarelli (exh. cat., Perugia, 1992) and Guido Johannes Joerg's 'Rossini a Londra' and 'La cantata Il pianto delle Muse in morte di Lord Byron' in *Bollettino del Centro rossiniano*, XXVIII (1988); the latter was also used for Act Three. The original score of *Il canto delle muse* is at the British Library, Music Manuscript no. 30246.

Bruno Cagli's 'Il risveglio magnetico e il sonno della ragione', *Accademia nazionale di Santa Cecilia*, XIV/1 (1985), is a jewel.

ACT THREE
BALZAC AND THE INTELLECT

Madame Girardin's correspondence of 1848–9, *Lettres Parisiennes*, ed. (Paris, 1987) and A. Bellessort's equally delightful 'La France et le pars de Balzac', *Revue Hebdomadaire* (1 March 1924) provided me with ideas. I read Pierluigi Petrobelli's 'Balzac, Stendhal e il Moisè di Rossini' in *Bolletino del Centro rossiniano* (1971) and 'Balzac et la musique', *Mercure de France*, (1922), both of which discuss aspects of Balzac's understanding of Rossini's music. I also consulted C. Bellaigue's 'Balzac et la musique', *Revue des deux mondes* (1 October 1924) and P. Cajole's *La Medicine et les medicins dans l'oeuvre de Balzac* (Lyons, 1901). For Olympe's background, 'Balzac, O. Péllissier et les courtisanes' by C. Mauray in *Année Balzacienne*, (1975) was essential. The description of the steam boat comes from Flaubert's *L'Educa-tion Sentimentale* in the translation by Robert Baldick (London, 1964). 'Rossini e Metternich' by Bernd-Rudiger Kerr, *Bollettino del Centro rossi-niano*, XLIX (1999) was a good guide for the political events, as indeed was *Histoire de la France*, Vol. II (Paris, 1947) by André Maurois and *La France des notables* by A. Jardin and A-J. Tudesq, 2 vols (Paris, 1973).

Andrew Porter's 'A Lost Opera by Rossini', *Music and Letters*, XLV (1964) is the article that solved the mystery of *Ugo, re d'Italia*. On *Guillaume Tell*, Giovanni Carlo Ballola wrote programme notes for the Rossini Opera Festival (1995), and Andrea Baggioli's 'Le fonti letterarie di Guillaume Tell' is in the *Bollettino del Centro rossiniano* XXXVII (1997). Also valuable for this act were *Honoré de Balzac* by Hubert J. Hunt (London, 1957), *The Memoirs of Hector Berlioz*, trans. and ed. David Cairns (London, 1969, 2/ 1977), (pen name) Marie d'Agoult's *Mémoires, souvenirs et journaux*, ed. Daniel Sterns, 2 vols (Paris, 1990) and P-Brighenti's *Della musica rossiniana e del suo autore* (Bologna, 1830). But it was Eugène Delacroix's *Journal*, ed. (Paris, 1932) which provided me with the most wide-ranging thoughts – and often moved me to tears.

Balzac's *La Peau de chagrin* (1831), *Gambara* (1837) and *Massimilla Doni* (1839) discuss Rossini's music and entourage. Maurice Serval's 'Une enigme balzacienne' in the *Bulletin de la Société Historique* (1925–6) supplied me with further details on the friendship between Rossini and Balzac. The letters to and from Balzac, also quoted in the next act, are in the Bibliothèque de la Maison Balzac, Paris.

ACT FOUR
VERDI AND REVOLUTIONS

This act focuses on the explosion of anger of the age, the distance that separated Rossini from the new Romantic era, his cool friendship with Verdi and his deepening depression. Mary Jane Phillips-Matz's biography *Verdi* (Oxford, 1993) was invaluable, while *Viva la libertà: Politics in Opera* by Anthony Arblaster (Oxford, 1992) and Folco Portinari's *Pari siamo!* (Turin, 1981) discuss politics and music. Harry Hearder's *Italy in the Age of the Risorgimento* (London, 1988) and Raffaello Montezosso's *La Musica nel Risongimento* (Milan, 1948) were also useful. *Lettere inedite e rare*, ed. Guiseppi Mazzatinti (Imola, 1892) was important for this and the previous act. *Filosofia della musica* (Milan, 1870) by Giuseppe Mazzini spells out the politician's thoughts on music and *Metternich: Der Staatsman und der Mensch* (Munich, 1925) provided some important details.

For Verdi, Marcello Conati's *Verdi: Interviste e incontri* (Turin, 1980), my own *Traviata* (London, 1994), Lorenzo Arruga's *Medaglie incomparabili* (Milan, 2001), Luzio's *Il pensiero artistico e politico di Verdi* (Milan, 1901) and *Il salotto della Contessa Maffei* by Raffaella Barbiera (Sesto San Giovanni, 1914) have interesting stories.

Arnold Whittall's *Romantic Music* (Oxford, 1987) is a lovely book while Bruno Cagli's *L'ultima stagione* (Pesaro), and *G. Rossini Lettere*, ed. Enrico Castiglione (Rome, 1992) gave me further information.

For details of Balzac's Italian visit, I read G Gigli, *Balzac in Italia* (Milan, 1892) and H. Prior, 'Balzac à Milan', *Revue de Paris*. Victor Hugo's description of Balzac's death is from *Choses vues* (1830–48), ed. (Paris, 1997). Quotations from Bellini's letters are my translations of *Vincenzo Bellini: Epistolario*, ed. Luisa Cambi (Verona, 1943), and Olympe Pélissier's from *Il Fondo francese dell'archivio rossiniano di Pesaro* (Pesaro, 1921).

Rossini's conversations with Filippo Mordani, also a victim of depression, are published in Mordani's *Della vita privata di Giovacchino Rossini: Memorie inedite* (Imola, 1871). On Rossini's illness I also consulted Bruno Riboli 'Profilo medico-psicologico di Gioachino Rossini', *Rassegna musicale*, III (1954) and Anthony Storr's *The Dynamics of creation*.

ACT FIVE
WAGNER AND DEATH

Richard Wagner's *Pagine d'arte italiana 1834–72* (Turin, 1915), his *Souvenirs 1884* and his *Eine Erinnerung an Rossini* (1868) were essential reading for this act, as was Charles Baudelaire's 'Richard Wagner et Tannhäuser à Paris', first published in 1861 and reprinted in *Critique d'art et critique musicale* (Paris, 1976). But the core of my story is based on Edmond Michotte's *Souvenirs Personels: La Visite de Richard Wagner à Rossini (Paris 1860)* (Paris, 1906); the translation by Herbert Weinstock, *Richard Wagner's Visit to Rossini* (London, 1982), also proved valuable for Rossini's visit to Beethoven. Massimo Mila's *Brahms e Wagner* (Turin, 1994) is a beautiful book. Leon Escudier's and Marie Escudier's *Rossini: Sa Vie* (London, 1824) was useful – and not as bitchy as what the brothers wrote about Rossini in their letters to Verdi. The invaluable *Dictionnaire du Second Empire*, ed. Jean Tulon (Paris, 1995) was a present from my son Orlando Mostyn-Owen.

ACKNOWLEDGEMENTS

And now, may I bow out of this story and give thanks to the many who have helped me in gathering the information I needed to build an understanding of the man to whom I have dedicated time and thoughts.

Among those whom I would like to thank are: Jean-Pierre Angremi, Director of the Bibliothèque Nationale de France; M. Bruno Blasselle and Mme Guibert, the curators of the Bibliothèque de l'Arsenal; Mathias Auclair of the Bibliothèque-Musée de l'Opéra and the curators of the Richelieu, Departement de Musique. As for the Maison Balzac and its attached Bibliothèque Balzac, I was even given a private room in which to work after closing time, thanks to its director and its curator.

In England, the staff of the London Library and the British Library as well as the Bodleian in Oxford were helpful. Simon Wessely, Professor of Epidemiological and Liaison Psychiatry, Academic Department of Psycho-logical Medicine and Institute of Psychiatry at Guy's, King's and St Thomas's School of Medicine in London, to whom I was introduced by my friend Professor John Studd, dedicated study and time to the complex question of 'translating' Rossini's symptoms into modern medical terms and diagnoses.

But most of all, in Pesaro, I want to express appreciation to Maestro Alberto Zedda in particular. As artistic director of the Rossini Opera Festival, he is a life-long Rossiniano and was the first to talk to me about Balzac and Rossini, their friendship and what Balzac had written on Rossini. Souvrintendente Gianfranco Mariotti, of the Rossini Opera Festival, was the first to speak to me about another Rossini, the person and the musician who had been hidden and had been hiding. As Mariotti said in 2002:

*The long battle waged by the Festival, together with the Rossini
Foundation, for over twenty years, aiming above all at the restoration
of Rossini's serious works to the stage, has put paid to this [Rossini's
silence, the subsequent neglect of most of his work] and to other
misunderstandings, and the revival of almost all Rossini's operas
allows us, today, to arrive at last at a balanced judgement on the
complete works of the composer.*

Philip Gossett of Chicago University answered all my emails and queries.
As for Bruno Cagli, whom I often quote in the course of my narrative, I owe
him more than I can express: first of all, the pleasure of reading and
absorbing his literary output which has wit, knowledge and breadth; also,
his friendship, help and generosity towards me has included not only
information on Rossini's disease but also the benefit of his extraordinary
memory and perception.

My husband Hugh Myddelton Biddulph has been looking at chapter after
chapter. For this and other things I thank him.

Ian Thompson looked at Chapter 5 and 6 of Act IV; Ian Buruma, the whole
of Act V. Paolo Terni chapters 1, 2, 3 and 4 of Act V, Alberto Zedda chapters
5 and 6 of Act III, Bruno Cagli the whole of Act IV, Cesare de Seta Act V –
and Simon Wessely read those chapters concerned with Rossini's nervous
crisis. I thank them all again. Thanks also to my literate children Allegra
Mostyn-Owen, who looked at Act IV and Orlando Mostyn-Owen at Act V.

The proofs were read by Dr Sergio Ragni a great Neapolitan musicologist
who has a superb collection of Rossiniana and whom I thank for his generosity
in allowing me to use the images from his collection. I also sent proofs to
Professor Bruno Cagli and Christopher Sinclair-Stevenson; Allegra Mostyn-
Owen dedicated time and knowledge to copy-edit the final version of this
book; something for which I thank her. Anna Williamson has been a fantastic
picture researcher and attentive editor together with Carol O'Brien whom I
thank elsewhere.

I also thank Lady Berlin for letting me use quotations from her husband's
The Power of Ideas and Romanticism; besides Alexander Herzen's *Diaries*
translated and edited by Isaiah Berlin.

I am indebted to the Museo Teatrale alla Scala and its director Maestro
Matteo Sartorio for allowing me to use various illustrations and for his
courtesy and solicitude; to Reto Muller who came to me as a wonderful
surprise, collector of rossiniana and a scholar whose total commitment to
Rossini and generosity to me was astonishing.

I would have liked to be able to thank the Fondazione Rossini from Pesaro
which, since it receives State money, is presumably meant to help.

Franca Mancini and her husband Cesare have given me not only wonderful hospitality in Pesaro but all the warmth they are capable of, a lot. Giorgio and Marina Forni were extremely kind in sending me the list of Rossini papers held at the Conservatorio Padre Martini in Bologna. Simona Barabesi and Sue Graham-Dixon made my path easy. The former, whose musical knowledge and taste is admirable, looked after me in Pesaro and made it possible for me to listen to superb performances of Rossini's operas.

Carol O'Brien is a friend and an attentive editor (if only English publishing could boast many more Carol O'Briens!).

As for the primary sources and later publications from which I have drawn, my Bibliography is not meant to be a guide for further reading, but simply indicates the journals and books consulted. Translations are mine unless otherwise stated.

INDEX